This is a beautifully written and compelling account of what it is like to work in the classical music profession. Written with admirable clarity and great insight, the book makes a major contribution to our understanding of gendered subjectivity in the workplace, and also to the growing field of studies of creative labour. A magnificent book that deserves to become essential reading.

Rosalind Gill, Professor of Cultural and Social Analysis,
City University of London, UK

This is a dazzling and important book. Meticulously researched, Scharff documents the ways in which female classical musicians experience their own professional identities and how they become 'entrepreneurial subjects'. Scharff plays close attention to the texture of inequities in this milieu, and to how competition takes specifically gendered forms. The book is a major contribution to creative economy studies, to sociology, social psychology and gender studies.

Angela McRobbie Professor of Communications,
Goldsmiths University of London, UK

Christina Scharff's book is a superbly thoughtful and insightful feminist study of women musicians in two contrasting cities, and it is also a major contribution to studies of creative labour. It shows how cultural workers are required to be entrepreneurs – and skilfully reveals how this contributes to workplace inequalities.

David Hesmondhalgh, Professor of Media, Music and
Culture, University of Leeds, UK

Gender, Subjectivity, and Cultural Work

What is it like to work as a classical musician today? How can we explain ongoing gender, racial, and class inequalities in the classical music profession? What happens when musicians become entrepreneurial and think of themselves as a product that needs to be sold and marketed?

Gender, Subjectivity, and Cultural Work explores these and other questions by drawing on innovative, empirical research on the working lives of classical musicians in Germany and the UK. Indeed, Scharff examines a range of timely issues such as the gender, racial, and class inequalities that characterise the cultural and creative industries; the ways in which entrepreneurialism – as an ethos to work on and improve the self – is lived out; and the subjective experiences of precarious work in so-called creative cities. Thus, this book not only adds to our understanding of the working lives of artists and creatives, but also makes broader contributions by exploring how precarity, neoliberalism, and inequalities shape subjective experiences.

Contributing to a range of contemporary debates around cultural work, *Gender, Subjectivity, and Cultural Work* will be of interest to scholars and students in the fields of sociology, gender, and cultural studies.

Christina Scharff is Senior Lecturer in Culture, Media, and Creative Industries at King's College London.

Routledge Research in Gender and Society

For a full list of titles in this series, please visit www.routledge.com

54 **Changing Names and Gendering Identity**
Social Organisation in Contemporary Britain
Rachel Thwaites

55 **Genealogies and Conceptual Belonging**
Zones of Interference between Gender and Diversity
Eike Marten

56 **Black Women, Agency, and the New Black Feminism**
Maria del Guadalupe Davidson

57 **Marginalized Masculinities**
Contexts, Continuities and Change
Edited by Chris Haywood and Thomas Johansson

58 **Equality Struggles**
Women's Movements, Neoliberal Markets and State Political
Agendas in Scandinavia
Mia Liinason

59 **Gender, Subjectivity, and Cultural Work**
The Classical Music Profession
Christina Scharff

60 **The Conundrum of Masculinity**
Hegemony, Homosociality, Homophobia and Heteronormativity
*Chris Haywood, Thomas Johansson, Nils Hammarén, Marcus Herz
and Andreas Ottemo*

61 **Body Image as an Everyday Problematic**
Looking Good
Félix Díaz Martínez

Gender, Subjectivity, and Cultural Work

The Classical Music Profession

Christina Scharff

Routledge
Taylor & Francis Group

LONDON AND NEW YORK

First published 2018
by Routledge
2 Park Square, Milton Park, Abingdon, Oxon OX14 4RN

and by Routledge
711 Third Avenue, New York, NY 10017

Routledge is an imprint of the Taylor & Francis Group, an informa business

British Library Cataloguing-in-Publication Data
A catalogue record for this book is available from the British
Library

Library of Congress Cataloging-in-Publication Data
A catalog record for this book has been requested

ISBN: 978-1-138-94256-1 (hbk)
ISBN: 978-1-315-67308-0 (ebk)

Typeset in Times New Roman
by Apex CoVantage, LLC

This is to Penelope and Philippa, with love

Contents

List of figures		x
List of tables		xi
Acknowledgements		xii
	Introduction	1
1	Setting the stage: the cultural and creative industries, entrepreneurialism, and the classical music profession	10
2	Documenting and explaining inequalities in the classical music profession	41
3	The silence that is not a rest: negotiating hierarchies of class, race, and gender	85
4	Entrepreneurialism at work: mapping the contours of entrepreneurial subjectivity	113
5	"Difficult, fickle, tumultuous" and yet "the best job in the world": analysing subjective experiences of precarious work	140
6	Structures of feeling in two creative cities: London and Berlin	170
	Conclusion: key contributions, directions for further research, and recommendations	194
	Index	204

Figures

2.1   Percentage of female students at five UK conservatoires   45

2.2   Percentage of students from low participation neighbourhoods
at five UK conservatoires   47

2.3   Percentage of privately schooled students at five
UK conservatoires   47

2.4   Percentage of black and minority ethnic students: i) at five
UK conservatoires and ii) doing a music degree across all
UK universities   48

2.5   Percentage of black and minority ethnic students at five
UK conservatoires   49

2.6   Gender breakdown by instrument among members of British
orchestras   51

2.7   Gender breakdown by instrument/subject taught by
conservatoire staff in the United Kingdom   52

2.8   Gender breakdown by instrument/subject taught by German
conservatoire staff   52

2.9   Gender profile of teaching staff at UK conservatoires   53

2.10 Gender profile of teaching staff at German conservatoires   54

Tables

2.1   Total number and percentage of women conductors and artistic
      directors in British orchestras   56
2.2   Total number and percentage of women in British orchestras
      for: i) all players and ii) principals; by instrument   56
2.3   Ethnic background of teaching staff at UK conservatoires   57
2.4   Ethnic background of teaching staff at German conservatoires   58

Acknowledgements

I am deeply grateful to the 64 female musicians who took part in this research. I would like to thank all research participants for taking the time to talk to me, share their views, beliefs, and feelings, as well as direct me to colleagues I could interview. It was a great privilege and pleasure to meet so many musicians and gain insight into their working lives. My thanks also go to Trudy White, Patrick Haighton, Anna Bull, Matthias Stoffels, Robin Hoffmann, and Annesley Black, who put me in touch with research participants at the beginning of the project and got the ball rolling.

I would not have been able to conduct this research without a small grant from the British Academy (SG120354) and the Economic and Social Research Council's (ESRC) Future Research Leaders scheme. The ESRC grant (ES/K008765/1) gave me the precious gift of research time, especially for the analysis, writing up, and dissemination of my findings. Both grants covered expenses occurring at various stages in the research, ranging from transcription and data collection to copy-editing. My special thanks go to Anne Koch and Anika Meier for transcribing the interviews; Brigid McClure and Fiona Wright for tirelessly clicking through websites to gain information about the demographic makeup of British orchestras and teaching staff at German and UK conservatoires; and to Patrizia Kokot-Blamey and John Kokot-Blamey for analysing the quantitative data featured in this book and generously sharing their expertise, wit, and insight. Towards the end of the project, Yvonne Ehrstein provided invaluable assistance with note taking, referencing, and copy-editing. I would not have been able to finish this book on time without her reliable help, attention to detail, as well as constructive and co-operative attitude. I really value and appreciate the hard work she has done, which I know requires a lot of technical knowhow, expertise, and concentration. I would also like to thank Sara De Benedictis for proofreading my manuscript so carefully and for accommodating my rather tight schedule. Finally, I have enjoyed co-operating with Routledge. It has been a real pleasure to work with my editors Emily Briggs and Elena Chiu and I am grateful for their support throughout the publication process.

Many colleagues and friends have supported and mentored me over the course of this research. At the early stages, I discussed the design of the project with

Angela McRobbie, who at the time was my mentor and whose vast amount of expertise, insight, and experience in the field provided an invaluable source of inspiration. Andy Pratt acted as my mentor during my ESRC Future Research Leaders grant and offered his time and thoughts on numerous occasions, providing vital guidance throughout. Stephanie Taylor and David Hesmondhalgh also played a key inspiring and supportive role, both through their excellent research on creative labour and the cultural industries, as well as by acting as mentors and referees on several occasions. Last but not least, my dear friend and colleague Rosalind Gill has supported me in this project in many, invaluable ways: by discussing and exchanging ideas, reading and commenting on my work, sharing the ups and downs of life in academia, acting as a mentor on numerous occasions, and being a wonderful friend.

This project has been inspired by contemporary, feminist cultural studies, research on cultural work, and analyses of the classical music sector. Thanking every inspiring colleague would exceed the scope of the acknowledgements, but I would like to mention a few by name. First, my thanks go to those who have read and commented on drafts of individual chapters. Catherine Rottenberg, Francesca Carpos, Melissa Nisbett, Bridget Conor, Rachel O'Neill, Anna Bull, Carolyn Pedwell, Stephanie Taylor, Rosalind Gill, Kirsten Forkert, and Sara De Benedictis provided insightful and constructive comments. Thank you for taking the time to read and offer feedback on my work. Collaborating with Anna Bull, particularly through ongoing conversations about the classical music world, co-organising several conferences, and co-authoring an article has also nourished my research. In the fields of cultural work and music, Mark Banks and Daniel Leech-Wilkinson have provided manifold insights and generously shared these at conferences and beyond. More generally, Tim Jordan, Elisabeth Kelan, and Mary Evans have offered crucial support over recent years in their capacities as mentors and referees.

My research has benefitted from the many, stimulating exchanges I have had with current and former PhD students, Yvonne Ehrstein, Catherine Elzerbi, Brigid McClure, Natalie Wreyford, Simidele Dosekun, Ana Sofia Elias, Rachel O'Neill, Anna Watts, and Birgit Wildt. I also appreciate the various opportunities I have been offered for disseminating my findings within and beyond the world of classical music. In particular, I would like to thank Hannah Kendall and Robert Adediran at London Music Masters for giving me a platform to share and discuss my ideas on several occasions. In this context, I would also like to express my gratitude to Krystyna Budzynska from the Advance Network, Louise Blackwell from Fuel Theatre, Jeff Brown at VAN magazine, Jacob Thompson-Bell at The Sampler, Tom Service and the team at BBC Radio 3's Music Matters, as well as Lyndon Jones and colleagues who worked on the BBC Radio 4 programme 'Black, White and Beethoven'. Lastly, I would like to thank Erin Johnson-Williams and Sophie Fuller for inviting me to discuss my findings with a group of postgraduate students and aspiring musicians at Trinity Laban Conservatoire of Music and Dance.

My special thanks go to my friends and family who have sustained this research through their love and support. In particular, I would like to thank our daughters Penelope and Philippa for coming into this world and bringing us so much pleasure, fulfilment, and joy. This book is dedicated to you, with love.

Acknowledgement of sources

Please note that a shorter and earlier version of chapter four was published by Sage in 2016 as 'The psychic life of neoliberalism: Mapping the contours of entrepreneurial subjectivity' in the journal *Theory, Culture & Society*, *33*(6), 107–122. Reprinted with permission.

Section four in chapter two was published by John Wiley & Sons in 2015 as 'Blowing your own trumpet: Exploring the gendered dynamics of self-promotion in the classical music profession' in the journal *The Sociological Review*, *63*, 97–112. Reprinted with permission.

Introduction

This book is based on innovative, empirical research on the working lives of classical musicians[1] in Germany and the United Kingdom. It explores a range of timely issues, such as the gender, racial, and class inequalities that characterise the classical music profession; the ways in which entrepreneurialism – as an ethos to work on and improve the self – is lived out; the subjective experiences of precarious work; and how urban settings affect the feelings associated with work in the cultural and creative industries. Indeed, questions of subjectivity[2] are at the heart of this book. How do classical musicians negotiate ongoing hierarchies, privileges, and exclusions? What happens if the self is turned into a business that demands constant work and cannot get sick? How is the often-precarious nature of the classical music profession experienced? And is life and work as a classical musician easier in London or Berlin?

To answer these and other questions, *Gender, Subjectivity, and Cultural Work* draws on over 60 in-depth interviews with female, early career, classical musicians based in London and Berlin. It also provides a limited amount of new, quantitative data on the demographic makeup of the classical music profession in Germany and the United Kingdom. Theoretically, the book employs Foucauldian governmentality theory and is embedded in cultural studies, gender studies, and sociology. Analytically, it is informed by a range of critical, interdisciplinary perspectives on the cultural and creative industries, 'cultural work', inequalities in the cultural sector, neoliberalism, entrepreneurialism, precarity, and the rise of the 'creative city'.

The book's analysis of work in the classical music profession speaks to a growing interest in the working conditions characterising the cultural sector. While the cultural and creative industries have been discussed variously in public, policy, and academic debates, the question of what it is actually like to work in these industries has only attracted sustained scholarly attention in the last few years. Today, there is a rich body of research on cultural work, which is "broadly defined as symbolic, aesthetic or creative labour in the arts, media and other creative or cultural industries" (Banks et al., 2013: 4; see also Banks, 2007). Recent studies have explored work in various cultural industries, ranging from screenwriting (Conor, 2014; Wreyford, 2015), black British Jazz (Banks et al., 2014), fashion

(McRobbie, 2015), and web design (Kennedy, 2012) to research that focuses on a mix of sectors (Hesmondhalgh and Baker, 2011; Taylor and Littleton, 2012). By analysing the classical music profession, *Gender, Subjectivity, and Cultural Work* sheds light on an industry that has not been studied extensively, particularly in research on cultural work.

Apart from its focus on the working conditions in the classical music sector, the book makes a range of other significant contributions. First, it sheds light on the experiences of female classical musicians about whom, to date, we know comparatively little. The study thus gives voice to a previously under-researched group.[3] Second, *Gender, Subjectivity, and Cultural Work* offers a detailed analysis of the lack of diversity in the classical music profession. As part of this analysis, it presents original quantitative data on the demographic backgrounds of classical musicians in Germany and the United Kingdom. Third, I explore how musicians negotiate ongoing inequalities. Research participants talked openly about classed exclusions and, albeit to a lesser extent, racial hierarchies. However, they frequently disavowed gender imbalances. By employing several analytical frameworks, such as theories of individualisation, postfeminism, and neoliberalism, I demonstrate why gendered power relations tend to be silenced and rendered 'unspeakable' (Gill, 2014).

Fourth, my analysis seeks to explain the lack of diversity in the classical music profession by drawing on, and adding to, the wider literature on inequalities in cultural work. In particular, I build on research that has foregrounded the role of subjectivity and shown that the ideal cultural worker is a gendered, classed, and racialised figure (e.g. Allen et al., 2013; Conor, 2014; Conor et al., 2015; Gill, 2014; Taylor and Littleton, 2012; Wreyford, 2015). For instance, many of my research participants argued that self-promotion was important to secure work and to progress in one's career. Yet, female musicians face a range of gendered challenges when engaging in this practice, demonstrating that the figure of the self-promoting, cultural worker is not gender neutral. By foregrounding the dimension of subjectivity, my analysis advances our understanding of inequalities in the classical music profession. Indeed, I believe that my insights also speak to research on other work settings where similar dynamics are at play, both within and beyond the cultural and creative industries.

In addition to its focus on working conditions and inequalities, *Gender, Subjectivity, and Cultural Work* examines entrepreneurialism and how it is lived out on a subjective level. Writers in the Foucauldian tradition have explored how subjectivities are reconstituted under neoliberalism, showing that the neoliberal self is an entrepreneurial subject (Brown, 2003; Foucault, 2008; Lemke, 2001; Rose, 1992). Based on in-depth interviews with young, female classical musicians, my analysis offers insight into the accounts of individuals who appear to be entrepreneurial subjects par excellence. As research in cultural studies and gender studies has shown (e.g. McRobbie, 2009; 2015; Gill and Pratt, 2008; Gill and Scharff, 2011; Ringrose and Walkerdine, 2008; Ross, 2008), public and media discourses have positioned young women and cultural workers as ideal entrepreneurial subjects. By exploring the accounts of individuals who, as cultural workers and young women, are twice positioned as entrepreneurial, this book traces how entrepreneurial subjectivity is registered and negotiated.

My analysis maps and examines ten contours of entrepreneurial subjectivity. For instance, I demonstrate that entrepreneurial subjects relate to themselves as if they were a business, are active and in a constant mode of becoming, hide injuries, and disavow structural constraints. While some of my insights chime with existing research on the ways in which entrepreneurialism is lived out, I also make several important interventions, both methodologically and analytically. The majority of existing research tends to be theoretical in perspective. However, my analysis is empirically based and examines entrepreneurial subjectivity from the ground up. Analytically, my discussion of the contours of entrepreneurial subjectivity reframes existing accounts, for example in relation to the ways in which competition manifests itself in neoliberalism. I show that competition is not only other-directed, but also self-directed. This means that competition is potentially boundless; if there are no external limits, we can always try to outperform ourselves. In addition, competition may work at a 'deeper' level because it is not imposed upon us, but is taken on, seemingly voluntarily. In reframing existing accounts based on empirical analysis, *Gender, Subjectivity, and Cultural Work* expands the scope of contemporary debates on the interplay between neoliberalism and subjectivity, both methodologically and analytically.

Another key contribution relates to the book's exploration of the subjective experiences of precarious work. Musicians, like many other cultural workers, tend to be self-employed and have working lives that are marked by low incomes, uncertainty, and a lack of workplace benefits such as sick pay or pensions (e.g. Bennett, 2008; Musicians' Union, 2012; Schulz, 2013). By illustrating how musicians discuss and negotiate the insecurity that characterises their working lives, *Gender, Subjectivity, and Cultural Work* engages with yet another set of contemporary issues. It sheds light on a range of dimensions of precarious work, such as the reshaping of time, subjective responses, and coping mechanisms. For instance, I show that feelings about insecure, cultural work fluctuate. Instead of associating precarious work with constant anxiety, the research participants also talked about excitement. Significantly, I argue that the positive and negative aspects of cultural work, such as the pleasures and uncertainties associated with it, are inextricably intertwined. The research participants often described the hardships associated with casualised work in tandem with the joy they derived from playing music. Given that cultural workers have been positioned as being "at the centre of an ongoing transformation of work" (Banks et al., 2013: 3), this book's analysis of negotiations of precarious work may have implications that reach beyond the cultural and creative industries and speak to debates on the changing world of work more generally.

Finally, *Gender, Subjectivity, and Cultural Work* is international in scope because it explores the working lives of musicians in London and Berlin. I chose these two cities as research sites because they feature vibrant cultural and classical music sectors, but also very different housing costs. These distinctive material conditions give rise to the question of how cultural work is experienced in London and Berlin. By animating Raymond Williams's (1977) notion of 'structures of feeling', *Gender, Subjectivity, and Cultural Work* examines the affective register that underpins cultural work in two different, urban settings. I show that life in the two sites is marked by a cosmopolitan flair, but that feelings of hardship are more present in London, mainly due to its high housing costs. Berlin, by contrast, is experienced as almost luxuriously cheap, but there is also a sense of immanent change, which gives rise to insecurity.

Through its focus on London and Berlin, *Gender, Subjectivity, and Cultural Work* variously explores the dynamics of cultural work in different, national settings. In addition to focusing on 'structures of feeling' in the two cities, it sketches briefly the characterising features of the classical music profession in Germany and the United Kingdom. Equally important, it sheds light on the demographic makeup of the classical music sector in both countries. To be sure, the book's international scope does not mean that the analysis presented here is comparative. The data necessary for such an undertaking is not available. As an illustration, German labour market statistics do not commonly include data on the racial and ethnic backgrounds of workers. And while I collected some of this data in relation to the classical music profession, my aim has not been to conduct comparative research. Instead, my project could be more usefully described as a 'two-city study' (Forkert, 2011; 2013), which explores particular phenomena in two capitals.

This book thus approaches the interplay between gender, subjectivity, and work in the classical music profession from various angles. My analysis of inequalities in cultural work homes in on the dimensions of gender and subjectivity by exploring the gendered dynamics of self-promotion. However, I also examine processes of subjective meaning making by investigating how musicians negotiate ongoing exclusions in the classical music industry, especially in relation to gender. Likewise, my analysis of entrepreneurialism brings together the dimensions of gender, subjectivity, and cultural work. More specifically, it builds on the positioning of young women and cultural workers as entrepreneurial to map the contours of entrepreneurial subjectivity and explore how it is lived out. In addition, I examine female musicians' subjective experiences of precarious work, looking in particular at the complex affective dynamics associated with insecure work in the cultural and creative industries. Last but not least, I embed the research participants' accounts in their wider, urban settings in order to trace how subjective experiences of cultural work intersect with particular, geographical contexts. In order to give the reader a clearer sense of the structure of this book and focus of each chapter, I provide an outline in the following section.

Outline of the chapters

The first chapter, *'Setting the stage'*, contextualises the analysis presented in this book by introducing existing research on the cultural and creative industries, cultural work, entrepreneurialism, and the classical music profession in Germany and the United Kingdom. It begins with a discussion of the cultural and creative industries and subsequently outlines the rationale for embedding my study of the classical music profession in wider research on cultural work. The second section of the chapter introduces the study's Foucauldian theoretical framework and discusses the positioning of cultural workers and young women as entrepreneurial subjects. Finally, the third section contains a concise discussion of my methodology, including information on the research participants, research ethics, and the study's interpretative framework, discourse analysis.

Chapter two, 'Documenting and explaining inequalities in the classical music profession', discusses existing and new research on the lack of diversity in the classical music sector. By presenting both qualitative and quantitative data, the analysis makes visible a range of patterns, such as under-representation, as well as vertical and horizontal segregation. The chapter then sets out to explain why inequalities persist. More specifically, it draws on existing research to highlight the role of subjectivity in constructions of the ideal, classical musician, which seem to be gendered, racialised, and classed. The last section of the chapter applies the focus on subjectivity by exploring the gendered dynamics of self-promotion in the classical music profession. Research participants encountered several gendered dilemmas when engaging in self-promotion. They were afraid of being regarded as lacking in modesty, taken less seriously as artists, and felt that 'selling themselves' in a sexualised environment was not an easy undertaking.

The following chapter, 'The silence that is not a rest', examines how the research participants negotiated inequalities and shows that they talked about class, racial, and gender issues differently. The middle-class culture of the classical music profession was most openly discussed and some research participants also drew attention to ongoing racial inequalities. White privilege, however, remained unnamed and several research participants disarticulated racial inequalities by using individualist rhetoric. In comparison to issues around class and race, gender inequalities were negotiated most ambivalently. Many research participants used a range of rhetorical moves, such as trivialisation or normalisation, to argue that gender inequalities did not affect their working lives. The chapter makes sense of disarticulations of gender inequalities by drawing on theories of individualisation and postfeminism as well as the positioning of young women as entrepreneurial subjects. The disavowal of inequalities matters because it makes it more difficult to name and discuss ongoing issues, and to find ways of addressing them.

Chapter four, 'Entrepreneurialism at work', begins with a discussion of the frequently used, and yet contested term, neoliberalism. It subsequently adopts a Foucauldian perspective, which has shown that neoliberalism constructs individuals as entrepreneurial actors in every sphere of life. Having laid the theoretical groundwork, the chapter explores the accounts of the research participants who, as cultural workers and young women, are twice positioned as entrepreneurial. The main part of the chapter maps the contours of entrepreneurial subjectivity. It shows, for example, that entrepreneurial subjects relate to themselves as if they were a business, embrace risks, and engage in various forms of self-optimisation. My analysis resonates with the wider literature in various ways, but also reframes existing accounts. I argue that competition in neoliberalism is not only other-directed, but also self-directed. In addition, I intervene in existing debates by demonstrating that there is no one dominant feeling, such as anxiety, which characterises the affective register of entrepreneurial subjects. Lastly, I expand our understanding of the workings of exclusionary processes in relation to entrepreneurialism by suggesting that exclusions lie at the heart of constitutions of entrepreneurial subjectivity. Arguably, entrepreneurial subjectivity constitutes itself through the repudiation of racialised and classed others.

'"Difficult, fickle, tumultuous" and yet "the best job in the world"', the fifth chapter, explores how the research participants experienced precarious work. It shows that time is reshaped in crucial ways under precarity and that the feelings associated with insecure, cultural work change, ranging from fear and anxiety to excitement. Far from being homogenous, feelings about precarious work fluctuate and depend on the degree of freedom associated with particular forms of work, and the wider positioning of the worker, such as their class background. The research participants responded to uncertainty in a range of ways. One prevalent reaction was to emphasise their flexibility, ability to plan financially, and willingness to take risks; in short, adopting an entrepreneurial attitude. This entrepreneurial response took place in the wider context of an ambivalent relationship with work in the classical music profession, where the research participants discussed its negative components at the same time as highlighting the immense pleasure they derived from it. As the final two sections of the chapter demonstrate, the positive and negative aspects of precarious, cultural work are deeply intertwined and neither can be dismissed in analyses of cultural workers' experiences.

The final chapter, 'Structures of feeling in two creative cities', asks what it feels like to pursue cultural work in London and Berlin. The chapter begins with a brief discussion of Berlin's particularity and then moves on to an overview of the cultural and classical music sectors in the two cities. In part related to the size and importance of their cultural sectors, London and Berlin have been branded as 'creative cities' and the second section explores this policy discourse critically. Against this backdrop, the substantial parts of the chapter animate Raymond Williams's (1977) notion of 'structures of feeling' to explore the emotional underpinnings of doing cultural work in specific urban settings. London's structure of feeling was characterised by a sense of hardship, insecurity, inescapability, and excitement. By contrast, life in Berlin was portrayed as affordable. However, many research participants felt that change was immanent referring, among other issues, to rising rents. Thus, a sense of insecurity also featured in the structure of feeling in Berlin.

In the conclusion, I review Gender, Subjectivity, and Cultural Work's main arguments and contributions. In addition, I discuss directions for further analysis by highlighting several issues, such as the work on the body that musicians may engage in and the various gendered forms it takes. Drawing on existing and recent research on 'aesthetic labour' (e.g. Elias et al., 2017; Entwistle and Wissinger 2006; Warhurst et al., 2000), I chart ways in which my ideas and arguments could be taken forward. I conclude the book by discussing the wider concerns that my analysis has raised and by exploring how these can be addressed, particularly in relation to ongoing inequalities. Based on my findings, I lay out several recommendations for tackling the lack of workforce diversity in the classical music profession and the cultural sector more generally.

Notes

1 I define classical musicians as individuals who play a classical instrument and who have perfected their training in the context of higher education (Bork, 2010). As Steve Cottrell (2004: 8) has argued, this classical training tends to involve "learning an instrument from an early age, and gradually specializing more and more in music as one progresses through the educational system, often finishing with a university degree or equivalent conservatoire qualification". Of course, most classically trained musicians do not solely engage with classical music but also have to know other genres (Bennett, 2007; Bork, 2010; Cottrell, 2004). Equally important, by using the term 'classical music' in this book, I depart from the terminology preferred by many academic music departments, which is 'Western art music'. This is because my research participants used the term 'classical music' (see also Bull, 2015).
2 Henrietta Moore (2013: 203) has defined subjectivity as "the term we use to refer both to the process and the form of the relation of the individual to the social, and it remains a contested term by virtue of the fact that there is no possible resolution to the debate as to how the two definitely interrelate". In line with previous work with Rosalind Gill (Gill and Scharff, 2011: 8), I employ the notion of subjectivity "to signal the extent to which we see contemporary modes of power operating increasingly on and through the making and remaking of subjectivities, and through 'governing the soul' (Rose, 1989)". Power, then, does not work through top-down imposition, but through "negotiation, mediation, resistance, and articulation" (Gill, 2008: 11) and, as Gill continues to point out, affective investments. By introducing and applying my Foucauldian, theoretical framework (see chapters one and four) and methodological perspective (see chapter one), I clarify my use and understanding of subjectivity.
3 By exploring the views of female, classical musicians, my analysis of gender focuses on femininities.

References

Allen, K., Quinn, J., Hollingworth, S., & Rose, A. (2013). Becoming employable students and 'ideal' creative workers: Exclusion and inequality in higher education work placements. *British Journal of Sociology of Education*, *34*(3), 431–452.

Banks, M. (2007). *The politics of cultural work*. Basingstoke: Palgrave Macmillan.

Banks, M., Ebrey, J., & Toynbee, J. (2014). *Working lives in Black British jazz: A report and survey*. Accessed 1 December 2016. Available at: www.cresc.ac.uk/sites/default/files/WLIBBJ%20NEW%20FINAL.pdf

Banks, M., Gill, R., & Taylor, S. (2013). *Theorizing cultural work: Labour, continuity and change in the creative industries*. London: Routledge.

Bennett, D. (2007). Utopia for music performance graduates. Is it achievable, and how should it be defined? *British Journal of Music Education*, *24*(2), 179–189.

Bennett, D. (2008). *Understanding the classical music profession: The past, the present and strategies for the future*. Farnham: Ashgate.

Bork, M. (2010). *Traumberuf Musiker? Herausforderungen an ein Leben für die Kunst*. Mainz: Schott.

Brown, W. (2003). Neo-liberalism and the end of liberal democracy. *Theory & Event*, 7(1), 37–59.

Bull, A. (2015). *The musical body: How gender and class are reproduced among young people playing classical music in England*. Unpublished PhD thesis, Goldsmiths, University of London.

Conor, B. (2014). *Screenwriting: Creative labour and professional practice*. London: Routledge.

Conor, B., Gill, R., & Taylor, S. (Eds.). (2015). *Gender and creative labour* (Vol. 63). Chichester: Wiley.

Cottrell, S. (2004). *Professional music-making in London: Ethnography and experience*. Farnham: Ashgate.

Elias, A. S., Gill, R., & Scharff, C. (Eds.). (2017). *Aesthetic labour: Rethinking beauty politics in neoliberalism*. Basingstoke: Palgrave Macmillan.

Entwistle, J., & Wissinger, E. (2006). Keeping up appearances: Aesthetic labour in the fashion modelling industries of London and New York. *The Sociological Review*, 54(4), 774–794.

Forkert, K. (2011). *Artistic Labour and the changing nature of work: A two-city study*. Unpublished PhD thesis, Goldsmiths, University of London, London.

Forkert, K. (2013). *Artistic lives: A study of creativity in two European cities*. Farnham, Surrey: Ashgate.

Foucault, M. (2008). *The birth of biopolitics: Lectures at the Collège de France, 1978–79* (M. Senellart, Ed.). Basingstoke: Palgrave Macmillan.

Gill, R. (2008). Culture and subjectivity in neoliberal and postfeminist times. *Subjectivity*, 25(1), 1–19. Accessed 11 December 2016. Available at: http://openaccess.city.ac.uk/4113/2011/culture%2020and%2020subjectivity.pdf

Gill, R. (2014). Unspeakable inequalities: Post feminism, entrepreneurial subjectivity, and the repudiation of sexism among cultural workers. *Social Politics: International Studies in Gender, State and Society*, 21(4), 509–528.

Gill, R., & Pratt, A. C. (2008). In the social factory? Immaterial labour, precariousness and cultural work. *Theory, Culture & Society*, 25(7–8), 1–30.

Gill, R., & Scharff, C. (2011). Introduction. In R. Gill & C. Scharff (Eds.), *New femininities: Postfeminism, neoliberalism and subjectivity* (pp. 1–17). Basingstoke: Palgrave Macmillan.

Hesmondhalgh, D., & Baker, S. (2011). *Creative labour: Media work in three cultural industries*. London: Routledge.

Kennedy, H. (2012). *Net work: Ethics and values in web design*. Basingstoke: Palgrave Macmillan.

Lemke, T. (2001). 'The birth of bio-politics': Michel Foucault's lecture at the Collège de France on neo-liberal governmentality. *Economy and Society*, 30(2), 190–207.

McRobbie, A. (2009). *The aftermath of feminism: Gender, culture and social change*. London: Sage.

McRobbie, A. (2015). *Be creative: Making a living in the new culture industries*. Cambridge: Polity.

Moore, H. (2013). Subjectivity. In M. Evans & C. L. Williams (Eds.), *Gender: The key concepts* (pp. 203–208). London: Routledge.

Musicians' Union (2012). *The working musician.* London: Musicians' Union. Accessed 1 December 2016. Available at: www.musiciansunion.org.uk/Files/Reports/Industry/The-Working-Musician-report

Ringrose, J., & Walkerdine, V. (2008). Regulating the abject: The TV make-over as site of neo-liberal reinvention toward bourgeois femininity. *Feminist Media Studies, 8*(3), 227–246.

Rose, N. (1992). Governing the enterprising self. In P. Heelas & P. Morris (Eds.), *The values of the enterprise culture: The moral debate.* London: Routledge.

Ross, A. (2008). The new geography of work: Power to the precarious? *Theory, Culture & Society, 25*(7–8), 31–49.

Schulz, G. (2013). Bestandsaufnahme zum Arbeitsmarkt Kultur. In G. Schulz, O. Zimmermann, & R. Hufnagel (Eds.), *Arbeitsmarkt Kultur: Zur wirtschaftlichen und sozialen Lage in Kulturberufen* (pp. 27–201). Berlin: Deutscher Kulturrat.

Taylor, S., & Littleton, K. (2012). *Contemporary identities of creativity and creative work.* Farnham: Ashgate.

Warhurst, C., Nickson, D., Witz, A., & Cullen, A. M. (2000). Aesthetic labour in interactive service work: Some case study evidence from the "new" Glasgow. *Service Industries Journal, 20*(3), 1–18.

Williams, R. (1977). *Marxism and literature.* Oxford: Oxford University Press.

Wreyford, N. (2015). *The gendered contexts of screenwriting work: Socialized recruitment and judgments of taste and talent in the UK film industry.* Unpublished PhD thesis, King's College London.

Chapter 1

Setting the stage

The cultural and creative industries, entrepreneurialism, and the classical music profession

This chapter contextualises the analysis presented in this book by introducing wider debates and existing research on the cultural and creative industries, cultural work, entrepreneurialism, and the classical music profession in Germany and the United Kingdom. It begins with a critical discussion of the rise of the 'creative industries' concept (Hesmondhalgh et al., 2015) and subsequently demonstrates why I embed my analysis of the classical music profession in wider research on the cultural and creative industries and cultural work (e.g. Banks, 2007; Banks et al., 2013; Conor et al., 2015; Conor, 2014; Gill, 2002; 2014; Gill and Pratt, 2008; Hesmondhalgh and Baker, 2011; McRobbie, 1998; 2002; 2015; Ross, 2003: 2; 2008; Taylor and Littleton, 2012; Wreyford, 2015). This body of work has highlighted various features of work in the cultural and creative industries, which are pertinent to my inquiry, ranging from the prevalence of inequalities and entrepreneurialism to the joys and pleasures associated with cultural work.

The second section of the chapter homes in on the notion of entrepreneurialism by introducing Foucauldian perspectives (e.g. Brown, 2003; 2015; Burchell, 1993; du Gay, 1996; Foucault, 2008; Gordon, 1987; Lemke, 2001). These approaches to entrepreneurialism have argued that the enterprise form is extended to all forms of conduct, inciting individuals to become autonomous, and to demonstrate self-initiative and self-improvement. Due to the cultural sector's emphasis on autonomy, self-application, and competition, cultural workers seem to be paradigms of entrepreneurial selfhood (McRobbie, 2002; 2015; Gill and Pratt, 2008; Ross, 2008). Crucially, 'young women' have been positioned in similar ways in media, public, and policy discourses (e.g. Baker, 2008; Gill and Scharff, 2011; Gonick, 2006; McRobbie, 2009; Ringrose and Walkerdine, 2008). By revisiting these debates on entrepreneurialism, cultural work, and young femininities, the second section introduces the theoretical framework that underpins this book's focus on early career, female, and classically trained musicians. As cultural workers and young women, my research participants were twice positioned as entrepreneurial.

The third section turns a critical eye on the classical music profession by exploring the working conditions prevalent in the sector. Resonating with wider research on cultural work, the classical music profession can be experienced as intensely fulfilling, especially during moments of 'being in the zone' (Banks, 2014; Jordan et al., 2017), but it is also precarious and characterised by ongoing inequalities and an ethos of entrepreneurialism. Moving away from theoretical and analytical considerations, the fourth and final section of this chapter introduces the research methodology underpinning the study presented in this book. This section provides detailed information on the qualitative in-depth interviews that I conducted, the composition of the sample, as well as my interpretative framework, discourse analysis. As such, the chapter lays the theoretical and methodological groundwork for the ensuing analysis of inequalities, entrepreneurial subjectivity, and precarious work in the classical music profession in London and Berlin.

The cultural and creative industries, cultural work, and inequalities

The cultural and creative industries

In many contemporary Western societies, the 'creative industries' have been hailed as a key growth sector of the economy, source of future employment, driver of urban regeneration, and promoter of inclusivity. Cultural policy conceived and conceptualised under the 'New Labour Government' (1997–2010) in the United Kingdom played a key role in this development. In 1998, the Department for Culture, Media and Sport (DCMS) defined the creative industries as "those industries which have their origin in individual creativity, skill and talent and which have a potential for wealth and job creation through the generation and exploitation of intellectual property" (DCMS, 1998, cited in DCMS, 2001: 5). According to this definition, the creative industries include several subsectors, ranging from advertising and designer fashion, film, video, software, and computer services, to television, radio, music, and the performing arts. The mapping exercise thus brought together a range of sectors under the heading 'creative industries'.

The creative industries concept has been adopted internationally, albeit with local variations (Hesmondhalgh et al., 2015). According to the Creative Economy report 2010, published by UNCTAD,[1] "an increasing number of governments, in developing and developed countries alike, are identifying the creative industries as a priority sector in their national development strategies" (UNCTAD, 2010: xix). In Germany too, the creative industries concept has proven influential and continues to inform cultural policy (German Federal Ministry of Economics and Technology, 2009; Berlin Senate, 2014b). A look at recent statistics supports this positive outlook on the creative industries. In the United Kingdom, the number of jobs in the creative industries increased by 15.8 per cent since 2011 and accounted for one in eight jobs in London in 2014 (DCMS, 2015). In Germany, employment in the cultural and creative industries grew by almost 2 per cent in 2014 (BMWi, 2015; see also Zimmermann and Geißler, 2012). The cultural and creative industries are particularly vibrant in Berlin. Twenty per cent of Berlin businesses are active in the creative industries and, with around 186. 000 people employed in Berlin's creative industries, the sector is a crucial factor in the city's employment market (Berlin Senate, 2014a; see chapter six).

Academic research, and particularly approaches informed by cultural studies and sociology, has however critiqued this positive narrative about the creative industries. Researchers have commented on the shift in terminology away from 'cultural industries' to 'creative industries'. In the United Kingdom, sociologists and progressive policy makers used the term 'cultural industries' from the 1960s onwards, but in the 1990s policy makers began to prefer the formulation 'creative industries' (Hesmondhalgh and Baker, 2011; see also Garnham, 2005). According to David Hesmondhalgh (2008), the term 'creative industries' represents a refusal of the forms of critical analysis associated with the cultural industries approach. Researchers have further pointed to the problematic ways in which the creative industries concept conceives of the relationship between culture and the economy, and highlighted the policy's failure to understand the particular ways in which the cultural industries operate (Hesmondhalgh et al., 2015; see also Eikhof and Warhurst, 2013). Given these and other critiques of the creative industries concept, I refer in this book to the 'cultural and creative industries' to signal a critical distance to overly celebratory policy discourses.[2]

Most crucial to the concerns discussed in this book, the creative industries concept has also been criticised for its lack of attention to working conditions in the cultural sector (e.g. Banks and Hesmondhalgh, 2009; Conor et al., 2015; Hesmondhalgh et al., 2015). In relation to the classical music profession, the failure to consider working conditions is evident in a report on the economic impact of three London conservatoires[3] on the UK and London economies (LSE, 2012). Echoing the cheerful positivity of the creative industries policy discourse, the report draws attention to the conservatoires' economic contributions. And while it does refer to some of the characterising features of musicians' working lives, such as having a portfolio career involving a breadth of activities, the report does not critically discuss the often-precarious nature of work in the classical music sector.

Paying attention to working conditions in the cultural and creative industries, including the classical music profession, is however crucial. First, the promotion of the cultural and creative industries in national and international policy discourses begs the question of what it is like to work in these fields. As David Hesmondhalgh and Sarah Baker (2011), among others, have pointed out, positive representations of work in the cultural and creative industries abound, which portray it as particularly desirable and offering greater fulfilment than other kinds of work. Second, and as I discuss in detail in chapters two and three, work in the cultural and creative industries is characterised by a range of inequalities. Contrary to common portrayals of the cultural and creative industries as meritocratic, work in these fields is not open to all (e.g. Allen et al., 2013; Banks et al., 2013; Conor, 2014; Conor et al., 2015; Gill, 2002; 2014; Oakley, 2013; Oakley and O'Brien, 2016; Taylor and Littleton, 2012; Warwick Commission, 2015; Wreyford, 2015).

Third, recent research, particularly in the social sciences, has positioned cultural workers as "role model subjects of contemporary capitalism" (de Peuter, 2014: 264; see also the introduction). According to this body of work, artists and 'creatives' embody the "new form of constantly labouring subjectivity required for contemporary capitalism, in which the requirements for people fully to embrace risk, entrepreneurialism and to adopt a 'sacrificial ethos' are often linked to an artistic or creative vocation" (Banks et al., 2013: 3). Indeed, as Angela McRobbie (2015: 11) has argued, the imperative to 'be creative' does some of the work of labour reform where cultural work provides a "future template for being middle class and learning to live without welfare protection and social security". Research on work in the cultural and creative industries thus provides an important critical challenge to celebratory policy discourses, especially with regards to the representation of these industries as meritocratic, and may advance our understanding of contemporary work conditions more broadly (Hennekam and Bennett, 2016). If cultural workers are at the cutting edge of transformations in work, analyses of their working lives may generate insights that are more widely applicable.

Cultural work

Several years ago, researchers still pointed to a lack of scholarly research, and particularly qualitative studies, on work in the cultural and creative industries (see for example Hesmondhalgh and Baker, 2010). However, the working lives of cultural workers are now firmly on the agenda due to a rich body of literature on cultural work (Banks et al., 2013). To be sure, there continues to be difficulties in defining cultural work and distinguishing it from other kinds of work (Neilson, 2013). Equally important, various terms have been deployed to describe work in the cultural and creative industries. Apart from 'cultural work', Hesmondhalgh and Baker (2011: 9) have coined the alternative and also frequently used term 'creative labour' "to refer to those jobs, centred on the activity of symbol-making, which are to be found in large numbers in the cultural industries". As the title of this book suggests, I use the term 'cultural work'. This is because Banks's (2007) *The Politics of Cultural Work* played a key role in the conception and design of my research. Exploring the politics of cultural work, and looking in particular at the ways in which it is constructed, managed, and performed, his book was a key inspiration for this project on the working lives of classical musicians.

Research on work in the cultural and creative industries (e.g. Banks, 2007; Banks et al., 2013; Conor, 2014; Gill, 2002; 2014; Gill and Pratt, 2008; Hesmondhalgh and Baker, 2011; Kennedy, 2012; McRobbie, 1998; 2002; 2010; 2015; Ross,

2003; 2008; Taylor and Littleton, 2012; Wreyford, 2015) has painted a relatively consistent picture of cultural work, demonstrating its positive and negative components. Resonating with some of the celebratory policy discourses, work in the cultural and creative industries has been described as pleasurable, intensely gratifying, and offering a high degree of autonomy (Banks and Hesmondhalgh, 2009; Gill, 2002; Gill and Pratt, 2008; Hesmondhalgh and Baker, 2011; Kennedy, 2012; Ross, 2003; 2008; Taylor and Littleton, 2012). Andrew Ross (2009) has for example drawn attention to the appeal of self-employment, self-direction, and autonomy, cautioning against understanding the appetite for "free agency as a mere product of market ideology" and arguing instead that it reflects employee demand (2009: 46). In this context, it is worth pointing out that, historically, cultural work has appealed to both sides of the political spectrum. The right saw it as big business and beneficial for capital, and the left hoped it would offer the opportunity for non-alienating employment (Banks and Hesmondhalgh, 2009).

However, and as Ross (2008: 18), among others, has reminded us, "[j]ob gratification, for creatives, has always come at a heavy sacrificial cost." Cultural workers frequently work long hours and the passion for their work involves the risk of self-exploitation "where the love of art can lead workers to neglect the care of the self" (Banks, 2007: 58). Boundaries between work and leisure easily get blurred, especially in contexts where 'network sociality' (Wittel, 2001) is prevalent which is, in part, characterised by the association between work and play. The use of new media technology can further exacerbate the tendency to collapse the boundaries between leisure and work (Gregg, 2011; see chapter five).

Doing the job you love often goes hand in hand with low earnings, project-based and irregular work, short-term contracts, uncertain career prospects, and little job protection (Banks and Hesmondhalgh, 2009; Gill and Pratt, 2008). Employment and income insecurity thus permeate the lifestyle of people working in the cultural and creative industries (see also Blair, 2003; Dex et al., 2000). In short, cultural work is precarious (de Peuter, 2014; Gill and Pratt, 2008; Neilson and Rossiter, 2008; see chapter five). What is more, cultural work "is increasingly *individualized* labour, operating in industries that stress the virtues of self-reliance, unique talent and personalized, performative modes of work (emphasis in original)" (Banks and Hesmondhalgh, 2009: 420; see also McRobbie, 2015). The prevalence of self-employment, small firms, and the lack of work hierarchies adds to the individualised nature of cultural work. Where there is no management but instead an ethos of individual, creative effort, cultural workers may only have themselves to blame for the failures and difficulties they experience at work (Banks, 2007; Gill, 2002; McRobbie, 2002; see chapter four).

Inequalities

The cultural and creative industries are further characterised by a substantial lack of workforce diversity in terms of gender, race, class, age, and disability, to name just a few. Pioneering studies challenged common depictions of cultural work as 'cool, creative and egalitarian' (Gill, 2002), drew attention to the underrepresentation of black and minority ethnic workers (e.g. Oakley, 2006; Thanki and Jefferys, 2007), pointed to ongoing gender imbalances (e.g. Bielby and Bielby, 1996), including women's difficulties of combining cultural work with caring responsibilities (Bain, 2004; Perrons, 2003; Pohlman, 1996), and suggested ways for increasing diversity (e.g. Randle et al., 2007). In the United Kingdom, New Labour's enthusiasm for measurement produced statistics on cultural labour markets (Hesmondhalgh et al., 2015), which, for example, highlighted the underrepresentation of women in the creative media industries (Skillset, 2010). In Germany, a report from 2003 (Leberl and Schulz, 2003) documented gender inequalities in the cultural sector.

The last few years have witnessed an increased media and policy interest in inequalities in the cultural workforce (Oakley and O'Brien, 2016), as well as a flurry of writings, including cultural sector reports (e.g. ACE, 2014; DCMS, 2015; Schulz et al., 2016; Warwick Commission, 2015) and academic research (e.g. Allen et al., 2013; Banks and Oakley, 2015; Conor, 2014; Conor et al., 2015; Gill, 2014; Eikhof and Warhurst, 2013; Grugulis and Stoyanova, 2012; Hesmondhalgh and Saha, 2013; Manske, 2015; McRobbie, 2015; O'Brien et al., 2016; Oakley and O'Brien, 2016; Randle et al., 2015; Taylor and Littleton, 2012; Wreyford, 2015). This body of work has continued to document the complex barriers that female and/or disabled cultural workers, as well as workers from black and minority ethnic and working-class backgrounds face in accessing, but also succeeding in, the cultural and creative industries.

Inequalities in the cultural and creative industries workforce matter for a range of reasons. First, the lack of diversity among cultural workers is a social justice issue and one, as Kate Oakley (2013: 56) has pointed out, that has effects on our self-understanding as a society: "Who gets to make culture, in its widest sense from advertisements to TV news bulletins and situation comedies, matters, because it is how we understand ourselves as a society." Certainly, the links between production, consumption, and representation are complex and need to be researched in more detail (Oakley and O'Brien, 2016). Arguably, however, cultural production is distinctive because it places more emphasis on communicating ideas, knowledge, values, and beliefs and therefore has the potential to influence societies and peoples (Hesmondhalgh and Saha, 2013).

Second, and against commonly shared perceptions (see for example Edley and Wetherell, 2001; chapter three), progress does not happen automatically where inequalities simply decrease over time. As the Warwick Commission (2015: 35) has pointed out, the "diversity of the creative workforce in Britain has progressively contracted over the past five years in relation to gender, ethnicity and disability." Documenting inequalities in the cultural and creative industries therefore represents an important task. Third, the Warwick Commission (2015: 21) has further argued that the lack of diversity in the cultural workforce matters because it is "bad for business, diminishing the breadth and depth of creative perspectives, audiences and consumers".[4]

Fourth, and as previously mentioned, cultural work has been positioned as being at the centre of ongoing transformations in work. If inequalities are pronounced in the cultural and creative industries, then we have to document and analyse their persistence as such an understanding will have implications for other fields of work. According to Christine Williams (2013), we need new concepts to understand inequalities in work contexts that are no longer characterised by job-security, full-time schedules, and the availability of career ladders. Research on the lack of diversity in the cultural workforce can help us develop a more refined understanding of exclusionary processes in informal work settings. For instance, my analysis of self-promotion (see chapter two) demonstrates that women encounter gender-specific challenges when promoting their work. Arguably, these and similar dynamics do not only apply to the classical music profession, but may also be relevant in other sectors of the economy.

Entrepreneurialism: cultural workers and young women as ideal entrepreneurial subjects

Cultural work is characterised by an entrepreneurial ethos. Entrepreneurialism, in this context, is understood in Foucauldian terms[5] and refers to a process where the "schema of *enterprise* is presented as a model not only for the conduct of economic activity, but for the totality of human action (emphasis in original)" (Gordon, 1987: 314; see also Brown, 2003; 2015; Burchell, 1993; du Gay, 1996; McNay, 2009). Enterprise discourses call on individuals to become an "active entrepreneur of the self" (Davies and Bansel, 2007: 252) and to structure their lives like an enterprise with endless potential for optimisation.

This Foucauldian approach regards entrepreneurialism as closely intertwined with neoliberalism. According to Michel Foucault (2008: 226), "in neo-liberalism – and it does not hide this; it proclaims it – there is also a theory of *homo oeconomicus*, but he is not at all a partner of exchange. *Homo oeconomicus* is an entrepreneur, an entrepreneur of himself (emphasis in original)." As I outline in chapter four, neoliberalism is a frequently used and yet also a deeply contested concept. I draw on Foucauldian approaches to neoliberalism, which regard it as a "mentality of government" (Rose, 1992: 145) that calls upon individuals to manage their lives self-responsibly and use their entrepreneurial skills to produce the best outcomes for themselves (Davies and Bansel, 2007). According to this perspective, the neoliberal self is an entrepreneurial subject (Brown, 2003; Foucault, 2008; Lemke, 2001; Rose, 1992), which is encouraged to become autonomous, creative, demonstrate self-initiative, self-improvement, and self-belief (Bröckling, 2005; 2007). Foucauldian approaches to neoliberalism focus on the constitution of subjectivity and therefore resonate with the wider focus of this book.

In relation to work in the cultural and creative industries, McRobbie (2002: 516) argued many years ago that "[c]reative work increasingly follows the neo-liberal model, [and is] governed by the values of entrepreneurialism" (see also McRobbie, 2015). As Mark Banks (2007: 64) has pointed out, both policy discourses and the situated practices of cultural work exhibit the values of entrepreneurialism: "techniques of governmentality have been doubly evidenced, first, in the construction of cultural policy (and other supporting) enterprise discourses and second, in the situated practice of constructing the entrepreneurial, creative self." Indeed, and as Rosalind Gill and Andy Pratt (2008: 2) have argued, "[a]rtists, (new) media workers and other cultural labourers are hailed as 'model entrepreneurs' by industry and government figures." They are "paradigms of entrepreneurial selfhood" (Ross, 2008: 32) due to the emphasis on autonomy, self-realisation, self-application, and competition in the context of creative fulfilment (see also Entwistle and Wissinger, 2006; Neff et al., 2005; Ursell, 2000). There is thus a link between cultural work, cultural policy discourse, and neoliberalism that becomes visible through the discourse of entrepreneurialism.

While it has been demonstrated that cultural work is characterised by entrepreneurialism, there appears to be little empirical research, which explores how cultural workers negotiate entrepreneurial discourses (but see Storey et al., 2005, discussed below). The empirical work that does exist tends to focus on other spheres of work, such as education (Alexiadou, 2001; Davies and Bansel, 2007; Usher and Garrick, 2000; Peters, 2001), management (Gray, 2003; Prichard, 2002), health (Doolin, 2002; Halford and Leonard, 2006), self-employed women (Fenwick, 2002), and retailing (du Gay, 1996). Many of these studies demonstrate that entrepreneurialism is not a unitary discourse and can be resisted in different ways (Fenwick, 2002). While some workers may adopt the enterprise discourse enthusiastically, others may subvert it or quietly re-construct practices that fit traditional models of professional practice (Alexiadou, 2001). Most importantly, individuals draw on a range of discourses in constructing, and negotiating, their work identities (Doolin, 2002; Halford and Leonard, 2006; Fenwick, 2002). As I demonstrate in chapter four, which explores the ways in which the research participants registered, negotiated, and lived out entrepreneurial subjectivity, workers can subvert entrepreneurial models by taking recourse to discourses of disinterested, autonomous art, or a sense of community (Coulson, 2012; Taylor and Littleton, 2008).

While the image of the 'autonomous artist' can provide an alternative discourse, it can also facilitate self-abjection and feelings of failure (Banks, 2007). If the "self-resourcing 'creative' is widely promoted as the standard and necessary mode of being" (Banks, 2007: 43), cultural workers may too readily blame themselves for failure and accept responsibility for circumstances not of their making. As John Storey et al.'s (2005) research has shown, freelancers in the new media industry experienced their work as intensely personal, which meant that experiences of success and failure were closely linked to personal identity and esteem. And because such forms of self-directed, autonomous, and independent work can feel intensely gratifying, power and 'discipline' become less visible (Usher and Garrick, 2000).

These findings, and reflections on the ways in which workers respond to entrepreneurialism, indicate the need for more research on subjective experiences of entrepreneurialism. Apart from the empirical studies discussed here, psychoanalytic research (Layton, 2009; 2010; 2013a; b; Saleci, 2010), social theorists and scientists (Berardi, 2009; Bröckling, 2007; Dardot and Laval, 2013; Ehrenberg, 2010; Hall and O'Shea, 2013; Swan, 2008; Sennett, 1998), and Foucauldian thinkers (Binkley, 2009; 2011a; b; Davies, 2005; McNay, 2009) have engaged with the ways in which entrepreneurial subjectivity is lived out. As I show in chapter four, these perspectives have provided a range of important insights. However, most of this work is theoretical in perspective, rests on textual readings, and does not explicitly focus on cultural workers' experiences. By exploring the contours of entrepreneurial subjectivity in chapter four, I provide systematic, empirical research on the ways in which entrepreneurial subjectivities are negotiated in the context of cultural work, looking in particular at the ways in which entrepreneurialism is lived out on a subjective level.

Interestingly, the features of entrepreneurialism, such as the emphasis on self-improvement, responsibility, and flexibility, have not only been discussed in relation to cultural work, but have also been the focus of feminist debates about young women in contemporary Western societies. In parallel to cultural workers' positioning as model entrepreneurs, feminist research has demonstrated that media, public, and policy discourses have portrayed young women as ideal, entrepreneurial subjects (Baker, 2008; Gill and Scharff, 2011; Gonick, 2006; McRobbie, 2009; Ringrose and Walkerdine, 2008). As McRobbie (2009: 15) has shown, young women have become "privileged subjects of social change" and are depicted as benefitting from late modern conditions by, for example, being able to work and control reproduction (Baker, 2008; Kagerbauer, 2010; Nayak and Kehily, 2008). Indeed, young women are presented as capably maximising the opportunities now offered to them and hailed as 'top girls' (McRobbie, 2007) and 'can-do girls' (Harris, 2004). By positioning young women as entrepreneurial subjects, this body of work departs from perspectives that have highlighted the links between masculinity and entrepreneurialism (see for example, Bruni et al., 2004; Lewis, 2014).

Indeed, in her recent book *Be Creative: Making a living in the new cultural industries*, McRobbie (2015) draws attention to the links between young women, cultural work, and entrepreneurialism. She (2015: 11) argues that the imperative to be creative constitutes a form of governmentality that incites young people, and "especially young women", to pursue self-entrepreneurship in the context of work in the cultural and creative industries. McRobbie (2015: 90) sees this as a distinctly gendered process where young women are "lifted out of the entanglements of race, ethnicity and class, and addressed simply as a population of women". Importantly, McRobbie does not suggest that race, ethnicity, and class no longer affect the working lives of young, female cultural workers. In relation to class, for example, she (2015: 94–95) argues that the coming forward of young women into the cultural and creative industries constitutes a process where "class is displaced and relegated to a twilight zone" to produce an aspirational, female workforce and expanded middle-class that can, however, no longer fall back on historic forms of protection and security. According to McRobbie,

> [n]eoliberalism succeeds in its mission in this respect if a now very swollen youthful middle class bypasses mainstream employment with its trade unions and its tranches of welfare and protection in favour of the challenge and excitement of being a creative entrepreneur.
>
> (2015: 11)

As such, McRobbie's analysis highlights the links between cultural work, young women, entrepreneurialism, and neoliberalism.[6]

Accordingly, the hopeful positioning of young women as subjects of capacity has to be located in the broader, neoliberal context that incites individuals to work on, and improve, the self. This incitement to self-transform is gendered and associated with femininity:

> If we think about what is and has been demanded of women, who have always had to be desirable, presentable, consumable, we can think about what is happening under neo-liberalism as an intensification of feminine as site (both subject and object) of commodification and consumption.
>
> (Ringrose and Walkerdine, 2008: 230)

As Bronwyn Davies (2005) has reminded us, the neoliberal self is defined by its capacity to consume, which further privileges the feminine through the long-standing association between women and consumption (see also Nayak and Kehily, 2008). Indeed, it is mainly women who are called on to work on and transform the self, which becomes particularly visible with regard to the management of the body and appearance (see for example Elias et al., 2017; Gill and Scharff, 2011; Tyler, 2011). Thus, and paralleling my discussion of the links between cultural work, entrepreneurialism, and neoliberalism, I place the links between femininity, youth, and entrepreneurialism in a wider, neoliberal context.

By focusing on young, female cultural workers, I take gender as my epistemological starting point. I also discuss issues of race and class, especially in chapter two which documents inequalities in the classical music profession. Chapter three, which looks at the ways in which classical musicians make sense of ongoing hierarchies and exclusions, also explores how class and racial inequalities, in addition to gender imbalances, are negotiated by the research participants. Nevertheless, this study's focus is on the gendered aspects of cultural work and work in the classical music profession more specifically. This is not to relegate issues of race and class or to reject an intersectional framework (Brah and Phoenix, 2004; Crenshaw, 1991; see chapter three). Instead, it is to be clear about the limitations of my research. In this context, it is also crucial to point out that my analysis of inequalities is limited to what Dave O'Brien and Kate Oakley (2015) have recently called the " 'big three' issues of inequality – race, class and gender". However, inequalities in cultural work, and beyond, also pertain to other axes of differentiation, such as age or disability. The Arts Council England (ACE, 2014) has drawn attention to the predominantly young composition of the cultural sector workforce. And in relation to disability, the Warwick Commission (2015) has highlighted that cultural workers who are classified as disabled under the Disability Discrimination act definition remain underrepresented (see also ACE, 2014). My exploration of the interplay between gender, subjectivity, and cultural work in the classical music profession should thus be regarded as presenting a starting point for future analyses of inequalities in the cultural and creative industries.

The classical music profession

There have been various studies of the classical music world, including research on higher education (Kingsbury, 1988; Nettle, 1995); the technical and social conventions of classical music (Small, 1977); the Institute for Research and Coordination in Acoustics/Music, Paris (Born, 1995); local music making (Finnegan, 1989); female musicians in the nineteenth and early-twentieth centuries (Macleod, 2001); as well as music, gender, and education (Green, 1997). More recent years have seen critical research on different aspects of the classical music sector, including studies of nineteenth century institutions in London (Johnson-Williams, 2014; 2015); international competitions (McCormick, 2009; 2015); higher education (Born and Devine, 2015; Perkins, 2013), race and classical music practice (Kok, 2006; Leppänen, 2014; Wang, 2009; Yang, 2007; Yoshihara, 2007); classical musicians' professional lives (Armstrong, 2013; Bennett, 2008; Bork, 2010; Cottrell, 2004; Gembris and Langner, 2005); classical music education (Baker, 2014; Bennett, 2016; Bull, 2015a; 2015b; 2016; Rimmer, 2014; Wagner, 2015); ethnomusicological approaches to classical music (Nooshin, 2011; 2014); performance practice (Leech-Wilkinson, 2016; Wilson, 2013); the world of opera (Atkinson, 2006); and orchestral culture (Bartleet, 2008; Beckles Willson, 2009a; b; Carpos, 2014; 2016; Osborne and Conant, 2010; Paternoga, 2005; 2006). These studies have provided a range of perspectives that have informed my research. Indeed, they generated a wealth of findings that I draw on throughout my analysis.

Gender, Subjectivity, and Cultural Work adds to this body of literature by embedding my analysis in wider research on cultural work. As I have shown in the introduction, this field has covered a range of sectors. However, the classical music profession has not yet been explored from a critical, cultural work perspective. I address this gap by applying the tools from research on cultural work to my analysis of the classical music profession. My study further contributes to existing research on the classical music sector by analysing the experiences of female, classically trained musicians, who have been under-researched so far. Finally, I add to our knowledge of the classical music industry by documenting ongoing inequalities, both through qualitative and quantitative analysis.

Existing research on the classical music profession in Britain (Cottrell, 2004), the United States (Yoshihara, 2007), Germany and Austria (Bork, 2010; Gembris and Langner, 2005), Australia, and internationally (Bennett, 2008) has painted a relatively consistent picture of the working lives of classical musicians, which resonates with wider trends in cultural work. Most are wholly or partly self-employed (Bennett, 2007; Bennett, 2008; Musicians' Union, 2012). Indeed, it is very common for classical musicians to hold multiple jobs, ranging from teaching to performing (Bennett, 2007; Gembris and Langner, 2005; HEFCE, 2002; Musicians' Union, 2012). The scarcity of full-time and permanent employment makes it a necessity to pursue several lines of work (Bossen, 2012), often outside the music industry (Bennett, 2007). Many musicians have portfolio careers, which are marked by low incomes, uncertainty, and lack of workplace benefits such as pensions (Bossen, 2012; Musicians' Union, 2012; Schulz, 2013; see chapter five).

One possible way of gaining economic stability in the classical music profession is to obtain a job in an orchestra.[7] However, few orchestras in the United Kingdom offer full-time, permanent employment. Orchestras tend to operate on a freelance basis, which means that players who are appointed as members are generally guaranteed first refusal of all work, subject to certain conditions (Cottrell, 2004; Gembris and Langner, 2005). Germany, by contrast, has a comparatively large number of orchestras and opera houses that offer permanent employment. Currently, there are 111 publicly funded orchestras, eight chamber orchestras, and 11 radio orchestras offering around 9,816 posts (DOV, 2016). This compares to 61 orchestras listed as full members of the Association of British Orchestras in 2014 (ABO, 2014).[8] However, many orchestras in Germany have been closed since the early 1990s, down from 168 (Mertens, 2012 [2005]). At the same time, numbers of music graduates have risen steadily, creating a labour market where permanent employment is the exception (Gembris and Langner, 2005; Mertens, 2012 [2005]).

A further way of gaining economic stability for classical musicians is to become a member of the faculty at a university or conservatoire (Yoshihara, 2007). However, work in academia is increasingly precarious as well (Ross, 2009). In Germany, workers on fixed-term contracts carry out almost half of the teaching in higher education in music (HfMDK, 2011). In the United Kingdom, "[w]hen the use of atypical academic staff is factored in, 54% of all academic staff and 49% of all academic teaching staff are on insecure contracts" (UCU, 2016: 1). Paralleling trends in cultural work more generally, work in the classical music profession is precarious (see chapter five).

Similar to other cultural workers, many classical musicians derive great pleasure from their work (Cottrell, 2004), placing passion at the core of their personal attributes (Bennett, 2008). As I demonstrate in chapter five, the research participants found their work intensely gratifying, especially in moments of 'being in the zone' (Banks, 2014; Jordan et al., 2017). According to Banks (2014: 241), being in the zone "describes the ideal fusion of the intensively productive mind and the labouring body". These moments of intense absorption and pleasure, however, also mean that musicians tend to find it difficult to separate themselves from their work (Bork, 2010). Frequently, the boundaries between leisure and work become blurred and, as I further demonstrate in chapter five, many musicians seem to pursue their work with a sense of constantly having to prove themselves. Indeed, the sense that 'you are only as good as your last job' is widespread in the classical music sector (Cottrell, 2004), mirroring trends in other cultural industries (Blair, 2001). Resonating with Andreas Wittel's (2001) reflections on network sociality and the reliance on informal networks to obtain work in the cultural and creative industries (Conor et al., 2015; Eikhof and Warhurst, 2013; see chapter two), musicians must also have strong networks in order to secure future gigs (Cottrell, 2004).

The term 'musician' is frequently understood in narrow terms as only referring to a performer, creating a hierarchy where performing is situated at the top and other frequently pursued activities, such as teaching, located at the bottom (Bennett, 2008; HEFCE, 2002; Mills, 2005; see chapter two). This view can cause a disjuncture between musicians' ambitions and the fact that performing often only constitutes a small component of their work. According to Dawn Bennett (2008), the gap between musicians' aspirations and the realities of working life may lead to feelings of anxiety, a sense of failure, and attrition. Typically, careers in classic music are intense but short and factors contributing to musicians leaving the profession include "family commitments, low and irregular salary, sporadic work, unsociable hours, prolonged periods of travel, managing multiple employments, and injury" (Bennett, 2008: 45). Many musicians experience health problems from the high physical and psychological demands of their profession (Alford and Szanto, 1996; Gembris and Heye, 2012; Help Musicians UK, 2014; Zaza et al., 1998; see chapter four). There is a higher rate of injury among musicians than athletes (Bennett, 2008; see also Bork, 2010; Paternoga, 2006); substance abuse (Lander, 2014; Tindall, 2005) and mental illness (Yoshihara, 2007) are also common. These negative components of work in classical music are exacerbated by the fact that many classically trained musicians start at an early age (sometimes at age 3; Bork, 2010; Wagner, 2015) and devote a considerable amount of time, effort, and money (Yoshihara, 2007) to their training.

Having trained in classical music for many years, passed an audition to get into a conservatoire, and finished a degree, music graduates "enter ill-defined, complex labour markets with rapidly transforming employment contexts" (Bennett, 2016: 386). Studies suggest that music graduates are aware of the difficulties associated with a career in music (Comunian et al., 2014). However, they still struggle with the transition into work because they feel unprepared (Bennett, 2007; 2008; Bork, 2010; Gembris and Langner, 2005), lacking, for example, small business skills (Bennett, 2016). In response to this, there have been calls to change the learning cultures at conservatoires (e.g. Perkins, 2013) and to broaden the curriculum to include entrepreneurial skills (Bennett, 2007; 2008; 2016; Gembris and Langner, 2005; Myles Beeching, 2010). Many universities and conservatoires have picked up on this trend and now offer training in relevant areas (Bennett, 2007; 2016),

including the institutions in London and Berlin that most of my research participants had attended.

While the teaching of business skills responds to students' needs and provides
useful training, it does not address the underlying problem of a shrinking job
market and simultaneously increasing numbers of graduates. Against this backdrop, the shift towards entrepreneurialism in classical music education could be
seen as part of the infiltration of neoliberalism into various domains of activity
(Brown, 2015), and as a form of governmentality that calls on musicians to cul-
tivate an entrepreneurial attitude to navigate precarious work. In her self-help
book on how to create a successful career in music, Angela Myles Beeching
(2010), an arts career specialist, warns against a passive approach to one's career
and instead tells musicians that they are in charge of their future. Reiterating
entrepreneurial discourse, Myles Beeching (2010: 11) encourages musicians to
"[t]hink like an entrepreneur"; "[y]ou are the architect of your future. Through
your attitude and actions, you can determine your luck and success (emphasis in
original)" (2). Resonating with wider trends in the cultural and creative industries
and beyond, musicians are incited to adopt an entrepreneurial attitude – both in
the conventional and Foucauldian sense – in order to navigate their careers. As
I demonstrate in chapters four and five, this entrepreneurial outlook also came
to the fore in the research participants' accounts. For instance, they responded to
precarious work by emphasising their flexibility, ability to plan financially, and
willingness to take risks.

The quest to be entrepreneurial, and the associated belief in self-application,
hard work, and individual merit, is pronounced, even though the field of classical music is marked by inequalities along the lines of gender, race, and class.
Indeed, identities – in relation to gender, race, and class – intersect with music
on various levels. Music is "socially mediated" (Born, 2012: 263) and can construct new identities or reflect existing ones (Born and Hesmondhalgh, 2000). As
Mari Yoshihara (2007: 7) has shown in her study of Asian[9] and Asian Americans
who pursue classical music in the United States, "classical music is the medium
through which they experience the social meanings of their racial, gender, sexual,
or class identities". While this body of work (in relation to gender, see also Maus,
2012; McClary, 1991; Solie, 1993) points to the complex interplay between social
identities and music, my book has a more narrow focus and explores gender, race,
and class primarily in the context of work in the classical music industry.

As I demonstrate in chapter two, the classical music profession is characterised
by a range of gender, racial, and class inequalities, such as underrepresentation as
well as horizontal and vertical segregation. Critically, inequalities in the classical
music sector are not limited to these issues. In the context of gender, they also
relate to a pay gap and the particular challenges that female musicians encounter
when negotiating a range of contradictory expectations around femininity, sexuality, and appearance (e.g. Bartleet, 2008; Green, 1997; McCormick, 2009; 2015),
which also intersect with race (Yoshihara, 2007) and class (Bull, 2015a). As such,
and as I argue in the subsequent chapter, the subjectivities required to work and

succeed in the classical music profession are gendered, classed, and racialised. The constantly available and fully committed musician does not seem to have any caring responsibilities and is therefore a gendered figure. Similarly, attributions of musicality in classical music, which are key to succeed in the profession, seem to be racialised and associated with whiteness (Leppänen, 2014; Wang, 2009; Yang, 2007). Equally important, the actively networking and well-connected musician appears to be from a middle-class background (see also Scharff, 2017). These persisting, complex, and intersecting inequalities do not mean that it is impossible for female musicians or musicians from a black and minority ethnic background and/or working-class background to take part and succeed in the profession. An analysis of wider patterns does not amount to a deterministic argument. Against the backdrop of celebratory discourses about cultural work, the silencing of inequalities in the cultural and creative industries (Gill, 2014; see chapter three), as well as the relative lack of data about inequalities in the classical music sector, I however argue that it is crucial to document existing patterns and to explain their persistence.

A further parallel between the classical music sector and the cultural and creative industries is that they are strongly, although not exclusively, centred in urban areas (Pratt, 2009). By exploring the experiences of female, classical musicians working in Berlin and London, this study focuses on two cities that are characterised by a vibrant cultural and classical music sector, but that also have quite distinctive material conditions (Forkert, 2013; McRobbie, 2015; McRobbie et al., 2016). As chapter six explores in detail, cultural work is experienced differently in these specific urban settings, marked by a sense of hardship, insecurity, inescapability, and excitement in London, and feelings of affordability, but also insecurity, in Berlin.

While the research participants' experiences of pursuing cultural work in particular urban contexts differed, their accounts were remarkably similar in relation to the other issues addressed in this book. National differences did not strongly come to the fore in the research participants' negotiations of inequalities, entrepreneurial subjectivity, and precarious work. This is not to diminish the importance of spatial context. Indeed, chapter two documents that inequalities manifest themselves differently in the classical music profession in Germany and the United Kingdom and issues around precarious work are not the same in both countries (O'Reilly et al., 2009; Weinkopf, 2009). By foregrounding common themes in my analysis of the research participants' negotiations of inequalities (see chapter three), entrepreneurial subjectivity (see chapter four), and precarious work (see chapter five), but also drawing attention to national specificities (see chapter two and chapter six), I highlight both differences *and* similarities in processes of subjective meaning making and the ways in which they intersect with national contexts. Intriguingly, other studies on the negotiation of inequalities (e.g. Erel, 2009; Scharff, 2012) or precarious work (Hennekam and Bennett, 2017) in various Western contexts have suggested the presence of similar themes across multiple locations. In relation to the specific, subjective dynamics investigated in this book, national differences came to the fore most strongly in the research participants' discussion about their working lives in London and Berlin. By contrast, I found that they negotiated inequalities, entrepreneurial subjectivity, and precarious work in similar ways.

Researching gender, subjectivity, and work in the classical music profession

In this final section, I outline the methodology underpinning this study to further contextualise the accounts of the research participants and the findings presented in this book. After having obtained ethical approval, I conducted 64 in-depth interviews with early career, female, classically trained musicians in London (n = 32) and Berlin (n = 32). Given my focus on the interplay between subjectivity and cultural work, the use of qualitative interviews was most suitable. Interviews provide insight into subjective experiences and meanings (Rubin and Rubin, 1995); they enabled me to learn about the research participants' thoughts and feelings, and the ways in which they experienced and interpreted work in the classical music profession. The interviews that I conducted were semi-structured. Asking different interviewees the same questions offered an important point for comparison. Each interview began with inquiries about the research participant's training and education, and then covered a range of issues, relating to the ups and downs of the profession, views on inequalities, entrepreneurialism, and precarious work, as well as what it is like to work in London or Berlin. On the whole, the interviews addressed practical concerns, such as the research participants' ways of making a living, but also covered the emotional aspects of doing cultural work.

My sample consisted of musicians who played a range of instruments (string, woodwind, brass, piano, organ, percussion), as well as singers, conductors, opera directors, and composers. Participants were invited to provide me with demographic information – such as age, class, racial and ethnic background, and nationality – during our conversation. Reflecting the underrepresentation of working-class and black and minority ethnic players in the classical music profession, 44 musicians in my sample identified as middle-class, seven as working-class, and two as lower middle-class. 11 were not sure how to describe their socio-economic background, which resonates with broader arguments that popular awareness of class seems to wane (Bennett et al., 2009). 56 described their racial background as white, four as mixed-raced, two as East Asian, one as black and one as Asian. Also resonating with wider trends in the industry, the sample was international with participants from former West and East Germany, Britain, the Netherlands, Finland, Turkey, Poland, Serbia, Lithuania, Spain, Ireland, Italy, Singapore, Japan, Australia, New Zealand, and the United States. At the time of interview, all participants were based in either London or Berlin. In line with the features of cultural work discussed above, the majority were self-employed and held multiple jobs. Their work was overwhelmingly precarious and only a handful had permanent positions in orchestras or at teaching institutions.

Most research participants were in their late twenties/early thirties at the time of interview in 2012 and 2013. As such, they were at a relatively early stage in their career. Some were still students or had recently returned to higher education, but most had graduated within the last five years. My focus was on early career musicians for two reasons: first, and due to my interest in entrepreneurial subjectivity, I wanted to speak to musicians who would fall into the category of 'young women' and who would thus be twice positioned as entrepreneurial (as young women and as cultural workers). Second, the transition from higher education into work is an important stage for musicians (Cottrell, 2004; Gembris and Langner, 2005). During this phase, musicians evolve from being students/ amateurs to being professionals. This transition is often key for their future musical development as well as the shaping of their artistic identity and career path (Gembris and Langner, 2005).

I recruited research participants by using personal and professional contacts and subsequent snowballing. Each interviewee was given an information sheet, which included details about my project, but also covered important ethical issues such as the right to withdraw, confidentiality, anonymity, and the use of pseudonyms. Prior to each interview, I discussed these issues with the research participants and obtained their informed consent. On average, interviews lasted an hour and fifteen minutes. They were conducted in English or German, recorded, and subsequently transcribed in their original language. All translations are mine and I analysed the data by using NVivo software for initial coding and discourse analysis.

There are many different types of discourse analysis (Wetherell, 2003). I use an approach informed by Jonathan Potter and Margaret Wetherell's early writings (Potter and Wetherell, 1987), critical discursive psychology (e.g. Edley, 2001; Edley and Wetherell, 2001; Wetherell, 1998; 2003; 2005), and more recent modifications of this work (Taylor and Littleton, 2006; 2008; 2012). According to Rom Harré and Grant Gillett (1994: 32), discursive psychology is concerned with "language in use as the accomplishment of acts or as attempts at their accomplishment". It seeks to demonstrate how social order is produced through discursive interaction. Consequently, social and particularly psychological phenomena – such as the ways in which the research participants lived out entrepreneurial subjectivity – are interpreted as features of discourse. Discourse is regarded as constructing both social *and* psychological processes. Rather than positing an internal psychic reality, discursive psychologists argue that psychology should study "outward activity" (Cameron and Kulick, 2003: 119). Discursive psychology thus offers useful analytical tools for this study's focus on musicians' subjective experiences and the ways these intersect with the wider social context (for use of discursive psychology in the field of music see also Wilson and MacDonald, 2005).

In using this approach, I analysed the interviews looking for patterns found in the data relating, for example, to the ways in which the research participants talked about and negotiated precarious work (see chapter five) or inequalities (see chapter three). In each chapter, I illustrate these patterns by providing short extracts from the larger dataset. As Stephanie Taylor and Karen Littleton (2012: 44–45) have emphasised,

> although any example of talk is from an individual speaker, a woman, a man, a certain age and so on, they are not approached as 'types'. For this reason, speakers are labelled minimally in the data extracts which are presented [. . .] The extracts from their interviews are illustrative examples of features of the talk of many speakers, although, of course, their circumstances were specific to themselves in the detail.

Following this approach, I refrain from providing demographic information about each participant when I discuss individual statements, unless it is absolutely necessary to make sense of their claims. More generally, this approach has enabled me to preserve the anonymity of the research participants. Given the lack of women in various roles in the profession (see chapter two), it would be easy to identify a female, Italian bassoonist who plays for a prestigious London orchestra. This entirely fictitious example demonstrates why I only provide the demographic information that is absolutely necessary to make sense of particular statements. While I am aware that this decision on data presentation risks decontextualising the participants' accounts, it does ensure their anonymity is protected.

Conclusion

By introducing a wide range of literature on the cultural and creative industries, cultural work, entrepreneurialism, young femininities, and the classical music sector, this chapter has outlined the theoretical and analytical context of my study. More specifically, my discussion focused on the working conditions characterising the cultural and creative industries and has foregrounded the pleasurable and precarious nature of cultural work, as well as persisting inequalities and an ethos of entrepreneurialism. As I have shown, my understanding of entrepreneurialism is embedded in a Foucauldian framework and is informed by research on cultural work and young femininities. These bodies of work have demonstrated that cultural workers and young women have been positioned as entrepreneurial subjects. My empirical analysis focuses on early career, female classical musicians in order to grasp the experiences of individuals who may be entrepreneurial subjects par excellence.

The third section of this chapter homed in on the classical music sector and outlined my study's contributions to existing research in the field. By embedding my analysis in wider research on cultural work, I approach the classical music profession from a different angle than previous studies. In addition, my focus on female musicians and particularly my analysis of inequalities and entrepreneurial subjectivity add new dimensions to existing research on the classical music industry. Indeed, and as I outline in the subsequent chapter, there has been a dearth of research on inequalities in the classical music profession. By documenting existing hierarchies and exclusions, especially in relation to gender, race, and class, the subsequent chapter addresses this gap. However, it does not only map ongoing inequalities, but also presents existing and original insights to make sense of their persistence. Building on groundbreaking research (e.g. Allen et al., 2013; Conor, 2014; Conor et al., 2015; Gill, 2002; 2014; Taylor and Littleton, 2012; Wreyford, 2015), I argue that constructions of ideal worker subjectivities play a role in maintaining and fostering complex and intersecting inequalities. The self-promoting cultural worker, for example, seems to be a gendered figure, raising particular dilemmas for female musicians.

Notes

1 United Nations Conference on Trade and Development.
2 However, I use alternative terms, such as 'creative industries' when citing or referring to sources that use such terminology.
3 Conservatoires offer education and training in the performing arts, including music, and offer a key entry point into the profession. According to Perkins (2013: 196), "[m]any of the most pre-eminent musicians in the classical music profession begin their career at a conservatoire of music."
4 The Warwick Commission (2015) has also argued that the lack of diversity in the cultural and creative industries damages the United Kingdom's international reputation as a tolerant society. In this context, the 2016 vote in the United Kingdom to leave the European Union raises questions about the new challenges posed by 'Brexit', which pertain to the United Kingdom's international reputation, but also a range of other issues, including access to specialist workers, EU funding, the single market, and relevant regulatory frameworks (Creative Industries Federation, 2016).
5 I do not draw on alternative, theoretical frameworks, such as the Italian Operaismo School (e.g. Hardt and Negri, 2000; Virno and Hardt, 1996; Lazzarato, 1996; Virno, 2004). At first glance, this school of thought may provide a useful theoretical perspective given its focus on subjectivity and immaterial labour, defined as "labour that produces an immaterial good, such as a service, a cultural product, knowledge, or communication" (Hardt and Negri, 2000: 290). However, the Operaismo work has been variously critiqued. Most pertinent to my analysis are criticisms that the approach uses class as a defining meta-concept and underplays the importance of gender (McRobbie, 2010; 2015); elides profound differences between different kinds of workers (Gill and Pratt, 2008); and lacks an empirical engagement with the specifics of cultural production (Hesmondhalgh and Baker, 2008; 2011). Given these critiques, I found the Foucauldian perspective, as outlined in this section, more suitable.
6 Through her discussion of the intersections between class and gender in the context of entrepreneurialism and cultural work, McRobbie (2015) points to the important issue that the resources to become an entrepreneurial subject are unevenly distributed. As I discuss in chapter four, they do not only intersect with gender and class, but also with race.
7 Some studies have demonstrated that orchestral musicians are dissatisfied with their jobs due to, for example, the patriarchal culture in orchestras (Levine and Levine, 1996), poor working conditions (Price, 2006), or fear of worsening technical skills, intonation, tone, and precision (Bork, 2010; see also Allmendinger et al., 1996; Cottrell, 2004). Other studies, however, have shown that orchestral musicians are satisfied with their jobs overall (Paternoga, 2006; Gembris and Heye, 2012). I therefore do not refer to orchestral

jobs to suggest that they provide ideal career paths, but as one possible way, especially in Germany, to gain permanent employment.

8 Note, however, that the "ABO does not represent all British orchestras though it does include most of the best known" (LSE, 2012: 23).

9 Commonly referred to as 'East Asian' in the United Kingdom. I use the term Asian when discussing literature and research on the US context, and East Asian when referring to the UK or European contexts.

References

ABO (2014). *Directory*. London: Association of British Orchestras. Accessed 1 June 2014. Available at: www.abo.org.uk/members/directory.aspx

ACE (2014). *Equality and diversity within the arts and cultural sector in England*. Accessed 1 December 2016. Available at: www.artscouncil.org.uk/publication/equality-and-diversity-within-arts-and-cultural-sector-england

Alexiadou, N. (2001). Management identities in transition: A case study from further education. *Sociological Review*, *49*(3), 412–435.

Alford, R. R., & Szanto, A. (1996). Orpheus wounded: The experience of pain in the professional worlds of the piano. *Theory and Society*, *25*(1), 1–44.

Allen, K., Quinn, J., Hollingworth, S., & Rose, A. (2013). Becoming employable students and 'ideal' creative workers: Exclusion and inequality in higher education work placements. *British Journal of Sociology of Education*, *34*(3), 431–452.

Allmendinger, J., Hackman, J. R., & Lehman, E. V. (1996). Life and work in symphony orchestras. *Musical Quarterly*, *80*(2), 194–219.

Armstrong, V. (2013). Women's musical lives: Self-managing a freelance career. *Women: A Cultural Review*, *24*(4), 298–314.

Atkinson, P. (2006). *Everyday arias: An operatic ethnography*. Lanham, MD: AltaMira Press.

Bain, A. L. (2004). Female artistic identity in place: The studio. *Social & Cultural Geography*, *5*(2), 171–193.

Baker, G. (2014). *El Sistema: Orchestrating Venezuela's youth*. New York: Oxford University Press.

Baker, J. (2008). The ideology of choice. Overstating progress and hiding injustice in the lives of young women: Findings from a study in North Queensland, Australia. *Women's Studies International Forum*, *31*(1), 53–64.

Banks, M. (2007). *The politics of cultural work*. Basingstoke: Palgrave Macmillan.

Banks, M. (2014). Being in the zone of cultural work. *Culture Unbound: Journal of Current Cultural Research*, *6*(1), 241–262.

Banks, M., Gill, R., & Taylor, S. (2013). *Theorizing cultural work: Labour, continuity and change in the creative industries*. London: Routledge.

Banks, M., & Hesmondhalgh, D. (2009). Looking for work in creative industries policy. *International Journal of Cultural Policy*, *15*(4), 415–430.

Banks, M., & Oakley, K. (2015). The dance goes on forever? Art schools, class and UK higher education. *International Journal of Cultural Policy*, *22*(1), 41–57.

Bartleet, B-L. (2008). Women conductors on the orchestral podium: Pedagogical and professional implications. *College Music Symposium*, *48*, 31–51.

Beckles Willson, R. (2009a). The parallax worlds of the West-Eastern divan orchestra. *Journal of the Royal Musical Association*, *134*(2), 319–347.

Beckles Willson, R. (2009b). Whose utopia? Perspectives on the West-Eastern divan orchestra. *Music and Politics, 3*(2), 1–21.

Bennett, D. (2007). Utopia for music performance graduates: Is it achievable, and how should it be defined? *British Journal of Music Education, 24*(2), 179–189.

Bennett, D. (2008). *Understanding the classical music profession: The past, the present and strategies for the future.* Farnham: Ashgate.

Bennett, D. (2016). Developing employability in higher education music. *Arts & Humanities in Higher Education, 15*(3–4), 386–413.

Bennett, T., Savage, M., Bortolaia Silva, E., Warde, A., Gayo-Cal, M., & Wright, D. (2009). *Culture, class, distinction.* Abingdon, Oxon; New York: Routledge.

Berardi, F. (2009). *The soul at work.* Cambridge, MA: MIT Press.

Berlin Senate (2014a). *Third creative industries report: Development and potential.* Accessed 1 December 2016. Available at: www.berlin.de/projektzukunft/uploads/tx_news/KWB13_Inhalt_engl.pdf

Berlin Senate (2014b). *Kulturförderbericht 2014 des Landes Berlin.* Accessed 1 December 2016. Available at: www.berlin.de/sen/kultur/kulturpolitik/www.berlin.de/sen/kultur/kulturpolitik/

Bielby, D. D., & Bielby, W. T. (1996). Women and men in film: Gender inequality among writers in a culture industry. *Gender & Society, 10*(3), 248–270.

Binkley, S. (2009). The work of neoliberal governmentality: Temporality and ethical substance in the tale of two dads. *Foucault Studies, 6* (February), 60–78.

Binkley, S. (2011a). Psychological life as enterprise: Social practice and the government of neo-liberal interiority. *History of the Human Sciences, 24*(2), 83–102.

Binkley, S. (2011b). Happiness, positive psychology and the program of neoliberal governmentality. *Subjectivity, 4*(4), 371–394.

Blair, H. (2001). 'You're only as good as your last job': The labour process and labour market in the British film industry. *Work, Employment & Society, 15*(1), 149–169.

Blair, H. (2003). Winning and losing in flexible labour markets: The formation and operation of networks of interdependence in the UK film industry. *Sociology, 37*(4), 677–694.

BMWi (2015). Monitoring zu ausgewählten wirtschaftlichen Eckdaten der Kultur- und Kreativwirtschaft 2014. Berlin: Bundesministerium für Wirtschaft und Energie. Accessed 1 December 2016. Available at: www.kultur-kreativ-wirtschaft.de/KuK/Redaktion/PDF/monitoring-wirtschaftliche-eckdaten-kuk-2014,property=pdf,bereich=kuk,sprache=de,rwb=true.pdf

Bork, M. (2010). *Traumberuf Musiker? Herausforderungen an ein Leben für die Kunst.* Mainz: Schott.

Born, G. (1995). *Rationalizing culture: IRCAM, Boulez, and the institutionalization of the musical avant-garde.* Berkeley, CA: University of California Press.

Born, G. (2012). Music and the social. In M. Clayton, T. Herbert, & R. Middleton (Eds.), *The cultural study of music: A critical introduction* (2nd ed., pp. 261–274). New York: Routledge.

Born, G., & Devine, K. (2015). Music technology, gender, and class: Digitization, educational and social change in Britain. *Twentieth-Century Music, 12*(2), 135–172.

Born, G., & Hesmondhalgh, D. (2000). *Western music and its others: Difference, representation and appropriation in music.* Berkeley, CA; London: University of California Press.

Bossen, A. (2012). *Einkommenssituation und Arbeitsbedingungen von Musikschullehrkräften und Privatmusiklehrern 2012.* Berlin: Verdi Fachgruppe Musik. Accessed 1 December 2016. Available at: www.miz.org/dokumente/2012_verdi_umfrage.pdf

Brah, A., & Phoenix, A. (2004). "Ain't I a woman?": Revisiting intersectionality. *Journal of International Women's Studies*, *5*(3), 75–86.

Bröckling, U. (2005). Gendering the enterprising self: Subjectification programs and gender differences in guides to success. *Distinktion: Scandinavian Journal of Social Theory*, *6*(2), 7–25.

Bröckling, U. (2007). *Das unternehmerische Selbst: Soziologie einer Subjektivierungsform*. Berlin: Suhrkamp.

Brown, W. (2003). Neo-liberalism and the end of liberal democracy. *Theory & Event*, *7*(1), 37–59.

Brown, W. (2015). *Undoing the demos: Neoliberalism's stealth revolution*. New York: Zone Books.

Bruni, A., Gherardi, S., & Poggio, B. (2004). Doing gender, doing entrepreneurship: An ethnographic account of intertwined practices. *Gender, Work & Organization*, *11*(4), 406–429.

Bull, A. (2015a). *The musical body: How gender and class are reproduced among young people playing classical music in England*. Unpublished PhD thesis, Goldsmiths University of London.

Bull, A. (2015b). Reproducing class? Classical music education and inequality. *Discover Society*, 14. Accessed 1 December 2016. Available at: http://discoversociety. org/2014/2011/2004/reproducing-class-classical-music-education-and-inequality/

Bull, A. (2016). El Sistema as a bourgeois social project: Class, gender, and Victorian values. *Action, Criticism, and Theory for Music Education*, *15*(1), 120–153.

Burchell, G. (1993). Liberal government and techniques of the self. *Economy and Society*, *22*(3), 267–282.

Cameron, D., & Kulick, D. (2003). *Language and sexuality*. Cambridge: Cambridge University Press.

Carpos, F. (2014). *The London orchestra as a prestige economy*. Paper presented at the conference Classical Music as Contemporary Socio-Cultural Practice, 23rd May 2014, King's College London.

Carpos, F. (2016). *The London orchestra as a prestige economy*. Unpublished PhD thesis, University College London.

Comunian, R., Faggian, A., & Jewell, S. (2014). Exploring music careers: Music graduates and early career trajectories in the UK. In N. Crossley, S. McAndrew, & P. Widdop (Eds.), *Social networks and music worlds* (pp. 165–188). Abingdon, Oxon: Routledge.

Conor, B. (2014). *Screenwriting: Creative labour and professional practice*. London: Routledge.

Conor, B., Gill, R., & Taylor, S. (Eds.). (2015). *Gender and creative labour* (Vol. 63). Chichester: Wiley.

Cottrell, S. (2004). *Professional music-making in London: Ethnography and experience*. Farnham: Ashgate.

Coulson, S. (2012). Collaborating in a competitive world: Musicians' Working lives and understandings of entrepreneurship. *Work, Employment & Society*, *26*(2), 246–261.

Creative Industries Federation (2016). *Brexit report: The impact of leaving the EU on the UK's arts, creative industries and cultural education – and what should be done*. London: Creative Industries Federation. Accessed 1 December 2016. Available at: www. creativeindustriesfederation.com/assets/userfiles/files/Brexit%20Report%20web.pdf

Crenshaw, K. (1991). Mapping the margins: Intersectionality, identity politics, and violence against women of color. *Stanford Law Review*, *43*(6), 1241–1299.

Dardot, P., & Laval, C. (2013). *The new way of the world: On neoliberal society*. London: Verso.

Davies, B. (2005). The (im)possibility of intellectual work in neoliberal regimes. *Discourse: Studies in the Cultural Politics of Education, 26*(1), 1–14.

Davies, B., & Bansel, P. (2007). Neoliberalism and education. *International Journal of Qualitative Studies in Education, 20*(3), 247–259.

DCMS (1998). *Creative industries mapping documents*. London: Department for Culture, Media and Sport. Accessed 1 December 2016. Available at: www.gov.uk/government/publications/creative-industries-mapping-documents-1998

DCMS (2001). *Creative industries mapping documents*. London: Department for Culture, Media and Sport. Accessed 1 December 2016. Available at: www.gov.uk/government/publications/creative-industries-mapping-documents-2001

DCMS (2015). *Creative industries: Focus on employment*. London: Department for Culture, Media & Sport. Accessed 1 December 2016. Available at: www.gov.uk/government/uploads/system/uploads/attachment_data/file/439714/Annex_C_-_Creative_Industries_Focus_on_Employment_2015.pdf

de Peuter, G. (2014). Beyond the model worker: Surveying a creative precariat. *Culture Unbound: Journal of Current Cultural Research, 6*(1), 263–284.

Dex, S., Willis, J., Paterson, R., & Sheppard, E. (2000). Freelance workers and contract uncertainty: The effects of contractual changes in the television industry. *Work, Employment & Society, 14*(2), 283–305.

Doolin, B. (2002). Enterprise discourse, professional identity and the organizational control of hospital clinicians. *Organization Studies, 23*(3), 369–390.

DOV (2016). *Alphabetische Aufstellung der deutschen Kulturorchester mit Einstufung und Planstellen*. Berlin: Deutsche Orchestervereinigung. Accessed 1 December 2016. Available at: www.dov.org/tl_files/pdf/Infos%20&%20Publikationen/Planstellenstatistik%20dasOrchester%202016.pdf

du Gay, P. (1996). *Consumption and identity at work*. London: Sage.

Edley, N. (2001). Analysing masculinity: Interpretative repertoires, ideological dilemmas and subject positions. In M. Wetherell, S. Taylor, & S. Yates (Eds.), *Discourse as data: A guide for analysis* (pp. 189–228). London: Sage.

Edley, N., & Wetherell, M. (2001). Jekyll and Hyde: Men's constructions of feminism and feminists. *Feminism and Psychology, 11*(4), 439–458.

Ehrenberg, A. (2010). *The weariness of the self: Diagnosing the history of depression in the contemporary age*. Quebec: McGill-Queen's University Press.

Eikhof, D. R., & Warhurst, C. (2013). The promised land? Why social inequalities are systemic in the creative industries. *Employee Relations, 35*(5), 495–508.

Elias, A. S., Gill, R., & Scharff, C. (Eds.). (2017). *Aesthetic labour: Rethinking beauty politics in neoliberalism*. Basingstoke: Palgrave Macmillan.

Entwistle, J., & Wissinger, E. (2006). Keeping up appearances: Aesthetic labour in the fashion modelling industries of London and New York. *The Sociological Review, 54*(4), 774–794.

Erel, U. (2009). *Migrant women transforming citizenship: Life-stories from Britain and Germany*. Farnham: Ashgate.

Fenwick, T. J. (2002). Transgressive desires: New enterprising selves in the new capitalism. *Work, Employment & Society, 16*(4), 703–723.

Finnegan, R. (1989). *The hidden musicians: Music-making in an English town*. Cambridge: Cambridge University Press.

Forkert, K. (2013). *Artistic lives: A study of creativity in two European cities*. Farnham, Surrey: Ashgate.

Foucault, M. (2008). *The birth of biopolitics: Lectures at the Collège de France, 1978–79* (M. Senellart, Ed.). Basingstoke: Palgrave Macmillan.

Garnham, N. (2005). From cultural to creative industries: An analysis of the implications of the "creative industries" approach to arts and media policy making in the United Kingdom. *International Journal of Cultural Policy*, *11*(1), 15–29.

Gembris, H., & Heye, A. (2012). *Älter werden im Orchester: Eine empirische Studie zu Erfahrungen, Einstellungen, Performanz und Lebensperspektiven von professionellen Orchestermusikern*. Paper presented at the symposium Musikalische Begabung und Alter(n), 21st and 22nd September 2012, Institut für Begabungsforschung in der Musik, Paderborn.

Gembris, H., & Langner, D. (2005). *Von der Musikhochschule auf den Arbeitsmarkt: Erfahrungen von Absolventen, Arbeitsmarktexperten und Hochschullehrern*. Augsburg: Wißner.

German Federal Ministry of Economics and Technology (2009). *Gesamtwirtschaftliche Perspektiven der Kultur- und Kreativwirtschaft in Deutschland. Forschungsbericht Nr. 577*. Accessed 1 December 2016. Available at: https://kreativgesellschaft.org/assets/files/doku box/4/Gesamtwirtschaftliche_Perspektiven_Kreativwirtschaft_Deutschland_2009.pdf

Gill, R. (2002). Cool, creative and egalitarian? Exploring gender in project-based new media work in Europe. *Information, Communication & Society*, *5*(1), 70–89.

Gill, R. (2014). Unspeakable inequalities: Post feminism, entrepreneurial subjectivity, and the repudiation of sexism among cultural workers. *Social Politics: International Studies in Gender, State and Society*, *21*(4), 509–528.

Gill, R., & Pratt, A. C. (2008). In the social factory? Immaterial labour, precariousness and cultural work. *Theory, Culture & Society*, *25*(7–8), 1–30.

Gill, R., & Scharff, C. (Eds.). (2011). *New femininities: Postfeminism, neoliberalism and subjectivity*. Basingstoke: Palgrave Macmillan.

Gonick, M. (2006). Between "girl power" and "reviving ophelia": Constituting the neoliberal girl subject. *NWSA Journal*, *18*(2), 1–23.

Gordon, C. (1987). The soul of the citizen: Max Weber and Michel Foucault on rationality and government. In S. Lash & S. Whimster (Eds.), *Max Weber, rationality and modernity* (pp. 293–316). London: Allan & Unwin.

Gray, A. (2003). Enterprising femininity: New modes of work and subjectivity. *European Journal of Cultural Studies*, *6*(4), 489–506.

Green, L. (1997). *Music, gender, education*. Cambridge: Cambridge University Press.

Gregg, M. (2011). *Work's intimacy*. Cambridge: Polity.

Grugulis, I., & Stoyanova, D. (2012). Social capital and networks in film and TV: Jobs for the boys? *Organization Studies*, *33*(10), 1311–1331.

Halford, S., & Leonard, P. (2006). Place, space and time: Contextualising work-place subjectivities. *Organisation Studies*, *27*(5), 657–676.

Hall, S., & O'Shea, A. (2013). Common-sense neoliberalism. *Soundings: A Journal of Politics and Culture, Special Issue: After neoliberalism? The Kilburn manifesto* (S. Hall, D. Massey, & M. Rustin, Eds.), 1–16. Accessed 11 December 2016. Available at: www. lwbooks.co.uk/sites/default/files/2003_commonsenseneoliberalism.pdf

Hardt, M., & Negri, A. (2000). *Empire*. Cambridge, MA; London: Harvard University Press.

Harré, R., & Gillett, G. (1994). *The discursive mind*. Thousand Oaks, CA; London: Sage.

Harris, A. (Ed.). (2004). *All about the girl: Culture, power, and identity*. New York: Routledge.

HEFCE (2002). *Creating a land with music: The work, education, and training of professional musicians in the 21st century.* Bristol; London: Higher Education Funding Council for England. Accessed 1 December 2016. Available at: www.hanze.nl/assets/kc-kunst—samenleving/lifelong-learning-in-music/Documents/Public/273creatingalandwithmusic.pdf

Help Musicians UK (2014). *Professional music in the UK: Health and wellbeing survey.* London: Help Musicians UK. Accessed 1 December 2016. Available at: https://issuu.com/helpmusiciansuk/docs/help_musicians_uk_health_and_wellbe?e=10405134/8971874

Hennekam, S., & Bennett, D. (2016). Self-management of work in the creative industries in the Netherlands. *International Journal of Arts Managment, 19*(1), 31–41.

Hennekam, S., & Bennett, D. (2017). Creative industries work across multiple contexts: Common themes and challenges. *Personnel Review, 46*(1), 68–85.

Hesmondhalgh, D. (2008). Cultural and creative industries. In T. Bennett & J. Frow (Eds.), *The Sage handbook of cultural analysis* (pp. 552–569). London: Sage.

Hesmondhalgh, D., & Baker, S. (2008). Creative work and emotional labour in the television industry. *Theory, Culture & Society, 25*(7–8), 97–118.

Hesmondhalgh, D., & Baker, S. (2010). 'A very complicated version of freedom': Conditions and experiences of creative labour in three cultural industries. *Poetics, 38*(1), 4–20.

Hesmondhalgh, D., & Baker, S. (2011). *Creative labour: Media work in three cultural industries.* London: Routledge.

Hesmondhalgh, D., Oakley, K., Lee, D., & Nisbett, M. (2015). *Culture, economy and politics: The case of New Labour.* Basingstoke: Palgrave Macmillan.

Hesmondhalgh, D., & Saha, A. (2013). Race, ethnicity, and cultural production. *Popular Communication, 11*(3), 179–195.

HfMDK (2011). *Bundeskonferenz der Lehrbeauftragten an Musikhochschulen BKLM 22./23. Januar 2011 in der HfMDK Frankfurt am Main.* Frankfurt: Hochschule für Musik und Darstellende Kunst Frankfurt. Accessed 1 December 2016. Available at: www.bklm.org/archiv/statmr-bklm/151-ffr.html

Johnson-Williams, E. (2014). *Imperial surveillance: The origins of power formation in Victorian music education.* Paper presented at the conference Classical Music: Critical Challenges, October 17th, King's College London.

Johnson-Williams, E. (2015). *Re-examining the academy: Music institutions and empire in nineteenth-century London.* Unpublished PhD thesis, Yale University.

Jordan, T., Woodward, K., & McClure, B. (2017). *Culture, identity and intense performativity: Being in the zone.* London: Routledge.

Kagerbauer, L. (2010). Hier sind wir! Die Zukunft der Mädchenarbeit aus der Perspektive einer jungen Feministin: Herausforderungen und Anforderungen an einen Dialog der Generationen! In B. M. e.V. (Ed.), *Schriftenreihe zur Mädchenarbeit und Mädchenpolitik: Die Mädchen von heute sind die Frauen von morgen* (pp. 37–40). Berlin.

Kennedy, H. (2012). *Net work: Ethics and values in web design.* Basingstoke: Palgrave Macmillan.

Kingsbury, H. (1988). *Music, talent, and performance: A conservatory cultural system.* Philadelphia, PA: Temple University Press.

Kok, R-M. (2006). Music for a postcolonial child: Theorizing Malaysian memories. In S. Boynton & R.-M. Kok (Eds.), *Musical childhoods and the cultures of youth* (pp. 89–104). Middletown, CT: Wesleyan University Press.

Lander, R. (2014). Addiction in the orchestra: Classical music's drink and drugs problem. *The Guardian,* 26.08.2014. Accessed 1 December 2016. Available at: www.theguardian.com/music/2014/aug/2026/classical-music-alcohol-substance-abuse-addicts-symphony

Layton, L. (2009). Who's responsible? Our mutual implication in each other's suffering. *Psychoanalytic Dialogues, 19*(2), 105–120.

Layton, L. (2010). Irrational exuberance: Neoliberal subjectivity and the perversion of truth. *Subjectivity, 3*(3), 303–322.

Layton, L. (2013a). Editor's introduction to special section on the psychosocial effects of neoliberalism. *Psychoanalysis, Culture & Society 19*(1), 1–4.

Layton, L. (2013b). Psychoanalysis and politics: Historicising subjectivity. *Mens Sana Monographs, 11*(1), 68–81.

Lazzarato, M. (1996). Immaterial labor (P. Colilli & E. Emery, Trans.). *Generation Online*. Accessed 1 December 2016. Available at: www.generation-online.org/c/fcimmateriallabour2013.htm

Leberl, J., & Schulz, G. (2003). *Frauen in Kunst und Kultur II, 1995–2000.* Berlin: Deutscher Kulturrat. Accessed 1 December 2016. Available at: http://kulturrat.de/wp-content/uploads/altdocs/dokumente/studien/FraueninKunstundKultur2.pdf

Leech-Wilkinson, D. (2016). Classical music as enforced Utopia. *Arts and Humanities in Higher Education, 15*(3–4), 325–336.

Lemke, T. (2001). 'The birth of bio-politics': Michel Foucault's lecture at the Collège de France on neo-liberal governmentality. *Economy and Society, 30*(2), 190–207.

Leppänen, T. (2014). The west and the rest of classical music: Asian musicians in the Finnish media coverage of the 1995 Jean Sibelius Violin Competition. *European Journal of Cultural Studies, 18*(1), 1–16.

Levine, S., & Levine, R. (1996). Why they're not smiling: Stress and discontent in the orchestral workplace. *Harmony: Forum of the Symphony Orchestra Institute, 2*, 14–25.

Lewis, P. (2014). Postfeminism, femininities and organization studies: Exploring a new agenda. *Organization Studies, 35*(12), 1845–1866.

LSE (2012). *The impact of three London conservatoires on the UK and London economies: A project for the Royal Academy of Music, the Guildhall School of Music & Drama and the Royal College of Music, with Universities UK.* London: London School of Economics and Political Science. Accessed 1 December 2016. Available at: www.lse.ac.uk/geographyAndEnvironment/research/london/pdf/LSE-London-Conservatoires-Report-FINAL-July-2012.pdf

Macleod, B. A. (2001). *Women performing music: The emergence of American women as classical instrumentalists and conductors.* Jefferson, NC: McFarland.

Manske, A. (2015). *Kapitalistische Geister in der Kultur- und Kreativwirtschaft: Kreative zwischen wirtschaftlichem Zwang und künstlerischem Drang.* Bielefeld: Transcript.

Maus, F. E. (2012). Music, gender, and sexuality. In M. Clayton, T. Herbert, & R. Middleton (Eds.), *The cultural study of music: A critical introduction* (2nd ed., pp. 317–329). New York: Routledge.

McClary, S. (1991). *Feminine endings: Music, gender, and sexuality.* Minneapolis, MN: University of Minnesota Press.

McCormick, L. (2009). Higher, faster, louder: Representations of the international music competition. *Cultural Sociology, 3*(1), 5–30.

McCormick, L. (2015). *Performing civility: International competitions in classical music.* Cambridge: Cambridge University Press.

McNay, L. (2009). Self as enterprise: Dilemmas of control and resistance in Foucault's The Birth of Biopolitics. *Theory, Culture & Society, 26*(6), 55–77.

McRobbie, A. (1998). *British fashion design: Rag trade or image industry?* London: Routledge.

McRobbie, A. (2002). Clubs to companies: Notes on the decline of political culture in speeded up creative worlds. *Cultural Studies, 16*(4), 516–531.

McRobbie, A. (2007). Top girls? Young women and the post-feminist sexual contract. *Cultural Studies, 21*(4–5), 718–737.

McRobbie, A. (2009). *The aftermath of feminism: Gender, culture and social change*. London: Sage.

McRobbie, A. (2010). Reflections on feminism, immaterial labour and the post-Fordist regime. *New Formations, 70*, 60–76.

McRobbie, A. (2015). *Be creative: Making a living in the new culture industries*. Cambridge: Polity.

McRobbie, A., Strutt, D., Bandinelli, C., & Springer, B. (2016). *Fashion micro-enterprises in London, Berlin, Milan*. London: Goldsmiths University of London.

Mertens, G. (2012 [2005]). Philharmonisches Paradies? Arbeitsmarkt- und Berufssituation von Orchestermusikern. In O. Zimmermann & T. Geißler (Eds.), *Arbeitsmarkt Kultur: Vom Nischenmarkt zur Boombranche* (pp. 77–79). Berlin: Nachdruck von Beiträgen aus Politik & Kultur, Zeitung des Deutschen Kulturrates.

Mills, J. (2005). Addressing the concerns of conservatoire students about school music teaching. *British Journal of Music Education, 22*(1), 63–75.

Musicians' Union. (2012). *The working musician*. London: Musicians' Union. Accessed 1 December 2016. Available at: www.musiciansunion.org.uk/Files/Reports/Industry/The-Working-Musician-report

Myles Beeching, A. (2010). *Beyond talent: Creating a successful career in music*. Oxford: Oxford University Press.

Nayak, A., & Kehily, M. J. (2008). *Gender, youth and culture: Young masculinities and femininities*. Basingstoke; New York: Palgrave Macmillan.

Neff, G., Wissinger, E., & Zukin, S. (2005). Entrepreneurial labor among cultural producers: 'Cool' jobs in 'hot' industries. *Social Semiotics, 15*(3), 307–334.

Neilson, B. (2013). Logistics of cultural work. In M. Banks, R. Gill, & S. Taylor (Eds.), *Theorizing cultural work: Labour, continuity and change in the creative industries* (pp. 99–112). London: Routledge.

Neilson, B., & Rossiter, N. (2008). Precarity as a political concept, or, Fordism as exception. *Theory, Culture & Society, 25*(7–8), 51–72.

Nettle, B. (1995). *Heartland excursions: Ethnomusicological reflections on schools of music*. Urbana, IL: University of Illinois Press.

Nooshin, L. (2011). Introduction to the Special Issue: The ethnomusicology of Western art music. *Ethnomusicology Forum, 20*(3), 285–300.

Nooshin, L. (2014). *Classical music and its others: The view from Iran*. Paper presented at the conference Classical Music, Critical Challenges, 17th October 2014, King's College London.

O'Brien, D., Laurison, D., Miles, A., & Friedman, S. (2016). Are the creative industries meritocratic? An analysis of the 2014 British Labour Force Survey. *Cultural Trends, 25*(2), 116–131.

O'Brien, D., & Oakley, K. (2015). *Cultural value and inequality: A critical literature review*. Swindon, Wiltshire: Arts and Humanities Research Council. Accessed 1 December 2016. Available at: www.ahrc.ac.uk/documents/project-reports-and-reviews/cultural-value-and-inequality-a-critical-literature-review/

O'Reilly, J., MacInnes, J., Nazio, T., & Roche, J. M. (2009). The United Kingdom: From flexible employment to vulnerable workers. In L. F. Vosco, M. MacDonald, & I. Campbell (Eds.), *Gender and the contours of precarious employment* (pp. 108–126). London: Routledge.

Oakley, K. (2006). Include us out: Economic development and social policy in the creative industries. *Cultural Trends, 15*(4), 255–273.

Oakley, K. (2013). Absentee workers: Representation and participation in the cultural industries. In M. Banks, R. Gill, & S. Taylor (Eds.), *Theorizing cultural work: Labour, continuity and change in the creative industries* (pp. 56–68). London: Routledge.

Oakley, K., & O'Brien, D. (2016). Learning to labour unequally: Understanding the relationship between cultural production, cultural consumption and inequality. *Social Identities, 22*(5), 471–486.

Osborne, W., & Conant, A. (2010). *A survey of women orchestral players in major UK orchestras as of March 1, 2010.* Accessed 1 December 2016. Available at: www.osborne-conant.org/orch-uk.htm

Paternoga, S. (2005). Orchestermusikerinnen: Frauenanteile an den Musikhochschulen und in den Kulturorchestern. *Das Orchester, 5,* 8–14.

Paternoga, S. (2006). Was zufrieden macht: Eine repräsentative Studie zur Arbeits- und Berufszufriedenheit im Orchestermusikerberuf. *Das Orchester, 1,* 8–15.

Perkins, R. (2013). Learning cultures and the conservatoire: An ethnographically-informed case study. *Music Education Research, 15*(2), 196–213.

Perrons, D. (2003). The new economy and the work – life balance: Conceptual explorations and a case study of new media. *Gender, Work & Organization, 10*(1), 65–93.

Peters, M. (2001). Education, enterprise culture and the entrepreneurial self: A Foucauldian perspective. *Journal of Educational Enquiry, 2*(2), 58–71.

Pohlman, L. (1996). Creativity, gender and the family: A study of creative writers. *The Journal of Creative Behavior, 30*(1), 1–24.

Potter, J., & Wetherell, M. (1987). *Discourse and social psychology: Beyond attitudes and behaviour.* London: Sage.

Pratt, A. C. (2009). Cultural economy. In R. Kitchen & N. Thrift (Eds.), *International Encyclopedia of human geography* (pp. 407–410). Amsterdam; London; Oxford: Elsevier.

Price, A. (2006). Pit of despair. *The Guardian,* 02.02.2006. Accessed 1 December 2016. Available at: www.theguardian.com/music/2006/feb/2002/classicalmusicandopera2013

Prichard, C. (2002). Creative selves? Critically reading 'creativity' in management discourse. *Creativity and Innovation Management, 11*(4), 265–276.

Randle, K. R., Forson, C., & Calveley, M. (2015). Towards a Bourdieusian analysis of the social composition of the UK film and television workforce. *Work, Employment & Society, 29*(4), 590–606.

Randle, K. R., Kurian, J., & Leung, W. F. (2007). *Creating difference: Overcoming barriers to diversity in UK film and television employment.* Creative Industries Research & Consultancy Unit, Business School, University of Hertfordshire. Accessed 1 December 2016. Available at: http://uhra.herts.ac.uk/handle/2299/4575

Rimmer, M. (2014). *In 'harmony-Sistema England' and cultural value.* Paper presented at the conference Classical Music as Contemporary Socio-cultural Practice, 23rd May 2014, King's College London.

Ringrose, J., & Walkerdine, V. (2008). Regulating the abject: The TV make-over as site of neo-liberal reinvention toward bourgeois femininity. *Feminist Media Studies, 8*(3), 227–246.

Rose, N. (1992). Governing the enterprising self. In P. Heelas & P. Morris (Eds.), *The values of the enterprise culture: The moral debate.* London: Routledge.

Ross, A. (2003). *No-collar: The humane workplace and its hidden costs.* New York: Basic Books.

Ross, A. (2008). The new geography of work: Power to the precarious? *Theory, Culture & Society*, *25*(7–8), 31–49.

Ross, A. (2009). *Nice work if you can get it: Life and labor in precarious times*. New York; London: New York University Press.

Rubin, H. J., & Rubin, I. (1995). *Qualitative interviewing: The art of hearing data*. Thousand Oaks, CA: Sage.

Saleci, R. (2010). *The tyranny of choice*. London: Profile Books.

Scharff, C. (2012). *Repudiating feminism: Young women in a neoliberal world*. Farnham: Ashgate.

Scharff, C. (2017). Inequalities in the classical music industry: The role of subjectivity in constructions of the 'ideal classical musician'. In C. Dromey & J. Haferkorn (Eds.), *The classical music industry*. London: Routledge.

Schulz, G. (2013). Bestandsaufnahme zum Arbeitsmarkt Kultur. In G. Schulz, O. Zimmermann, & R. Hufnagel (Eds.), *Arbeitsmarkt Kultur: Zur wirtschaftlichen und sozialen Lage in Kulturberufen* (pp. 27–201). Berlin: Deutscher Kulturrat.

Schulz, G., Ries, C., & Zimmermann, O. (2016). *Frauen in Kultur und Medien: Ein Überblick über aktuelle Tendenzen, Entwicklungen und Lösungsvorschläge*. Berlin: Deutscher Kulturrat. Accessed 1 December 2016. Available at: www.kulturrat.de/publikationen/frauen-in-kultur-und-medien/

Sennett, R. (1998). *The corrosion of character: The personal consequences of work in the new capitalism*. New York; London: W. W. Norton.

Skillset. (2010). *Women in the creative media industries*. London: Skillset. Accessed 1 December 2016. Available at: www.ewawomen.com/uploads/files/surveyskillset.pdf

Small, C. (1977). *Music, society, education: A radical examination of the prophetic function of music in Western, Eastern and African cultures with its impact on society and its use in education*. London: Calder.

Solie, R. A. (1993). *Musicology and difference: Gender and sexuality in music scholarship*. Berkeley, CA: University of California Press.

Storey, J., Salaman, G., & Platman, K. (2005). Living with enterprise in an enterprise economy: Freelance and contract workers in the media. *Human Relations*, *58*(8), 1033–1054.

Swan, E. (2008). 'You make me feel like a woman': Therapeutic cultures and the contagion of femininity. *Gender, Work & Organization*, *15*(1), 88–107.

Taylor, S., & Littleton, K. (2006). Biographies in talk: A narrative-discursive research approach. *Qualitative Sociology Review*, *2*(2), 22–38.

Taylor, S., & Littleton, K. (2008). Art work or money: Conflicts in the construction of a creative identity. *The Sociological Review*, *56*(2), 275–292.

Taylor, S., & Littleton, K. (2012). *Contemporary identities of creativity and creative work*. Farnham: Ashgate.

Thanki, A., & Jefferys, S. (2007). Who are the fairest? Ethnic segmentation in London's media production. *Work Organisation, Labour & Globalisation*, *1*(1), 108–118.

Tindall, B. (2005). *Mozart in the jungle: Sex, drugs, and classical music*. New York: Grove Press.

Tyler, I. (2011). Pregnant beauty: Maternal femininities under neoliberalism. In R. Gill & C. Scharff (Eds.), *New femininiites: Postfeminism, neoliberalism and subjectivity* (pp. 21–36). Basingstoke: Palgrave Macmillan.

UCU (2016). *Precarious work in higher education: A snapshot of insecure contracts and institutional attitudes*. London: University and College Union. Accessed 1 December 2016. Available at: www.ucu.org.uk/media/7995/Precarious-work-in-higher-education-a-

snapshot-of-insecure-contracts-and-institutional-attitudes-Apr-16/pdf/ucu_precari
ouscontract_hereport_apr16.pdf

UNCTAD (2010). *Creative economy report 2010. Creative economy: A feasible development option.* Geneva: United Nations Conference on Trade and Development. Accessed
1 December 2016. Available at: http://unctad.org/en/Docs/ditctab20103_en.pdf

Ursell, G. (2000). Television production: Issues of exploitation, commodification
and subjectivity in UK television labour markets. *Media, Culture & Society, 22*(6),
805–825.

Usher, R., & Garrick, J. (2000). Flexible learning, contemporary work and enterprising
selves. *Electronic Journal of Sociology, 5*(1). Accessed 1 December 2016. Available at:
www.sociology.org/content/vol2005.2001/garrick-usher.html

Virno, P. (2004). *A grammar of the multitude: For an analysis of contemporary forms of
life.* Translated from the Italian: Isabella Bertoletti, James Cascaito, Andrea Casson. Los
Angeles, CA: Semiotexte.

Virno, P., & Hardt, M. (1996). *Radical thought in Italy: A potential of politics.* Minneapolis, MN: University of Minnesota Press.

Wagner, I. (2015). *Producing excellence: The making of virtuosos.* New Brunswick, NJ:
Rutgers University Press.

Wang, G. (2009). Interlopers in the realm of high culture: "Music moms" and the performance of Asian and Asian American identities. *American Quarterly, 61*(4), 881–903.

Warwick Commission (2015). *Enriching Britain: Culture, creativity and growth.* Coventry: University of Warwick. Accessed 1 December 2016. Available at: www2.warwick.
ac.uk/research/warwickcommission/futureculture/finalreport/warwick_commission_
report_2015.pdf

Weinkopf, C. (2009). Germany: Precarious employment and the rise of mini-jobs. In L. F.
Vosco, M. MacDonald, & I. Campbell (Eds.), *Gender and the contours of precarious
employment* (pp. 177–193). London: Routledge.

Wetherell, M. (1998). Positioning and interpretative repertoires: Conversation analysis and
post-structuralism in dialogue. *Discourse & Society, 9*(3), 387–412.

Wetherell, M. (2003). Racism and the analysis of cultural resources in interviews. In H. van
den Berg, M. Wetherell, & H. Houtkoop-Steenstra (Eds.), *Analyzing race talk: Multi-
disciplinary perspectives on the research interview* (pp. 11–30). Cambridge: Cambridge
University Press.

Wetherell, M. (2005). Unconscious conflict or everyday accountability? *British Journal of
Social Psychology, 44*(2), 169–173.

Williams, C. L. (2013). The glass escalator, revisited: Gender inequality in neoliberal
times, SWS feminist lecturer. *Gender & Society, 27*(5), 609–629.

Wilson, G. B., & MacDonald, R. A. R. (2005). The meaning of the blues: Musical identities
in talk about jazz. *Qualitative Research in Psychology, 2*(4), 341–363.

Wilson, N. (2013). *The art of re-enchantment: Making early music in the modern age.* New
York: Oxford University Press.

Wittel, A. (2001). Toward a network sociality. *Theory, Culture & Society, 18*(6), 51–76.

Wreyford, N. (2015). *The gendered contexts of screenwriting work: Socialized recruitment
and judgments of taste and talent in the UK film industry.* Unpublished PhD thesis,
King's College London.

Yang, M. (2007). East meets west in the concert hall: Asians and classical music in the century of imperialism, post-colonialism, and multiculturalism. *Asian Music, 38*(1), 1–30.

Yoshihara, M. (2007). *Musicians from a different shore: Asians and Asian Americans in classical music*. Philadelphia, PA: Temple University Press.

Zaza, C., Charles, C., & Muszynski, A. (1998). The meaning of playing-related musculoskeletal disorders to classical musicians. *Social Science & Medicine, 47*(12), 2013–2023.

Zimmermann, O., & Geißler, T. (Eds.). (2012). *Arbeitsmarkt Kultur: Vom Nischenmarkt zur Boombranche*. Berlin: Nachdruck von Beiträgen aus Politik & Kultur, Zeitung des Deutschen Kulturrates.

Chapter 2

Documenting and explaining inequalities in the classical music profession

This chapter begins with an overview of gender, racial, and class inequalities in the cultural and creative industries in order to set the context for my more detailed analysis of the classical music sector. I draw on existing and new quantitative research[1] to document the underrepresentation of women, black and minority ethnic players, as well as musicians from working-class backgrounds. In addition, my discussion highlights other patterns, including horizontal and vertical segregation, but also more complex issues such as the association of classical music with whiteness. Having documented a range of imbalances that characterise the classical music profession, I provide various explanations for their persistence. By drawing on existing research on inequalities in cultural work, I highlight the role of informal recruitment, networking, and education, as well as gendered, racialised, and classed constructions of who constitutes the ideal cultural worker and classical musician. The final section of the chapter maintains the focus on subjectivity to make sense of inequalities in cultural work. More specifically, it explores the gendered dynamics of self-promotion to demonstrate that the self-promoting, cultural worker is bound by particular gendered conventions that make it more difficult for female musicians to promote themselves. As such, the final section of this chapter adds a further dimension to our understanding of inequalities in the classical music profession by foregrounding the role of subjectivity in the interplay between gender and cultural work.

A quick glance at this chapter indicates that my documentation of inequalities in the classical music profession is quite extensive and includes a considerable amount of quantitative data. Given the overwhelmingly qualitative focus of the book, the inclusion and discussion of quantitative data may come as a surprise. When I conducted the research, I did, however, realise that there was a dearth of data on the demographic backgrounds of musicians. Apart from a few isolated studies and some historical data, we knew very little about the makeup of the profession in terms of gender, race, and class. This has changed slightly over the course of the study as several organisations – such as ACE (Arts Council England), ABRSM (Associated Board of the Royal Schools of Music), BASCA (The British Academy of Songwriters, Composers and Authors), and Deutscher Kulturrat – published relevant reports. In addition, a team of researchers under my supervision collected data on the demographic backgrounds of orchestral players in the United Kingdom and conservatoire teaching staff in Germany and the United Kingdom (McClure, Kokot and Scharff, 2014; Wright and Scharff, 2014). We also analysed data by the Higher Education Statistics Agency (HESA) to learn more about the demographic backgrounds of students doing a music degree in the United Kingdom (Blamey et al., 2014).

Of course, this quantitative analysis, along with the data from existing reports, does not give us a complete overview of the makeup of the classical music profession in Germany and the United Kingdom. It is limited in various ways, especially in relation to information on the class backgrounds of musicians or the comparability between data collected in Germany and the United Kingdom (see introduction). My analysis is thus not strictly comparative, but I hope that it provides a starting point for a more informed discussion of inequalities in the classical music sector. As Deborah Jones and Judith Pringle (2015: 39) have pointed out, "[t]he language of statistics is a key legitimating tool to make inequalities visible and speakable". Against the backdrop of the unspeakability of inequalities in the cultural and creative industries (Gill, 2014) and the classical music profession (see chapter three), this chapter makes an important intervention by documenting and analysing who is 'in' and who is 'out' in the classical music industry.

Inequalities in the cultural and creative industries

Before providing a detailed analysis of the ongoing hierarchies, privileges, and exclusions in the classical music sector, it is worth discussing these issues in the cultural and creative industries more generally. This is both to embed my analysis of the classical music sector in its wider context, but also to foreground common patterns, relating, for example, to underrepresentation and pay gaps. Although women make up a high proportion of students on artistic and creative subjects (Antrag der Abgeordneten, 2013; Allen et al., 2011), they are underrepresented in the cultural and creative industries. Data on the representation of women suggests that they represented 39.4 per cent of the cultural workforce in Germany in 2012 (BMWi, 2014) and held 36.7 per cent of jobs in the creative industries in the United Kingdom in 2014 (DCMS, 2015). This means that the representation of women is lower in the cultural and creative industries than in the overall economy, where, in the same years, they represented 46 per cent of the workforce in Germany and 47.2 per cent in the United Kingdom (DCMS, 2015). Apart from underrepresentation, the cultural and creative industries are marked by patterns of vertical and horizontal segregation (Coulangeon et al.,

2005). Vertical segregation refers to the over or underrepresentation of particular groups in positions of power and prestige, while the term horizontal segregation seeks to describe the concentration of particular groups in specific sectors of economic activity. In the cultural and creative industries, women are underrepresented in positions of authority and prestige (Antrag der Abgeordneten, 2013) and concentrated in particular sectors, such as museums, libraries, and archives in Germany (BMWi, 2014), as well as book publishing in the United Kingdom (Skillset, 2010).

Similar to other sectors in the economy, there is also a gender pay gap in the cultural and creative industries. Based on analysis of Labour Force Survey data in the United Kingdom in 2014, Dave O'Brien et al. (2016) have found that women employed in the cultural and creative industries earn about £5, 800 less a year than otherwise similar men. A report based on data by the German 'Künstlersozialversicherung'[2] has shown that the gender pay gap ranged from 22 per cent in music to 35 per cent in the performing arts in 2012 (Schulz, 2013b; see also MIZ, 2016). The gender pay gap seems to get more pronounced with age (Schulz, 2013b), supporting longer standing claims that women face cumulative disadvantage in the cultural and creative industries (Bielby and Bielby, 1996; Coulangeon et al., 2005). Relatedly, female cultural workers seem to be more likely to be in non-standard employment (Coulangeon et al., 2005; Antrag der Abgeordneten, 2013). Research on music teachers in Germany has, for example, demonstrated that male teachers tend to be in full-time employment more often than their female counterparts, even though there are more female teachers, many of who would like to have a full-time post (Bossen, 2012).

Workers from a minority ethnic and/or working-class background are also underrepresented in the cultural and creative industries.[3] According to the Warwick Commission:

> BAME workers represent 6% of workers in Design; 9.1% in Film, TV and radio; 6.7% in Music and Performing and Visual Arts, compared to 14.1% of the overall population in England and Wales and 40% in London where there is a high concentration of Cultural and Creative Industries.
>
> (2015: 35)

Annual pay also varies by ethnic origin. As Doris Eikhof's and Chris Warhurst's (2013: 501) analysis of 2010 Skillset data has shown, black and minority ethnic workers earn less than their white colleagues (£27, 200 p.a. versus £30, 600 p.a.).

In relation to class, the DCMS (2015: 7) published figures which demonstrate that "[m]ore advantaged groups make up 92.1 per cent of jobs in the Creative Industries". Exploring issues around class inequalities in the cultural and creative industries in more detail, O'Brien et al. (2016: 123) showed that workers from working-class origins are underrepresented:

> While 34.7% of the UK population aged 23–69 had a parent employed in a routine or semi-routine working-class occupation, the figure among those working in the CCIs is only 18%. This under-representation is mirrored by the comparative over-representation of those from professional and managerial backgrounds (that is, NS-SEC 1 and 2 combined: 50% in the CCIs vs. 29.1% in the population).

To be sure, the same study demonstrated that the cultural and creative industries showed significant variation in their openness towards workers from diverse class backgrounds. Underrepresentation of workers from working-class origins was particularly pronounced in publishing and music, but much less pronounced in craft. Equally important, O'Brien et al. (2016: 126) identified a 'class origin pay gap': "workers from working-class origins have earnings on average £157/week or over £8100 less per year than demographically similar people (working the same number of hours) from privileged backgrounds" (see also Friedman et al., 2016).

The finding that working-class cultural workers are underrepresented and that there is a 'class origin pay gap' resonates with the patterns identified in relation to racial and gender inequalities. Of course, inequalities in the cultural and creative industries (and beyond) are not limited to issues of underrepresentation, differences in pay, as well as vertical and horizontal segregation. Class background, for example, intersects in particular ways with the often-precarious nature of employment in the cultural and creative industries, where workers from privileged socio-economic backgrounds are better positioned to deal with insecurity, irregular incomes, and expectations to work for free (Friedman et al., 2016; see also chapter five). Racial inequalities too are not limited to the underrepresentation of black and minority ethnic workers in the cultural and creative industries. As David Hesmondhalgh and Anamik Saha (2013: 185) have shown, race and ethnicity also intersect with cultural production through the complex politics of appreciation and appropriation of cultural goods produced by ethnic minorities as well as "the failure of the cultural industries to create lasting and valuable spaces of cultural production that adequately embody the distinctive experiences and concerns of racialized communities". As the latter sections of this chapter demonstrate, gender imbalances also manifest themselves in complex ways. As such, my overview does not attempt to grasp inequalities in their complexity, but to contextualise my subsequent discussion of the classical music sector.

Inequalities in the classical music sector

Given that many musicians have to learn and practice their instrument from an early age onwards in order to enter the profession (Bork, 2010; Wagner, 2015), it is worth beginning with a discussion of music education. Reflecting trends in the wider cultural sector, women are overrepresented in music education and research demonstrates that there is a longer history to this trend. As Sabrina Paternoga (2005) has pointed out, women already constituted 47 per cent of the student body at conservatoires in West Germany in 1988. Lucy Green's (1997) historical research on gender, music, and education in the United Kingdom suggests an even longer trend by arguing that, by 1890, most conservatoire students were women. In 2014/2015, fewer women in Germany studied conducting (42 per cent) and composition (32 per cent), but they outnumbered men in instrument studies and orchestral music (54 per cent), as well as in music teaching at schools (61 per cent) (MIZ, 2015a). Overall, they constituted 54 per cent of the student body of all students studying a music-related subject (MIZ, 2015a).

Our research (Blamey et al., 2014)[4] on music students in the United Kingdom suggests a similar trend (see Figure 2.1): while women made up around half of the student population at five conservatoires in 2012/2013, they were overrepresented in the mid-1990s. However, it is interesting to look at these figures in the context of admissions data (CUKAS, 2013; UCAS Conservatoires, 2015). This data indicates that women apply to undergraduate courses at conservatoires in high numbers, but that more or less equal numbers of male and female students are accepted. This shows that "the acceptance rate for men has been consistently higher than that for women" (UCAS Conservatoires, 2015: 23), with 18 per cent for women and 26 per cent for men on undergraduate courses in 2014. The figure for postgraduate courses in the same year was 29 per cent for women and 37 per cent for men (UCAS Conservatoires, 2015). Overall, women are well represented in music education, including youth music in the United Kingdom (ABO, 2014). The admissions data to conservatoires does however raise questions about their lower acceptance rate.

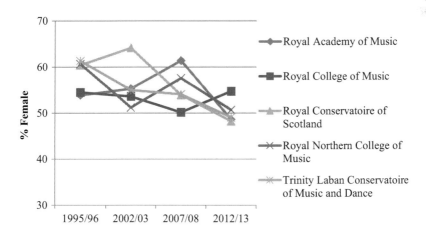

Figure 2.1 Percentage of female students at five UK conservatoires.

In relation to class and music education in the United Kingdom, research demonstrates that children from less privileged class backgrounds are underrepresented.

> [Ninety per cent] of children from AB backgrounds will have played an instrument, compared with 80% of children from other social grades. In addition, 74% of children from AB backgrounds have had instrumental lessons compared with only 55% of children from social grades C1 and DE.
>
> (ABRSM, 2014: 18)

Indeed, Anna Bull's (2015) in-depth study on youth music education in England has identified and traced continuities between middle-class culture and the culture of music education. These continuities manifest themselves in a range of ways, including, for example, the long-term investment required to learn classical music, which more readily resonates with middle-class values (see also Green, 2012; chapter three).

The middle-class culture of classical music education has also been documented in the sphere of UK Higher Education. Georgina Born and Kyle Devine (2015) compared the demographics of students on both traditional music and music technology degrees. Traditional music degrees, which are associated with classical music, draw students with higher social class profiles than the British national average, while music technology degrees are lower in terms of social class profile.[5] Reflecting a similar trend, data on applicants to undergraduate courses at conservatoires (UCAS Conservatoires, 2015: 27) shows that "young people aged 18 in 2013 from the most advantaged areas were 4.6 times more likely to apply through UCAS Conservatoires than those from the most disadvantaged areas." In addition, young people "from the most advantaged areas were more than 6.2 times as likely to be accepted through UCAS Conservatoires as those from the most disadvantaged areas" (28). In this context, and against the backdrop that "graduates from the three conservatoires [Royal Academy of Music; Guildhall School of Music & Drama; Royal College of Music] account for over half of players in the four major London orchestras" (LSE, 2012: 4), it is interesting to explore the class backgrounds of conservatoire students.

As seen in Figure 2.2, excluding unknowns and not applicable entries, 5.2 per cent of students across five UK conservatoires came from a 'low participation neighbourhood' in 2002/2003, which fell to only 3.2 per cent in 2007/2008 and slightly recovered to 3.9 per cent in 2012/2013 (Blamey et al., 2014). By comparison, the overall proportion of students from low participation neighbourhoods in UK higher education in 2011/2012 was above 10 per cent (Universities UK, 2013). In addition, as seen in Figure 2.3, a high proportion of conservatoire students attended a private school (Blamey et al., 2014). Excluding unknowns and not applicable entries, 24.4 per cent of students across five UK conservatoires in 2012/2013 had attended a private school. According to the Independent Schools Council (Independent Schools Council, 2016), the

> independent sector educates around 6.5% of the total number of school children in the UK (and over 7% of the total number of school children in

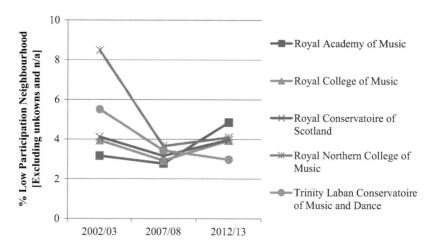

Figure 2.2 Percentage of students from low participation neighbourhoods at five UK conservatoires.

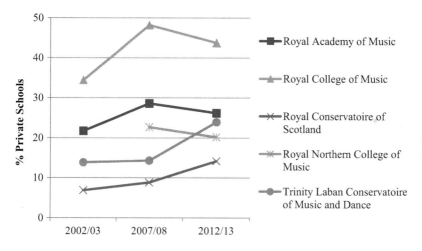

Figure 2.3 Percentage of privately schooled students at five UK conservatoires.

England) with the figure rising to more than 18% of pupils over the age of 16.

The proportion of privately schooled students at conservatoires is thus higher than the UK average.

Apart from class inequalities, there are also racial inequalities in music education. A qualitative study by Graham Welsh and Beverley Mason (2014) documented some of the barriers that black and minority ethnic youth face when engaging in classical music education in the United Kingdom, such as feeling like an outsider and lagging behind: "If you've come from a family that's very culturally aware (Western classical music), then from the age of three you're already one step ahead if you've had that cultural background your whole life." Analysis of the demographic backgrounds of conservatoire students demonstrates that students from black and minority ethnic backgrounds are underrepresented (see Figure 2.4). Among UK music students who disclosed their ethnicity, 10 per cent were from a black and minority ethnic background in 2012/2013. By contrast, the representation of black and minority ethnic students at five UK conservatoires, where data was available, was 8 per cent in 2012/2013 (Blamey et al., 2014).

Again, it is interesting to look at UK conservatoire admission data in this context. Data from 2013 (CUKAS, 2013) demonstrates that there were fewer applicants for undergraduate courses who were black, Asian, and mixed (238), excluding the category 'other', than white applicants (3447). Furthermore, 746 white applicants and no black, 13 Asian, and 26 mixed undergraduate applicants were offered a place. This raises the question of whether the acceptance rate for black and minority ethnic students is lower than that for white students. Between 2011–2013, 110 black undergraduate applicants applied (25 in 2011; 36 in 2012; and 49 in 2013) but none were accepted.

Crucially, black and minority ethnic groups are culturally and socially diverse. In the US context, for example, Asian and Asian American[6] musicians constitute a considerable presence in the world of classical music (League of American Orchestras, 2016; Wang, 2009; Yang, 2007; Yoshihara, 2007). The participation of

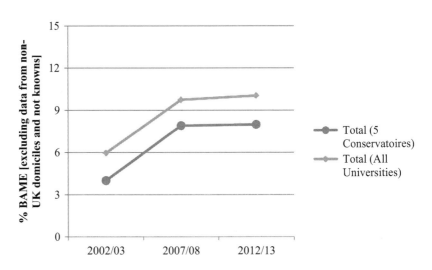

Figure 2.4 Percentage of black and minority ethnic students: i) at five UK conservatoires and ii) doing a music degree across all UK universities.

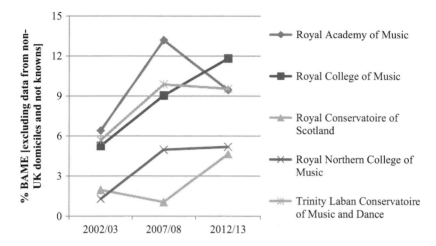

Figure 2.5 Percentage of black and minority ethnic students at five UK conservatoires.

Asians and Asian Americans in classical music can be linked to a range of factors, including "the history of Western imperialism in the nineteenth century, the push for modernization in East Asia from the late-nineteenth to mid-twentieth century, and the process of globalization in the late twentieth century" (Yoshihara, 2007: 6; see also Bates, 2014; Wang, 2009; Yang, 2007). Asians and Asian Americans constitute a large percentage of the student population at leading music schools and departments in the United States (Wang, 2009) and made up just over 9 per cent of players in US orchestras in 2014 (League of American Orchestras, 2016). Musicians of East Asian origin also take part in music competitions internationally, including Europe (Leppänen, 2014). More research needs to be done to explore the representation of this demographic in the classical music sector in Germany and the United Kingdom.

Shifting the focus from music education to the classical music profession, we find that women are underrepresented, despite their overrepresentation on relevant degree programmes. In 2011, women made up 35.5 per cent of the music workforce in Germany[7] (Schulz, 2013a), while the gender profile of artistic staff across the Arts Council England's 2012–2015 National Portfolio Organisations was 38.5 per cent female in music (ACE, 2014). In comparison to other sectors, music had the lowest representation of women, with the grand total of all sectors being 46.9 per cent women (ACE, 2014). The underrepresentation of women in the classical music profession has been made particularly visible in research on orchestral players. Historical data suggests that the number of female players in orchestras is increasing slowly. In 1990, the representation of women in British orchestras was 30 per cent, and 16 per cent in both West and East Germany (All-mendinger and Hackman, 1995). Data on the membership of German orchestras showed that the average percentage of female players in 2014 was around 30 per cent (DOV, 2014). Our study[8] of the membership of British orchestras suggests that women made up 43.2 per cent of players in 2014 (McClure et al., 2014).

Underrepresentation is not limited to orchestral players, but also applies to media coverage of classical and non-classical musicians (Schmutz, 2009), to composers whose work is performed in concerts (Bachtrack, 2014; see also Wimust, 2013), and to commissions for compositions (BASCA, 2016). According to a study[9] published by the British Academy of Songwriters, Composers and Authors (BASCA, 2016), the proportion of female, commissioned composers (21 per cent) was lower than that of men and does not reflect the proportion of female composition students (36 per cent). Women's underrepresentation is notable, given that significantly more women than men engage in the arts in the United Kingdom (Taking Part Survey, 2015). Indeed, women in Germany have more of a preference for classical music and opera than men (MIZ, 2015b).

As compared to research on the representation of women in music, there seems to be an absence of statistical data on the socio-economic background of musicians. In relation to the United Kingdom, the Warwick Commission (2015: 26) pointed out "that no in-depth statistical analysis of cultural and creative workforce data in terms of socio-economic backgrounds has been published". While existing data has recently been analysed (see, for example, O'Brien et al., 2016, discussed above), researchers have attributed the dearth of data on the class backgrounds of cultural workers to the fact that social class was not included as a 'protected characteristic' in the 2010 Equality Act (O'Brien and Oakley, 2015). Looking specifically at the classical music profession, the Musicians' Union (Musicians' Union, 2012) has shown that 56 per cent of surveyed musicians earned less than £20, 000 a year in 2012 (see also Creative Blueprint, 2012). This information does not, however, tell us something about the class backgrounds of musicians. And yet, the available information on music education (ABRSM, 2014; UCAS Conservatoires, 2015), as well as our research on conservatoire students' class backgrounds, highlights the lower representation of children from less privileged socio-economic backgrounds. This suggests that musicians from working-class and/or lower middle-class backgrounds are underrepresented in the profession.

Similar to musicians' class backgrounds, there seems to be a lack of information on the racial backgrounds of cultural workers, including musicians. As shown by the Arts Council England's 2014 report on equality and diversity within the arts and cultural sector, there was an absence of data on the racial background of almost a quarter of staff surveyed, equating to nearly 19,000 people (ACE, 2014). However, the few studies that exist point to an underrepresentation of black and minority ethnic musicians. Creative Blueprint (2012), which includes data on the entire music sector in the United Kingdom in 2010/2011, has shown that 96 per cent of workers in the industry were white and 4 per cent were from a black and minority ethnic background. In our 2014 study of the membership of British orchestras (McClure et al., 2014), it was possible to collect data on the racial backgrounds of the members of 17 orchestras. Of 629 orchestra players, only 11 (1.7 per cent) could be identified to be from a black and minority ethnic background. The study by BASCA (2016: 1), cited above, has also shown that the percentage of commissioned composers who are from a black and minority ethnic background was 7 per cent, which "is especially low if we consider that over half of composers live in London where the BAME population is 30%". These figures on the classical music sector, while limited to orchestral players and commissioned composers, suggest that the number of black and minority ethnic musicians working in this industry is low.

Apart from underrepresentation, the classical music sector also parallels wider trends in the cultural and creative industries in terms of horizontal segregation. Female and male musicians tend to be concentrated in particular fields of the profession, such as instrument groups (see Figure 2.6). Some instruments and instrumental groups are gendered, particularly harp (female), brass (male), and percussion (male) (McClure et al., 2014; see also Coulangeon et al., 2005). These more recent figures on British orchestras resonate with more dated research on the gendered composition of orchestral players in Germany. As Paternoga (2005) has shown, there were numerous female flautists and harpists, but hardly any female percussionists. Horizontal segregation also exists among teaching staff at UK and German conservatoires (see Figures 2.7 and 2.8). Women are particularly over-represented among staff that teach harp and underrepresented in conducting, percussion, and brass (McClure et al., 2014; Wright and Scharff, 2014).

Apart from men and women playing particular instruments, men are overrepresented in composition.[10] This can be gleaned from Figures 2.9 and 2.10, which

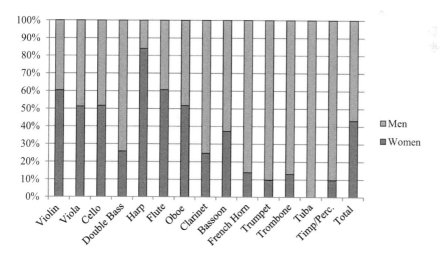

Figure 2.6 Gender breakdown by instrument among members of British orchestras.

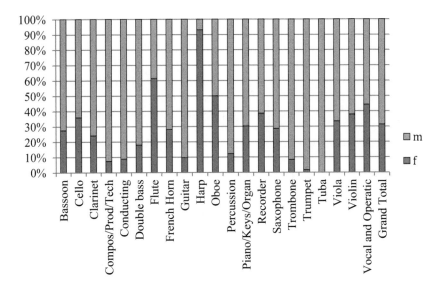

Figure 2.7 Gender breakdown by instrument/subject taught by conservatoire staff in the United Kingdom.

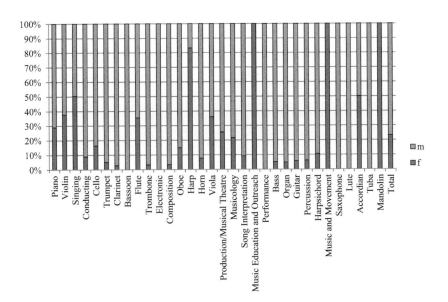

Figure 2.8 Gender breakdown by instrument/subject taught by German conservatoire staff.

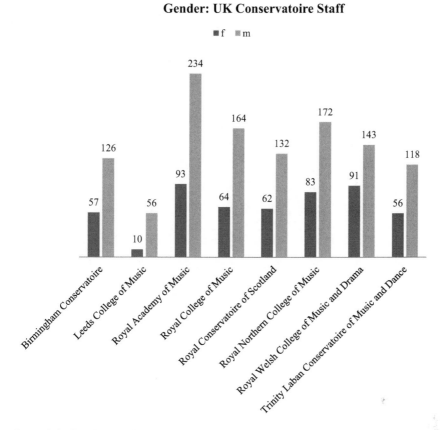

Gender: UK Conservatoire Staff

■ f   ▪ m

Figure 2.9 Gender profile of teaching staff at UK conservatoires.

document the low number of female composition teachers at UK and German conservatoires. Data by Künstlersozialversicherung suggests that the percentage of female composers in Germany has risen from 8 per cent in 1995 to 10 per cent in 2010 (Schulz, 2013b). Similarly, the female membership of the Performing Rights Society For Music in the United Kingdom, as well as its equivalent in Germany, GEMA, was only 14 per cent in Germany in 2013 and is currently 16 per cent in the United Kingdom (Klangzeitort, 2014; PRS for Music Foundation, 2016). Figures on new music festivals in Germany show that the percentage of works performed by female composers was 10 per cent in 2010 and 12 per cent in 2013 (Klangzeitort, 2014). The organisation Women in Music (2016) has surveyed women's participation in the BBC Proms, arguably the world's most significant classical music festival. According to this survey, 1 out of 103 (0.97 per

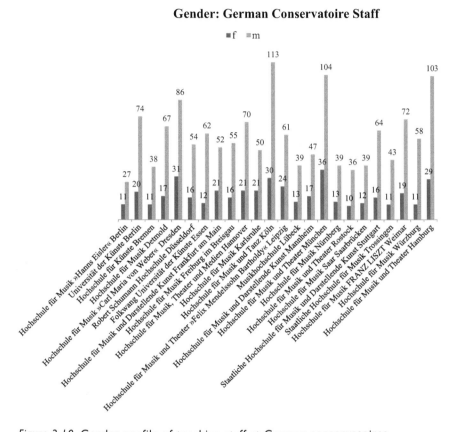

Figure 2.10 Gender profile of teaching staff at German conservatoires.

cent) composers were female in 1992; in 2016, the percentage of female composers had increased to 9.2 per cent (8 out of 116). As Siobhan McAndrew and
Martin Everett (2015) have shown, female composers are no less successful than
male composers in having their compositions featured by the BBC Proms; however, they are significantly less successful in terms of the number of recordings in
which they feature.

In contrast to composition, female musicians are overrepresented in teaching. According to Green (1997), women have dominated music teaching in
Britain and other nations, which provide systematic music education, throughout the twentieth century. In 2014, 71 per cent of music teachers in the United
Kingdom were female, 28 per cent male, and 1 per cent preferred not to say
(ABRSM, 2014). In Germany, more women than men studied music pedagogy
in 2014/2015 (MIZ, 2015a) and more than half of music teachers were female in

2012 (Bossen, 2012). Interestingly, however, music teaching is often considered a lesser form of music making (Bennett, 2008; Comunian et al., 2014; HEFCE, 2002; Mills, 2005). According to Janet Mills (2005), students often agree with statements consistent with a positive attitude to teaching. "However, they also tend to think that secondary class music teaching is not 'doing music'" (2005: 63). Dawn Bennett (2008: 1) echoes these findings by arguing that the term musician is still equated with performer, leading to "the unfortunate perception of music teachers as lesser beings". These reported views correspond to a hierarchy of achievement identified in research on the work, education, and training of professional musicians (HEFCE, 2002), which ranked solo performing highest, followed by ensemble musician, orchestral player, opera chorus, music therapist, teacher, and administrator. The overrepresentation of women in music teaching is not only significant as a feature of horizontal segregation within the classical music profession, but also because of the negative effect it can have on female musicians' career development (Mills, 2007) and the dissociation of teaching from 'true musicianship'.

Crucially, not all forms of music teaching are devalued. Teaching at conservatoires is considered more prestigious and, indicative of vertical segregation, men are overrepresented among conservatoire teachers in the United Kingdom and Germany (see Figures 2.9 and 2.10).[11] In 2014, around 30 per cent of conservatoire teachers in the United Kingdom were female and just over 23 per cent in Germany (McClure et al., 2014; Wright and Scharff, 2014). In Germany, this only represents an increase of around 1 per cent since 2000 (Leberl and Schulz, 2003). Reflecting the lack of women in positions of authority, few conductors are female (Bartleet, 2008; Bennett, 2008), and this seems to be changing slowly. Data collected by Women in Music (2016) has shown that only 5 out of 58 were female conductors (8.6 per cent) at the BBC Proms in 2016.

Women are also underrepresented among conductors, artistic leaders and principals in British orchestras (McClure et al., 2014; see Table 2.1). In 2014, women only made up 1.4 per cent of conductors and 2.9 per cent of artistic/musical directors. Publicly available German data is incomplete; out of 27 identified artistic directors/chief-conductors or conductors, none were female in 2014 (Schulz et al., 2016). Historically, the participation of women in leadership roles in German orchestras has been low (Leberl and Schulz, 2003). While women represented 43.2 per cent of players in British orchestras in 2014, only 26.8 per cent were principals (McClure et al., 2014; see Table 2.2). We also know that women only wrote 7 per cent of orchestral commissions in the United Kingdom, which are considered particularly prestigious (BASCA, 2016). In her less recent study of German orchestras, Paternoga (2005) correspondingly found that there were fewer women than men in better-paid positions. In addition, women tend to be underrepresented in prestigious orchestras, and this has been the case historically (Allmendinger and Hackman, 1995). While women made up 43.2 per cent in British orchestras, they only represented around 30 per cent in the London Symphony Orchestra in 2014 (McClure et al., 2014). Similarly, 19 women played for the

Table 2.1 Total number and percentage of women conductors and artistic directors in British orchestras

Position	Total	% women
Conductor	72	1.4
Artistic/Musical Director	35	2.9

Table 2.2 Total number and percentage of women in British orchestras for: i) all players and ii) principals; by instrument

Instrument	All players		Principals	
	Total	% women	Total	% women
Violin	729	60.4	87	41.4
Viola	244	51.2	33	36.4
Cello	238	51.7	38	28.9
Double Bass	151	25.8	34	17.6
Harp	25	84.0	12	83.3
Flute	94	60.6	44	50.0
Oboe	85	51.8	37	32.4
Clarinet	93	24.7	49	18.4
Bassoon	89	37.1	36	30.6
French Horn	144	13.9	42	14.3
Trumpet	92	9.8	36	5.6
Trombone	84	13.1	36	16.7
Tuba	22	0.0	13	0.0
Timp/Perc.	124	9.7	55	9.1
Total	**2214**	**43.2**	**552**	**26.8**

Berliner Philharmoniker in 2014 (Blech, 2014), which has 128 posts. The percentage of women was thus below the average of 30 per cent female players in German orchestras in the same year (DOV, 2014).

Apart from orchestras, women are poorly represented at board level. In the UK music sector, 65.3 per cent of board members were male and 34.7 per cent were female, as shown by research published in 2014 (ACE, 2014). The same study demonstrated that the grand total for board membership in the arts and cultural sector was 56.5 per cent (male) and 43.5 per cent (female) (ACE, 2014). Probably related to horizontal and vertical segregation, statistics on the UK music sector from 2010/2011 have established that there is a gender pay gap. Men earned £7.92 per hour while women's hourly pay was £6.92 (Creative and Cultural Skills, 2010). With regard to Germany, I have already shown that female freelance musicians earned 22 per cent less than their male counterparts in 2012 (Schulz, 2013b; see also Bossen, 2012). Equally important, earnings were highest in conducting and composing (Schulz, 2013b), which are male-dominated fields.

Women are not the only group who is affected by vertical segregation in the classical music profession. As seen in Table 2.3, our research shows that the representation of black and minority ethnic staff was also low among conservatoire staff in 2014 (McClure et al., 2014; Wright and Scharff, 2014). Out of 1787 staff in the United Kingdom, we could identify the ethnic background of 1345. Twenty-eight staff, or around 2 per cent, were from a black and minority ethnic background. In Germany, we could identify the ethnic background of 1862 staff, with 38 staff, or around 2 per cent, being from a black and minority ethnic background (see Table 2.4). In the arts and cultural sector in the United Kingdom, less than one in ten managers are from a black and minority ethnic background, as research published in 2014 has demonstrated (ACE, 2014). Class background may of course also affect workers' positioning within the classical music hierarchy, but I am not aware of any data on class and vertical segregation in the classical music profession.

Similar to the point I made earlier about the complexities of inequalities in the cultural and creative industries, issues of gender, race, and class in classical music exceed underrepresentation, vertical and horizontal segregation, and the gender pay gap. According to Lisa McCormick (2009: 16), "musical performance is at the same time a performance of race, ethnicity, gender and other social characteristics" (see also DeNora, 2002; McCormick, 2015). In the context of the performance of gender, women musicians encounter particular challenges in relation to negotiating appearance, femininity, and sexuality. As Brydie-Leigh Bartleet (2008) has discussed in her research on the gendered dimensions of conducting, female conductors have to navigate gendered conducting norms skilfully. Conductors' dress, for example, was designed for a male body and no such standard uniform has been developed for women. "As a result, women have had to dress cautiously, in a manner that avoids sexual objectification, but also conveys their own personal femininity" (Bartleet, 2008: 40).

Table 2.3 Ethnic background of teaching staff at UK conservatoires[i]

Conservatoire	BAME	White
Birmingham Conservatoire	<5	114
Leeds College of Music	<5	62
Royal Academy of Music	10	321
Royal College of Music	<5	198
Royal Conservatoire of Scotland	<5	95
Royal Northern College of Music	<5	204
Royal Welsh College of Music and Drama	<5	172
Trinity Laban Conservatoire of Music and Drama	<5	151
Total	28	1317
Grand Total		1345

i Numbers below five deleted to preserve anonymity. However, the totals have remained unchanged.

Table 2.4 Ethnic background of teaching staff at German conservatoires[i]

Conservatoire	BAME	White
Hochschule für Musik "Hanns Eisler" Berlin	<5	37
Universität der Künste Berlin	<5	92
Hochschule für Künste Bremen	<5	49
Hochschule für Musik Detmold	<5	84
Hochschule für Musik "Carl Maria von Weber" Dresden	<5	113
Robert Schumann Hochschule Düsseldorf	<5	68
Folkwang Universität der Künste Essen	<5	71
Hochschule für Musik und Darstellende Kunst Frankfurt am Main	<5	70
Hochschule für Musik Freiburg im Breisgau	<5	69
Hochschule für Musik, Theater und Medien Hannover	<5	89
Hochschule für Musik Karlsruhe	<5	68
Hochschule für Musik und Tanz Köln	<5	135
Hochschule für Musik und Theater "Felix Mendelssohn Bartholdy" Leipzig	<5	82
Musikhochschule Lübeck	<5	50
Hochschule für Musik und Darstellende Kunst Mannheim	<5	62
Hochschule für Musik und Theater München	7	131
Hochschule für Musik Nürnberg	<5	52
Hochschule für Musik und Theater Rostock	<5	46
Hochschule für Musik Saar Saarbrücken	<5	49
Staatliche Hochschule für Musik und Darstellende Kunst Stuttgart	<5	79
Staatliche Hochschule für Musik Trossingen	<5	52
Hochschule für Musik FRANZ LISZT Weimar	<5	90
Hochschule für Musik Würzburg	<5	66
Hochschule für Musik und Theater Hamburg	<5	120
Total	**38**	**1824**
Grand total		**1862**

i Numbers below five deleted to preserve anonymity. However, the totals have remained unchanged.

As McCormick (2015: 152) has shown, female musicians taking part in international music competitions "are well aware not only that their gender is 'visible' to the audience, but also that their physical attractiveness is factored into the listener's experience".

Indeed, female musicians' physical appearance often becomes the focus of media attention. Research on media representations of female and male musicians in the United States, Germany, France, and the Netherlands between 1955 and 2005 has demonstrated that "female musicians receive less media attention than their male counterparts and, when they do receive recognition, their physical appearance and their family lives often garner as much or more attention than their music" (Schmutz, 2009: 301). The representation of female musicians has been an issue historically (Macleod, 2001) and is also not a trivial matter. According to

Green (1997: 65), "femininity risks reducing the seriousness with which women's instrumental music-making is taken". This means that an emphasis on physical appearance can affect the reputation and credibility of female musicians, which is a point that I come back to when discussing the gendered dynamics of self-promotion at the end of this chapter.

Apart from tracing the ways in which gender affects classical music practice, Bull's (2015) study of youth music in England has also explored the interplay between class and classical music. As I have shown above, Bull has documented various links and overlaps between classical music and middle-class culture. She, for example, found that research participants who were from a lower middle-class background were more likely to experience bullying by instrumental teachers than their middle-class peers and generally felt less comfortable and confident in the classical music world. Interestingly, and as I demonstrate in the next chapter, research participants from a working-class background in my study also reported feeling like an outsider in the world of classical music.

Who is 'in' and who is 'out' in the classical music industry, at least in terms of subjective feelings, seems to depend on class background, but also relates to racial and ethnic background. Several studies on race, ethnicity, and classical music, particularly in relation to the status of East Asian players, have shown that Western classical music continues to be associated with whiteness (Leppänen, 2014): "Although Asians have been playing Western art music for over a century, and playing it well, the essentialist idea that this music by natural right belongs to Europeans – is on loan to Asians on an interim basis – prevails" (Yang, 2007: 16). These racialised dimensions of classical music practice also intersect with gender, as is evident in exoticist, visual coding of female Asian musicians. As Mari Yoshihara (2007) has observed, images of female Asian musicians generally fall into one of three categories: the innocent and somewhat alien child prodigy; the young, sensuous, sexy Asian; and the mature, slightly exotic woman. The sexualisation of female players thus intersects with racialised stereotypes. More generally, these insights in relation to gender, class, race, and classical music practice point to the question about the kinds of subjectivities required to becoming, and counting as, a 'classical musician'. This is an issue that I return to in the following section, which draws on existing research on the cultural and creative industries, and the classical music profession, to explain and make sense of the persistence of inequalities.

Making sense of the persistence of inequalities

Many sectors within the cultural and creative industries rely on informal recruitment and it has been well documented that these practices disadvantage women, black and minority ethnic workers, and individuals from working-class or lower middle-class backgrounds (Conor et al., 2015; Eikhof and Warhurst, 2013; Gill, 2002; Thanki and Jefferys, 2007; Wing-Fai et al., 2015). Instead of formal recruitment methods, reliance is placed "on contacts, on word of mouth and on recommendations" (Holgate and McKay, 2009: 159). Networking is thus crucial to finding employment in the cultural and creative industries (Conor et al., 2015; Eikhof and Warhurst, 2013; Grugulis and Stoyanova, 2012; Randle et al., 2015; Wing-Fai et al., 2015; Wreyford, 2015a; b), and this also applies to the classical music profession (Carpos, 2014; Cottrell, 2004). Most of the research participants that I interviewed worked as freelancers and heavily relied on their personal networks in order to get work (see chapter five). As McAndrew and Everett (2015) have shown in relation to composers and the BBC Proms, network connections are critical for achieving great success in having works performed because they act as pathways whereby 'raw talent' is converted into success.

The reliance on networks, however, tends to disadvantage women, as well as working-class and black and minority ethnic workers (Acker, 2006). Research on the UK film industry has shown that white, male, and middle-class workers are more likely to enjoy networks that can provide quality work (Grugulis and Stoyanova, 2012). Access to influential networks is not open to all, but tends to depend on a range of factors, such as educational background, knowing "the 'correct codes of behaviour'", and having the confidence to talk to people (Randle et al., 2015: 598). These factors often privilege workers from middle-class backgrounds because they are more likely to possess the required cultural capital in terms of education and habitus (Friedman et al., 2016; O'Brien and Oakley, 2015; Randle et al., 2015; Scharff, 2017). Gender also plays a role in terms of access to networks (Wreyford, 2015a; b). As Leung Wing-Fai et al. (2015) have pointed out, the spaces for networking, such as pubs, may form challenging environments for women and 'after-hours' socialising is not easily manageable for those with caring responsibilities. Importantly, networks do not only provide access to work, but also fulfil other functions, such as offering advice or featuring role models (O'Brien and Oakley, 2015).

Linked to the reliance on informal recruitment and networking, homophily also plays a role in excluding female workers and those from working-class and black and minority ethnic backgrounds (Koppman, 2015; Wing-Fai et al., 2015; Wreyford, 2015a). Homophily, which describes the tendency of individuals to form networking relationships with those who have a similar background in terms of gender (Ibarra, 1992), race, and class, means that exclusionary hiring practices persist, if unconsciously (Wing-Fai et al., 2015). As Natalie Wreyford (2015a: 117) has demonstrated in relation to the UK film industry, creative homophily is widely understood "as a path to successful collaboration, and since the numbers of women and BAME in the industry are far less than white men, it is very likely that a view of the industry as a meritocracy may not be entirely well founded."

According to Eikhof and Warhurst (2013), the project-based model of production, which is prevalent in the cultural and creative industries, means that there tends to be little time for recruitment and thus little room for error. This, along with the importance placed on reputation for securing and distributing work, adds to the reliance on homophily in hiring practices. Maintaining a good reputation is key to getting work in the cultural and creative industries (Blair, 2001) and the classical music profession (Cottrell, 2004). This makes it harder for cultural workers to raise issues around inequalities because of the "disciplining power of reputation" (O'Brien, 2015: 260) and the "view that resistance could adversely affect workers' careers" (Thanki and Jefferys, 2007: 117). As I discuss in detail in the next chapter, my research participants shared these fears which meant that inequalities often became unmanageable (Jones and Pringle, 2015) and, indeed, unspeakable (Gill, 2014).

Higher education also plays a key role in fostering inequalities in the cultural and creative industries (Oakley and O'Brien, 2016). Relevant factors include the increase in tuition fees, at least in the United Kingdom, but also apply to processes of admission (Burke and McManus, 2009), the importance attributed to work placements (Allen et al., 2013), as well as the development of social networks (Randle et al., 2015). While the United Kingdom has had a history of state-funded art and design training, which offered upwards social mobility to hitherto marginalised working-class youth, this has changed and working-class students are now more marginalised (Banks and Oakley, 2016). My earlier discussion of exclusions in classical music education has already highlighted the middle-class culture of early music training, the lower acceptance rate of women at UK conservatoires, as well as the comparatively low numbers of black and minority ethnic conservatoire students.

Notably, early music education seems to be as important as higher education in this context. Given the early age at which musicians have to commence their training in order to compete professionally, we (Bull and Scharff, forthcoming) would extend Kate Oakley's and Dave O'Brien's (2016) argument about the role of higher education in fostering inequalities to include early music training. This point is not only relevant in relation to the processes described above, such as the middle-class culture of youth music education (Bull, 2015), but becomes particularly important if we place music education in a more global context (see for example Baker, 2014). Erin Johnson-Williams's (2014) research has demonstrated that Victorian music education set in place the very ideologies of social status, class, and race associated with classical music making that still pervade musical practice in Britain and the Commonwealth to this day. According to Roe-Min Kok (2006), the examining boards, which evaluate skills in Western classical music on a scale from grade 1 (elementary) to grade 8 (challenging), were established in the Victorian era and subsequently transmitted to a range of non-Western contexts. Instead of adapting its methods to speak to the specificities of the contexts they were applied in, the "ABRSM directors seemed to have been contented to transfer its methods, created and practiced in culturally, politically, and economically different Britain, directly into a postcolonial setting" (Kok, 2006: 97). Kok's insightful and critical reflections on her experience of undergoing this kind of early music education in post-colonial Malaysia demonstrates the 'colonial violence' it wrought on young minds and psyches. Early music education, in addition to higher education, is thus another context that fosters inequalities in classical music practice.

A further issue that is frequently raised in debates about inequalities in the cultural and creative industries, especially in relation to gender, is that of parenting and, more specifically, mothering. Indeed, it is often argued that women are underrepresented in the cultural and creative industries because of difficulties reconciling managing a career with raising a family (Skillset, 2010; Leberl and Schulz, 2003; Schulz et al., 2016). Sometimes, it seems that the issue that 'women go off and have babies' figures as a convenient explanation for persisting gender inequalities, thus shutting down other avenues of inquiry and critique (Gill, 2014) which would, for example, highlight the exclusionary nature of informal recruitment practices. Feminist analyses of the role that parenting plays in perpetuating gender inequalities thus face a particular dilemma: there is a need to recognise that women overwhelmingly continue to act as primary care givers while avoiding re-cementing the link between women and childcare (Wing-Fai et al., 2015).

Bearing this dilemma in mind, I draw on analyses that highlight the construction of the 'ideal cultural worker' and how this intersects with gender, subjectivity, and parenting (Gill, 2014; Wreyford, 2013; 2015a). Wreyford's (2015a: 165) research on screenwriting in the UK film industry demonstrates that prevalent views of the ideal, creative individual as fully committed and driven have "the effect of excluding anyone with other responsibilities or demands on their time. It is therefore very difficult for women with children to present themselves as ideal screenwriters." As Stephanie Taylor and Karen Littleton (2012) have pointed out, the ideal of the selfish, creative pursuit, which prioritises work over other areas of life, makes it more difficult for women to attain this ideal. Similarly, Wing-Fai et al.'s (2015: 61) research on the UK film and television industries has shown that it was considered "more 'rational' in any given situation to hire a man, because he would be less likely to leave or to take time off". Due to the association between women and childcare, female creative workers may thus be perceived as less ideal in at least two ways: they may be seen to lack the full commitment required for cultural work and regarded as unreliable because of potential periods of maternity leave (Wing-Fai et al., 2015; Wreyford, 2013; 2015a). The subjectivity required for cultural work – that of a fully committed individual with an uninterrupted career – tends to position women at a disadvantage in the context of childcare. This seems to apply regardless of whether or not they are or will become mothers.

In emphasising the role of subjectivity in the context of cultural work, gender, and parenting, I do not seek to discount other important factors, such as the predominance of freelancing and the negative impact this has on entitlement to maternity benefits (Wing-Fai et al., 2015). Furthermore, there are also issues related to the flexible nature of work in the cultural and creative industries (Gill, 2002; Perrons, 2003). While this is frequently lauded, it may indeed make it more difficult for women to carve out the time (Rafnsdóttir and Heijstra, 2013; Edwards and Wajcman, 2005) and space (Bain, 2004; Pohlman, 1996) to work while negotiating domestic and caring responsibilities. In her research on female artists, Alison Bain (2004) showed that women artists working from home struggled to have an uninterrupted and undisturbed space to work, which echoes Livia Pohlman's (1996) earlier research on gender, creativity, and the family. According to

Wreyford (2015a: 184), "[f]ar from being viewed as a benefit, working from home was perceived as an obstacle to work for some of the women in my research." Many of the musicians that took part in my study were comparatively young and therefore did not yet have children. When I asked them about their views on having children, they spoke favourably about the flexibility of the work, including the ability to work from home. Interestingly, however, the few research participants who already had children painted a much more sombre picture of the ability to combine having a family with a career in classical music, pointing, for example, to the lack of childcare provision in the evenings. Gender inequalities in the context of work and parenting are thus not limited to constructions of women as (potential) mothers and caregivers, but also apply to access to maternity benefits and the challenges of flexible work.

Apart from the positioning of women as primary care givers, there are further intersections between subjectivity and inequalities in the cultural and creative industries. Pioneering research (Allen et al., 2013; Conor et al., 2015; Conor, 2014; Gill, 2014; Taylor and Littleton, 2012; Wreyford, 2015a) has highlighted the role that constructions of the ideal worker subjectivity play in maintaining inequalities. In her study on screenwriting, Bridget Conor (2014: 121) has identified the ideal subject positions for the screenwriter, such as the pioneer, egotist, or fighter, and demonstrated that these masculine figures point to "gendered understandings of heroic, individual creativity". Prevailing notions of creativity are certainly gendered. "In contemporary Western mythology, the artist is understood to be male" (Bain, 2004: 172). This myth risks marginalising women from creative processes (Proctor-Thomson, 2013) and roles (Hesmondhalgh and Baker, 2015). In the context of the classical music profession, the association of masculinity with creativity may explain why female artists tend to be overrepresented in supportive roles (such as teaching), while men inhabit roles that are considered more creative (such as composition). Having discussed the association of creativity with masculinity, McAndrew and Everett (2015: 64) point out that "male composers accordingly have an advantage because they look like people's preconceptions of what a composer looks like."

The ideal, classical musician is not only gendered, but also classed. As Bull (2015: 25) has argued, "the accumulative, resourced, entitled, middle-class self (Skeggs, 2003) is both *assumed* in classical music education, and also *actively formed* through its norms" (emphases in original). As aforementioned, this middle-class self comes to the fore in the future orientation of classical music education but also in the way the body is controlled and disciplined. Cultivating restraint is a key part of classical music practice, but also a cornerstone of bourgeois subjectivity. According to Bull (2015: 159–160), "[i]t is significant that this is occurring within a predominantly middle-class site, as this restraint or control is historically a valued trait of bourgeois identity, therefore it is important for young middle-class people to learn it." Through her focus on subjectivity and the body, Bull (2015) makes an important contribution, which highlights that the link between class and classical music education is more than just economic: classical music practice in itself is associated with key traits of bourgeois subjectivity; in reproducing classical music, we also reproduce classed (and gendered) subjectivities.

As I have alluded to in my earlier discussion of the status of East Asian musicians, the classical music profession is also characterised by racial hierarchies and the association of classical music with whiteness (Leppänen, 2014). In relation to subjectivity, this association manifests itself in constructions and perceptions of white musicians as creative and musical, and their 'others', particularly East Asian musicians, as robotic, technical, and lacking 'real artistry' (Yang, 2007; Leppänen, 2014). According to Taru Leppänen (2014: 10), "classical music has embraced the idea that music must spring from the musician's self". This self, however, seems to be racially marked as white. As Mina Yang (2007: 14) puts it, "Asians have the technique, Westerners have the heart, the soul. The image of Asians as automatons, robots without souls, appears frequently in the Western imagination." I also encountered these stereotypes in my interviews with the research participants, some of who described East Asian musicians as 'technically skilled' and yet 'robotic'. I discuss these constructions of East Asian musicians in detail elsewhere (Scharff, 2017). Here, I seek to draw attention to the role of race in constructions of musicality and the ways this maps onto the ideal worker subjectivity. If whiteness is associated with musicality, and musicality deemed a key marker of good musicianship, then the ideal classical musician appears to be white.

This does, of course, not mean that it is impossible for black and minority ethnic musicians to forge a career in classical music. There are several examples of successful minority ethnic musicians and Yoshihara's (2007) study describes beautifully the complex ways in which Asian and Asian American musicians navigate their racial and musical identities in the wider context of classical music practice. However, I believe that the suggested link between whiteness and musicality indicates some barriers that black and minority ethnic musicians may face, which for example affect the ways their musicianship is evaluated. As a study (Elliott, 1995) on the effects of race and gender on the evaluations of music performers by musician educators has shown, black musicians were consistently evaluated lower than white musicians, even though the musical performance was identical (videotapes of male and female, as well as black and white performers were synchronised to identical performances). Indeed, the same study also showed how gender, and more specifically associations of particular instruments (flute and trumpet) with women and men, affect evaluations of classical music performance. This finding resonates with Claudia Goldin's and Cecilia Rouse's (2000) study on the effects of the shift to blind auditions in US orchestras, which may explain 25 per cent of the increase in the percentage of female players in the orchestras from the 1970s to 1996. These studies, as well as the wider research on inequalities in cultural work, highlight the role that gender, race, and class play in constructions of the ideal classical musician. In keeping with the focus on subjectivity, the next and final section of this chapter homes in on the entrepreneurial subjectivity required to be a cultural worker (see chapter one). More specifically, I analyse the role that self-promotion plays in succeeding in the classical music profession and demonstrate its gendered dynamics.

Exploring the gendered dynamics of self-promotion

As I have argued in the previous chapter, cultural work is increasingly (though not exclusively) governed by the values of entrepreneurialism; the field of classical music is not exempt from this trend. This shift towards entrepreneurialism means that the worker

> must be enterprising about making herself enterprising: becoming in effect a microcosmic business; developing a strategy, marketing herself, developing 'products', establishing herself as a brand, understanding the market (for herself) and so on.
>
> (Storey et al., 2005: 1036; see also Brouillette, 2013; Haunschild and Eikhof, 2009; McRobbie, 2015)

If workers are businesses that have to be marketed, they have to promote themselves. "Promoting the self, then, refers to processes in which different forms of marketing and branding are combined with 'advancing the self' in one way or another" (Mäkinen, 2012: 16). Or, to use Laurie Rudman's definition (1998: 629), self-promotion includes "pointing with pride to one's accomplishments, speaking directly about one's strengths and talents, and making internal rather than external attributions for achievements".

Self-promotion constitutes a central aspect of the entrepreneurial work ethos and yet the gendered politics of self-promotion[12] and the link of the self-promotional subject to wider inequalities in the cultural and creative industries have not been examined in great detail. By exploring how the research participants talked and felt about self-promotion, I aim to deepen our understanding of the kinds of subjectivities that are forged in order to succeed in the cultural and creative industries. More specifically, I trace the gendered dynamics of self-promotion to highlight the ways in which the self-promoting, entrepreneurial subject is bound, but not determined by particular gendered conventions. Adding to my preceding discussion about the gendered, classed, and racialised constructions of the ideal cultural worker and classical musician, this section seeks to deepen our understanding of the ways in which constructions of ideal worker subjectivities are implicitly gendered.

Many research participants emphasised that "you have to be really proactive in kind of in selling yourself" (Rose) "and you just gotta sell yourself as much as possible" (Robyn) in order to find work. As Linda pointed out, "no one would know you existed, and it's very much about selling yourself as a product". Resonating with the preceding discussion of informal recruitment practices in the cultural and creative industries, the research participants stated that self-promotion was key to finding employment, especially in the freelance sector.

While they readily and frequently pointed to the need to self-promote, many participants emphasised that they disliked selling themselves. Some of these statements were unprompted, as in Amanda's case:

> And then there is also things like you know, these days working life of a musician it's also, it's meant to be you sell yourself and you promote yourself and you do this on Facebook, and I just hate all that. I hate it with a really, really passion. I just – I always say why can't I just play? So I really, really dislike that part of it.

When asked how they felt about self-promotion, several research participants used similar, affect-laden language:

CHRISTINA: And how do you feel about going out there and asking people to support a particular project, this kind of marketing yourself – I guess it is a bit like that. How do you like that, how do you feel about doing that?
HOLLY: I really don't like it. I really, really, really don't like it.

Apart from Holly, Amy described self-promotion as "repulsive" and Susan as "cringe worthy". Emilia admitted that she does not "find it easy at all" and three other participants felt "uncomfortable" with promoting their work. Claiming that she sometimes spends 80 per cent of her time on promotional activities, Christine stated: "I would definitely rather not do it if I didn't have to."

There were some exceptions with a few participants expressing more positive attitudes towards self-promotion. Talking about updating her website, Carolyn stated:

> Generally, if I am just adding concerts and things, or adding some sound clips to the website, it's quite like – like I said, I think it is nice to put yourself out there and kind of be proud of what you do.

And as other discourse analysts have shown (Potter and Wetherell, 1987), research participants sometimes change their attitudes during an interview when they discuss the same issue in a different discursive context. I cited Christine's statement above that she "would definitely rather not" promote her work. She subsequently described her feelings in different ways:

> You know, you have to kind of be – show your peacock feathers, you know, sort of fan out your tail a bit. And I think instead of trying to think: "I have got to constantly prove myself" I try to think of it in more of a fun way than that. And often people – you know, it can be fun, actually, because if people

reply and they say "I really love that bit of music", that's great, you know, that gives you a bit of a boost really.

By thinking of self-promotion "in more of a fun way", Christine discusses the practice in positive terms and subsequently adopts a more affirmative attitude. While stances towards self-promotion were overwhelmingly negative, these statements demonstrate that they were not predetermined and could shift over time.

Performing modesty and femininity

Interestingly, several research participants emphasised that they found it easy to promote *other* people's work. Alice stated: "If it was someone else, no problem. I could sell sand to the Egyptians [. . .] But it's really hard to sell yourself." Alice's rather offensive statement demonstrates that she did not feel she lacked the necessary skills, but that she struggled to promote her *own* achievements. Talking about her experiences of working part-time for a cultural organisation, Liz said that she was very good at marketing "but that wasn't really about myself, and that's where it becomes difficult". This finding resonates with Corinne Moss-Racusin's and Laurie Rudman's (2010) study on attitudes towards self-promotion. They found that female participants struggled to promote their own work in comparison to male participants, but that these gender differences disappeared when women acted on behalf of a peer. As Moss-Racusin and Rudman (2010: 187) have pointed out, "self-promotion is problematic for women because it violates female prescriptions to be helpful, supportive, and other-oriented." In the context of cultural work, Taylor (2011: 368) has equally shown that the selfishness demanded by creative working conflicts "with long-established gendered positionings of women as other-oriented, attending to the needs of others and heeding their preferences".

In support of these findings, several research participants pointed out that self-promotion might come more easily to men. Alice continued her statement on her difficulties with self-promotion:

> Sometimes I think it's harder for women. Girls aren't – we aren't as good at that sort of thing, men are much better at being cut-throat and straight to the point, whereas [. . .] I'll zigzag until I get to where I want to go.

Equally, Christine said that self-promotion was:

> Something that you have to do, you have to do it, so I think certainly being a confident person really does help, and you know, confidence in itself is important as well, definitely. Which I think sometimes can come to men easier than it comes to women.

In these statements, Alice and Christine orient to their positionings as women to discuss their difficulties with self-promotion and to point out that confidence is key. This reference to confidence is notable as it is illustrative of a wider cultural context, which "seeks to persuade us that women are being held back not by patriarchal capitalism or institutionalised sexism, but by their own lack of confidence" (Gill, 2016: paragraph 8). But, as Eve's statement demonstrates, acting confidently might not provide an easy solution for women:

> If you are confident in any way people will think that's a bit aggressive or whatever, you shouldn't act like this, and – again, I don't know whether that's a personal thing or whether people would say that because they wouldn't expect a woman to act like that.

Similar to Alice and Christine, Eve orients to her positioning as a woman but also points to gendered expectations about women's display of confidence.

Indeed, several studies have shown that women who self-promote violate gender prescriptions to be modest (Moss-Racusin and Rudman, 2010; Rudman, 1998; Williams et al., 2012; Steinpreis et al., 1999), also in the cultural and creative industries (O'Brien, 2015). While a self-confident demeanour might be helpful in the context of self-promotion, gendered expectations that women be modest mean that they may reject such behaviour. According to Nora:

> It just doesn't come naturally to me, certainly, to just try and shout out about my work or say: "I am really proud of this work, I'd really love for you to come and see it". I mean it just smacks of self-promotion and sort of lack of modesty.

By emphasising her natural predispositions, Nora orients to gendered expectations that women are modest. She subsequently rejects self-promotion and instead opts to perform modesty.

In negotiating the contradictory requests to engage in self-promotion on the one hand and coming across as modest on the other, female musicians do not only perform modesty, but also femininity (Butler, 1993; Scharff, 2012). This means that I do not read their statements as indicative of a 'feminine essence' that naturally predisposes women to be modest. Instead, modesty and femininity are performatively constituted in Nora's statement through her claim that shouting out about her work does not come to her "naturally". Equally, Jane performed femininity in her statement about self-promotion:

> I feel a bit awkward doing that I suppose, yeah, I don't like to be pushy. But I'll try and do it in a nice way, just being friendly and chatting to network with people and meet people, so – more trying to make friends with people rather than appear too pushy [. . .]. Perhaps I would have got further quicker in my career if I had been a bit more proactive and a bit pushier, but I guess I am not *naturally* like that, and I think that is the best way to be I suppose, to get further with your career – certainly people I know that are a bit more

pushy, proactive, do get more work. I guess it's a personality thing, and I'm not *naturally* like that.

Similar to Nora, Jane evokes naturalness in negotiating self-promotion. She rejects pushy behaviour by repeatedly emphasising that she is not "naturally" like that. The reiterative nature of her statement highlights its performative function if we recall that performatives rely on reiteration to succeed (Butler, 1993). My understanding of gender is thus different from the one put forward by some of the research participants. While Nora and Jane take recourse to notions of femininity as a 'natural' property, I am examining how femininity is produced performatively.

Resonating with Jane's statement, several participants did not want to be pushy and instead intended to do self-promotion "nicely" and "politely" (Janine). Indeed, a few participants mentioned that engaging in self-promotion was a tight balancing act. According to Sophie and Saaga, self-promotion is:

Kind of difficult cause sometimes you don't want to be saying you're fabulous because then you sound like an idiot and no one will work with you but then at the same time if you say "I'm not very good at that" then people will believe that you're not very good at that. So it's quite a fine line.

(Sophie)

Talking to another musician about yourself, what you do, is much more difficult [than talking to audience members] because you can't be general, you have to be very like, pushy, without seeming pushy.

(Saaga)

These statements demonstrate the fine line between being confident and pushy. They indicate that female musicians do not find it impossible to promote their work, but that they engage in a lot of boundary work to delineate acceptable forms of self-promotion. The interviews can actually be read as discursive sites where such boundary work is undertaken and femininity performed. Such a reading suggests that the accounts provided in the interviews figure as another instance where gender is done.

In addition to gender, racial background and language skills intersected with the musicians' confidence in promoting their work (see also Williams et al., 2012). As Kira stated:

I know many good and really great pianists, but they can't sell themselves well. So I'm not saying that I am good at it, but – yeah, I am Japanese, I have spent eight years, nine years here and my German is a catastrophe and it's really, really difficult to be on the phone. And then I'm also not good at spelling. But yes, I'm trying it a bit, so that I can play a bit.

Kira also performs modesty in her statement by saying that she is not very good at selling herself. At the same time, her remarks point to the fact that self-promotion relies on a range of skills – such as language skills – that may not be equally accessible to all.

Liz also referred to her ethnic background in discussing her feelings towards self-promotion:

> But I have a real problem with pushing myself out there in a publicity sense, which is I think largely connected to my dad who brought me up to think that you shouldn't say, go around saying how good you are – and almost feel ashamed of myself for doing that. Which is partly cultural, because he is Indian, there's a different sense of what's proper and not proper.

Similar to my analysis of femininity as performance, ethnicity is performed in Kira's and Liz's statements. Both participants evoke their ethnic background in negotiating their discomfort with self-promotion. These extracts demonstrate that self-promotion, which is part of the wider entrepreneurial ethos, posed particular dilemmas that were linked to ethnic background and language ability. Indeed, Kim Allen et al. (2013) also identified classed dynamics of self-promotion in their research on work placements, inequalities, and higher education. They found that class confidence enabled middle-class students to self-promote because the necessary feeling of entitlement was more easily accessible to them. The quest to promote one's work thus challenges gendered norms that women are modest, but also intersects with ethnic and class background.

Art, commerce, and femininity

In discussing their feelings towards self-promotion further, several musicians expressed a "strong desire for what you do to just speak for itself" (Amanda). The rejection of self-promotion was frequently justified by drawing on the commonly used discourse that art and commercial activities are incompatible. While this discourse does not hold absolutely (Taylor and Littleton, 2008), Yoshihara's (2007: 6–7) ethnographic study on Asian and Asian American musicians has shown that "[c]lassical musicians, Asians or not, continue to proudly cherish their anti-commercialist, anti-materialist, art-for-art's-sake ideals".

In this vein, Sonja stated that self-marketing "really has very little to do with art". Several participants echoed her claim by drawing a distinction between musical and artistic skills on the one hand, and entrepreneurial and business skills on the other. In discussing the relationship between music making and business, Zola said:

> I don't think that it [art] belongs to any kind of business. It's such a creative thing, it's a personal thing. I feel like it shouldn't have anything to do with business. But also of course it does have to have something to do with business so we can earn some money and make a living, but I just [. . .] I dislike it. Because it does include a lot of bragging about what you can do, what you

are capable of, what you have done, and [. . .] I want my work to speak for itself, but sadly that is not how the business works.

Equally referring to different mind-sets, Linda claimed that:

> It's quite hard to do both – you know, the creative playing stuff and then having the business mind. It's quite hard to do them both well, I suppose. There are obviously musicians who do that, but then – and there are so many people who are, they are either really good at business, but you know, fairly average musicians, and there are amazing musicians who just have no business mind and therefore can't quite get to where they sort of should be.

These negotiations of the relationship between creative and business skills highlight the musicians' positioning at the axis point "between the forces of art and commerce" (Banks, 2007: 8). In drawing a distinction between artistic and commercial activities, Sonja, Zola, and Linda evoke an "aura of specialness" (Toynbee, 2013: 96) where musicians, and other cultural workers, "revolt against instrumental rationality, market relations and industrial capitalism" (93). By claiming specialness, the research participants discursively secure their status as artists. In this context, the distinction between art and commerce fulfils a constitutive function and affirms the participants' positioning as artists.

Although the distinction between art and commerce helped the participants establish themselves as artists, the very same distinction also had its perils. Arguably, the art-commerce axis constitutes a fraught terrain for female artists because of their historical positioning as the artist's other, which I have discussed above. If self-promotion is associated with commerce and not art, and if women are always-already positioned as the artist's other, female musicians' engagements in entrepreneurial activities might threaten their credibility and status as artists.

Isabella's discussion of the difficulties of being a female artist captures these tensions well:

> I mean we know everything is now about marketing, in any profession [. . .]. Unfortunately, talking from an art point view, it cheapens it. Because I do not want to be a product; I want to be an artist. I am not interested in, you know, the way I look, okay, well I like to look good, but that is outside from my art, that is me being a girl. But it really cheapens you when they are trying to sell it, your art, through the way you look, or whatever, and, okay I do not mind, but I do not want to be portrayed as one of those girls who just look good and cannot do it, because that is not why I work so hard. And I absolutely would not want to do it that way, but unfortunately, everything happens this way right now.

Isabella's negotiations of her appearance and femininity, and the ways these intersect with racial and class background, merit closer analysis elsewhere. What

I would like to highlight here is Isabella's struggle to promote her work without jeopardising her status as an artist. She engages in a lot of discursive negotiations to stabilise her positioning as a female artist in spite of her good looks. By splitting her appearance and femininity from her art ("that is outside from my art, that is me being a girl"), Isabella attempts to rid herself from commercial preoccupations in order to affirm her status as an artist.

Female musicians' struggles to be regarded as artists also emerged from other statements. Eve recounted her experiences of being a female student at a brass department:

> People always called us together: "Oh, they are the two women [brass players]". I just wanted to break up that – just really push and be thought of as a musician, rather than as the token woman in the department.

By distancing herself from being the "token woman in the department", and wanting to be thought of as a "musician" instead, Eve attempts to occupy the positioning of an artist, one that is less fraught than that of a woman brass player.

In contexts where there are few women, such as in brass departments, it does, however, seem difficult to escape being positioned as female. Sasha, who played in an all-female brass ensemble, stated that they had to devise an innovative marketing strategy because they "did not want to be typecast as women that sort of played [brass instruments], we wanted to do something more". Lauren alluded to a similar dilemma when voicing her misgivings about self-promotion. Having stated that she just wants to play the piano, she went on to say:

> And I will do that in a place and a way where I am appreciated for my skills, I don't have to sell myself, because I am kooky or female or weird or different, you know? I wanna be good at what I'm doing, that's it.

These statements indicate that it is difficult for female musicians to promote their work in ways that affirm, rather than threaten, their positioning as artists. This means that practices of self-promotion may not only challenge the musicians' gendered subjectivities because they involve modes of behaviour that are cast as unfeminine. Through the association of self-promotion with commercial practices that are regarded as non-artistic, self-promotion may also threaten musicians' already tenuous status as female artists.

The spectre of prostitution

When discussing their work, a few research participants alluded to prostitution. Some references to prostitution worked as a metaphor to describe unpopular types of musical work, such as teaching. Kara observed:

> We want to make art, but often you're just being a prostitute, basically, I think that makes it difficult. I don't know many musicians that say: "I'm going

to teach today, all day! Yes! I'm looking forward to it!" [. . .] I think a lot of musicians just want to practice their instrument and play nice music, but that's just not life.

Astrid also referred to prostitution when reflecting on her experiences of freelancing as a singer. In this case, however, the reference to prostitution related to her position as a woman in music and related issues of sexualisation. Astrid told me that she had recently performed with a band that played popular music:

> I really liked playing with them, but it was still, it had an aura of – for example, at the end of one evening, a man approached me and was like: "How much do you cost?" And I thought: "No, really?" [laughs]. No, and I mean it does not happen to you at every gig, but somehow you easily get into a position – I think that it's clear to everybody who is involved that it's a form of prostitution, somehow, in one way or another, I had the feeling.

Interestingly, Astrid does not explicitly portray prostitution as a gendered phenomenon. Indeed, her statement disarticulates (McRobbie, 2009; Scharff, 2012) the gendered dimension of prostitution by using the indefinite pronoun 'everybody'.

A closer look at the interviews does however suggest that female musicians negotiate specifically gendered and sexualised connotations when selling themselves. Reflecting on the various aspects of her freelance work, Kim stated:

> I mean I do Bollywood gigs, which is quite different from doing orchestral – I mean lots of orchestral musicians or freelance musicians do play for weddings and things like that. And I do that as well as in normal quartets but also Bollywood music, and there I am dressing up in either a sari or this or that. But I'm not doing it all the time, and I'm not selling my body, as it were, in that way.

As Kim's emphasis on "not selling [her] body" indicates, the notion of selling yourself can take on sexual meanings. Discussing female musicians' self-presentation, Jeanette wondered:

> How do you present yourself as a woman on stage? And when you look at the covers [of CDs] – they all sit there with a cleavage and you can see their G-strings shine through and they sell themselves somehow, yes, and I find that unprofessional. So yes, there, the woman gets degraded to being a sex object. And I really don't like that.

Jeanette's statement establishes links between sexy self-presentation, self-selling, and women being degraded to sex objects. The sexual connotations of women selling themselves may make it more difficult for female musicians to engage in self-promotion. Discussing her experiences of playing in commercial women's bands, Sonja pointed out that "you then sell yourself as a woman, commercially, and I find that very, very difficult". While she did not explore her reasons for finding it difficult, I want to suggest that the notion of "selling yourself" is not gender neutral. On a global level, it is mainly women who sell their bodies, and many do so in the context of sex work (Outshoorn, 2004).

Although there were only a few participants such as Jeanette who overtly established a link between self-selling and sexualisation, there were numerous passages in the data where the sexualisation of female musicians was indirectly evoked and negotiated. In relation to female players' success, for example, there was gossip that "they had slept their way to the top" (Elena). As Yoshihara (2007: 110) has found, there are frequent rumours "about famous female musicians having sexual relations with powerful conductors or managers who helped them launch their careers". These rumours are gendered as it is mainly women's success that is represented, and devalued, in these ways.

Reflecting on her conduct in an orchestra she was trialling with, Judith pointed out that she tried to be nice, but not too nice because "I would hate to feel that I only got the job because people fancy me or because they think this could happen or whatever." Ricarda, who was exceptional in that she held a permanent position in a prestigious orchestra, reported that she sometimes made pre-emptive jokes about having a sexual relationship with the male conductor:

> Sometimes I try and say it myself to kind of prevent anyone from trying [to make a joke]. I sort of talk about how I, you know, how: "Well, you know me and [name of male conductor], I mean, how else do you think I got this job?"

In these statements, Judith and Ricarda orient to their positioning as females and actively seek to pre-empt rumours that their success is based on sexual relationships. Even though these statements are not directly related to prostitution, they highlight one of numerous instances where female musicians are sexualised. Against the backdrop of the sexualisation of female players and the gendered nature of sex work, the notion that female musicians sell themselves may evoke the spectre of prostitution. Arguably, female musicians have to perform an additional layer of discursive work when engaging in self-promotion. At stake are not only their positionings as women and artists, but also the recognition of their skills that easily get devalued through rumours that they slept with powerful men.

As this section has demonstrated, the requirement to self-promote is fraught with particular tensions for women. First, self-promotion is associated with pushy behaviour that conflicts with normative expectations that women be nice and modest, and gives rise to dilemmas in the performance of femininity. Second, self-promotion is regarded as a commercial activity and positioned as un-artistic. Taking into account that women have been constructed as the artist's other, engagement in self-promotion may threaten their already tenuous status as artists. Lastly, the notion of selling yourself may evoke the spectre of prostitution due to the sexualisation of female musicians and the fact that it is mainly women who sell their bodies.

As I have shown, these gendered dynamics do not mean that female musicians are unable to pursue self-promotion, but that they engage in a range of discursive strategies to negotiate and secure their status as female artists. This discursive work is required to bridge the gap between the ideal subjectivity of the self-promoting cultural worker, which is implicitly constructed as masculine, and the research participants' subject positions as women. My examination of the gendered politics of self-promotion thus identified another layer of the kinds of subjectivities that are required to succeed in the classical music profession and the cultural and creative industries. As I have argued, these subjectivities are constructed along gendered, racialised, and classed lines. Closer analysis of the intersections between cultural work and subjectivity thus adds to our understanding of the persistence of inequalities in the cultural and creative industries.

Conclusion

This chapter began with a brief discussion of inequalities in the cultural and creative industries to set the scene for a much more detailed analysis of gender, racial, and class issues in the classical music sector. My analysis set out with a focus on music education and then moved on to explore underrepresentation as well as vertical and horizontal segregation. Notably, I pointed out that inequalities in the classical music profession are not limited to these patterns. Gender imbalances, for example, also relate to the particular challenges that female musicians face in relation to appearance, femininity, and sexuality. Having documented a range of existing hierarchies and exclusions, the third section drew on wider research on cultural work, which has provided explanations for the persistence of inequalities. This work has foregrounded several factors, such as informal recruitment practices, the reliance on networking, and exclusionary constructions of who constitutes the ideal, cultural worker.

As the final section on the gendered dimensions of self-promotion has demonstrated, analyses of subjectivity add a crucial dimension to our understanding of the persistence of inequalities in the cultural and creative industries, including the classical music profession. The next chapter also focuses on subjectivity, but approaches it from a different angle by asking how musicians make sense of ongoing hierarchies, privileges, and exclusions in the classical music profession. By shedding light on cultural workers' subjective experiences and sense making, the following analysis complements this chapter's examination of the documentation and explanation of existing inequalities.

Notes

1 I presented some of this data in my 2015 research report *Equality and Diversity in the Classical Music Profession* available at: http://blogs.kcl.ac.uk/young-female-and-entrepreneurial/files/2014/02/Equality-and-Diversity-in-the-Classical-Music-Profession.pdf

2 The Künstlersozialversicherung offers freelance artists and publicists national insurance (see also conclusion). It provides a wealth of data on the social and economic

situation of freelance cultural workers. The data cited here has been collated and ana-lysed by Schulz (2013b) and relates to freelancers.

3 As I pointed out in the introduction to this book, statistics in Germany do not tend to include any data on racial and ethnic background.

4 These findings are based on data purchased from the Higher Education Statistics Agency (HESA). The data set included all students doing an undergraduate or post-graduate music degree in the United Kingdom in 1995/1996, 2002/2003, 2007/2008, and 2012/2013. The data contained information on the demographic backgrounds of the students, including gender, ethnicity, nationality, and class backgrounds (as com-posed of the fields 'state school marker', 'socio-economic classification', and 'low participation neighbourhood marker'). John Blamey and Patrizia Kokot analysed this data, looking in particular at the demographic backgrounds of students at the five conservatoires that were represented in the data, and how their demographic back-grounds compare to music students in the United Kingdom as a whole. Please see http://blogs.kcl.ac.uk/young-female-and-entrepreneurial/files/2014/02/Equality-and-Diversity-in-the-Classical-Music-Profession.pdf for more information on the research methodology.

5 Born and Devine (2015) also found that the demographic of traditional music degrees in terms of gender matched the wider student population, while music technology degrees are overwhelmingly male.

6 As outlined in the previous chapter, I use US terminology when discussing the North American context.

7 This relates to employees paying mandatory social security contributions.

8 Data on the British orchestral landscape/conservatoire staff is based on a study con-ducted by Brigid McClure, Patrizia Kokot, and myself. This study documented pub-licly available information on the demographic backgrounds of orchestral musicians and conservatoire staff. Please see http://blogs.kcl.ac.uk/young-female-and-entrepre neurial/files/2014/02/Equality-and-Diversity-in-the-Classical-Music-Profession.pdf for information on the research methodology.

9 The data on music commissions covers works by British composers (either born in the United Kingdom or resident in the United Kingdom for five years), which received their UK premiere between 1 April 2014 and 31 March 2015.

10 Green (1997: 88) attributes the underrepresentation of female composers to the 'cerebral' aspects of composition, "for composition involves a metaphorical display of the power of mind. This cerebral power conflicts with patriarchal constructions of femininity to the extent that, when it is harnessed by women, it produces a threat to the sexual order."

11 The data set for German conservatoires (Wright and Scharff, 2014) is based on the 24 conservatoires that are members of the German Association of Music Colleges (www.die-deutschen-musikhochschulen.de/ueber-uns/mitglieder/start/). Fiona Wright used publicly available staff listings to document the gender and ethnic backgrounds of teaching staff. For more information on how gender and ethnic backgrounds were attributed, see the methodology used in McClure et al., 2014, available at: http://blogs. kcl.ac.uk/young-female-and-entrepreneurial/files/2014/02/Equality-and-Diversity-in-the-Classical-Music-Profession.pdf

12 But see Mäkinen, 2012, on self-promotion in the context of coaching.

References

ABO (2014). *Youth ensembles survey report*. London: Association of British Orchestras. Accessed 1 December 2016. Available at: www.abo.org.uk/media/33505/ABO-Youth-Ensemble-Survey-Report-App.pdf

ABRSM (2014). *Making music: Teaching, learning and playing in the UK*. London: Associated Board of the Royal Schools of Music. Accessed 1 December 2016. Available at: http://gb.abrsm.org/fileadmin/user_upload/PDFs/makingMusic2014.pdfhttp://gb.abrsm.org/fileadmin/user_upload/PDFs/makingMusic2014.pdf

ACE (2014). *Equality and diversity within the arts and cultural sector in England*. London: Arts Council England. Accessed 1 December 2016. Available at: www.artscouncil.org.uk/publication/equality-and-diversity-within-arts-and-cultural-sector-england

Acker, J. (2006). Inequality regimes: Gender, class, and race in organizations. *Gender & Society, 20*(4), 441–464.

Allen, K., Quinn, J., & Hollingworth, S. (2011). Doing diversity and evading equality: The case of student work placements in the creative sector. In Y. Taylor (Ed.), *Educational diversity: The subject of difference and different subjects* (pp. 180–200). Basingstoke: Palgrave Macmillan.

Allen, K., Quinn, J., Hollingworth, S., & Rose, A. (2013). Becoming employable students and 'ideal' creative workers: Exclusion and inequality in higher education work placements. *British Journal of Sociology of Education, 34*(3), 431–452.

Allmendinger, J., & Hackman, J. (1995). The more, the better? A four-nation study of the inclusion of women in symphony orchestras. *Social Forces, 74*(2), 423–460.

Antrag der Abgeordneten (2013). *Für die tatsächliche Gleichstellung von Frauen und Männern auch im Kunst-, Kultur- und Medienbereich. Drucksache 17/13478*. Accessed 1 December 2016. Available at: http://dip21.bundestag.de/dip21/btd/17/134/1713478.pdf

Bachtrack (2014). *2014 in Statistiken: Eine Wachablösung der klassischen Art*. Accessed 1 December 2016. Available at: https://bachtrack.com/classical-music-statistics-2014

Bain, A. L. (2004). Female artistic identity in place: The studio. *Social & Cultural Geography, 5*(2), 171–193.

Baker, G. (2014). *El Sistema: Orchestrating Venezuela's youth*. New York: Oxford University Press.

Banks, M. (2007). *The politics of cultural work*. Basingstoke: Palgrave Macmillan.

Banks, M., & Oakley, K. (2016). The dance goes on forever? Art schools, class and UK higher education. *International Journal of Cultural Policy, 22*(1), 41–57.

Bartleet, B-L. (2008). Women conductors on the orchestral podium: Pedagogical and professional implications. *College Music Symposium, 48*, 31–51.

BASCA (2016). *Equality and diversity in new music commissioning*. London: British Academy of Songwriters, Composers & Authors. Accessed 1 December 2016. Available at: https://basca.org.uk/newsletter/BASCA_Music-Commissioning.pdf

Bates, V. C. (2014). Rethinking cosmopolitanism in music education. *Action, Criticism, and Theory for Music Education, 13*(1), 310–327.

Bennett, D. (2008). *Understanding the classical music profession: The past, the present and strategies for the future*. Farnham: Ashgate.

Bielby, D. D., & Bielby, W. T. (1996). Women and men in film: Gender inequality among writers in a culture industry. *Gender & Society, 10*(3), 248–270.

Blair, H. (2001). 'You're only as good as your last job': The labour process and labour market in the British film industry. *Work, Employment & Society, 15*(1), 149–169.

Blamey, J., Kokot, P., & Scharff, C. (2014). Demographic background of students doing a music degree in the UK. In C. Scharff (Ed.), *Equality and diversity in the classical music profession*. Accessed 1 December 2016. Available at: http://blogs.kcl.ac.uk/young-female-and-entrepreneurial/files/2014/02/Equality-and-Diversity-in-the-Classical-Music-Profession.pdf

Blech, V. (2014). Immer mehr Frauen spielen in deutschen Orchestern. *Berliner Morgenpost*, 29.01.2014. Accessed 1 December 2016. Available at: www.morgenpost.de/kultur/berlin-kultur/article124360716/Immer-mehr-Frauen-spielen-in-deutschen-Orchestern.html

BMWi (2014). *Monitoring zu ausgewählten wirtschaftlichen Eckdaten der Kultur- und Kreativwirtschaft 2012*. Berlin: Bundesministerium für Wirtschaft und Energie. Accessed 1 December 2016. Available at: www.kultur-kreativ-wirtschaft.de/KuK/Navigation/Mediathek/publikationen,did=625724

Bork, M. (2010). *Traumberuf Musiker? Herausforderungen an ein Leben für die Kunst*. Mainz: Schott.

Born, G., & Devine, K. (2015). Music technology, gender, and class: Digitization, educational and social change in Britain. *Twentieth-Century Music, 12*(2), 135–172.

Bossen, A. (2012). *Einkommenssituation und Arbeitsbedingungen von Musikschullehrkräften und Privatmusiklehrern 2012*. Berlin: Verdi Fachgruppe Musik. Accessed 1 December 2016. Available at: www.miz.org/dokumente/2012_verdi_umfrage.pdf

Brouillette, S. (2013). Cultural work and antisocial psychology. In M. Banks, R. Gill, & S. Taylor (Eds.), *Theorising cultural work* (pp. 30–43). London: Routledge.

Bull, A. (2015). *The musical body: How gender and class are reproduced among young people playing classical music in England*. Unpublished PhD thesis, Goldsmiths, University of London.

Bull, A., & Scharff, C. (2017). 'McDonalds' music' versus 'serious music': how production and consumption practices help to reproduce class inequality in the classical music profession. *Cultural Sociology*. Accessed 20 July 2017. Available at: http://journals.sagepub.com/doi/pdf/10.1177/1749975517711045

Burke, J. P., & McManus, J. (2009). *'Art for a few': Exclusion and misrecognition in art and design higher education admissions*. National Arts Learning Network. Accessed 1 December 2016. Available at: http://blueprintfiles.s3.amazonaws.com/1321362562-AFAF_finalcopy.pdf

Butler, J. (1993). *Bodies that matter: On the discursive limits of "sex"*. London; New York: Routledge.

Carpos, F. (2014). *The London orchestra as a prestige economy*. Paper presented at 'Classical music as contemporary socio-cultural practice: Critical perspectives', King's College London, May 2014.

Comunian, R., Faggian, A., & Jewell, S. (2014). Exploring music careers: Music graduates and early career trajectories in the UK. In N. Crossley, S. McAndrew, & P. Widdop (Eds.), *Social networks and music worlds* (pp. 165–188). Abingdon, Oxon: Routledge.

Conor, B. (2014). *Screenwriting: Creative labour and professional practice*. London: Routledge.

Conor, B., Gill, R., & Taylor, S. (Eds.). (2015). *Gender and creative labour* (Vol. 63). Chichester: Wiley.

Cottrell, S. (2004). *Professional music-making in London: Ethnography and experience*. Farnham: Ashgate.

Coulangeon, P., Ravet, H., & Roharik, I. (2005). Gender differentiated effect of time in performing arts professions: Musicians, actors and dancers in contemporary France. *Poetics, 33*(5), 369–387.

Creative Blueprint (2012). *The creative and cultural industries: Music*. Accessed 1 December 2016. Available at: http://creative-blueprint.co.uk/statistics/reports/industry-statistics

Creative and Cultural Skills (2010). *Sector Skills Assessment for the creative and cultural industries*. Accessed 1 December 2016. Available at: www.oph.fi/download/143169_LinkClick.pdf

CUKAS (2013). *Annual report*. Cheltenham: Conservatoires UK Admission Service. Accessed 1 December 2016. Available at: www.ucas.com/file/62801/download?token= PDgszI4r

DCMS (2015). *Creative industries: Focus on employment*. London: Department for Culture, Media & Sport. Accessed 1 December 2016. Available at: www.gov.uk/gov ernment/uploads/system/uploads/attachment_data/file/439714/Annex_C_-_Creative_ Industries_Focus_on_Employment_2015.pdf

DeNora, T. (2002). Music into action: Performing gender on the Viennese concert stage, 1790–1810. *Poetics*, *30*(1), 19–33.

DOV (2014). *Deutsche Orchester: Abbau Ost schreitet voran*. Berlin: Deutsche Orches- tervereinigung. Accessed 1 December 2016. Available at: www.dov.org/pressereader/ items/deutsche-orchester-abbau-ost-schreitet-voran-1260.html

Edwards, P., & Wajcman, J. (2005). *The politics of working life*. Oxford: Oxford University Press.

Eikhof, D. R., & Warhurst, C. (2013). The promised land? Why social inequalities are sys- temic in the creative industries. *Employee Relations*, *35*(5), 495–508.

Elliott, C. A. (1995). Race and gender as factors in judgments of musical performance. *Bulletin of the Council for Research in Music Education*, *127*, 50–56.

Friedman, S., O'Brien, D., & Laurison, D. (2016). 'Like skydiving without a parachute: How class origin shapes occupational trajectories in British acting. *Sociology*, published online before print.

Gill, R. (2002). Cool, creative and egalitarian? Exploring gender in project-based new media work in Europe. *Information, Communication & Society*, *5*(1), 70–89.

Gill, R. (2014). Unspeakable inequalities: Post feminism, entrepreneurial subjectivity, and the repudiation of sexism among cultural workers. *Social Politics: International Studies in Gender, State and Society*, *21*(4), 509–528.

Gill, R. (2016). Postfeminism and the new cultural life of feminism. *Diffractions: Gradu- ate Journal for the Study of Culture*, *6*. Accessed 1 December 2016. Available at: https:// lisbonconsortium.files.wordpress.com/2012/2012/rosalind-gill_postfeminism-and-the- new-cultural-life-of-feminism.pdf

Goldin, C., & Rouse, C. (2000). Orchestrating impartiality: The impact of "blind" audi- tions on female musicians. *The American Economic Review*, *90*(4), 715–741.

Green, L. (1997). *Music, gender, education*. Cambridge: Cambridge University Press.

Green, L. (2012). Music education, cultural capital, and social group identity. In M. Clay- ton, T. Herbert, & R. Middleton (Eds.), *The cultural study of music: A critical introduc- tion* (2nd ed., pp. 206–215). London: Routledge.

Grugulis, I., & Stoyanova, D. (2012). Social capital and networks in film and TV: Jobs for the boys? *Organization Studies*, *33*(10), 1311–1331.

Haunschild, A., & Eikhof, D. (2009). Bringing creativity to market: Actors as self-employed employees. In A. McKinlay & C. Smith (Eds.), *Creative labour: Working in the creative industries* (pp. 156–173). Basingstoke: Palgrave Macmillan.

HEFCE (2002). *Creating a land with music: The work, education, and training of pro- fessional musicians in the 21st century*. Bristol; London: Higher Education Funding Council for England. Accessed 1 December 2016. Available at: www.hanze.nl/assets/ kc-kunst—samenleving/lifelong-learning-in-music/Documents/Public/273creatingalan dwithmusic.pdf

Hesmondhalgh, D., & Baker, S. (2015). Sex, gender and work segregation in the cul- tural industries. In B. Conor, R. Gill, & S. Taylor (Eds.), *Gender and creative labour* (pp. 23–36). Chichester: Wiley Blackwell.

Hesmondhalgh, D., & Saha, A. (2013). Race, ethnicity, and cultural production. *Popular Communication*, *11*(3), 179–195.

Holgate, J., & McKay, S. (2009). Equal opportunities policies: How effective are they in increasing diversity in the audio-visual industries' freelance labour market? *Media, Culture & Society*, *31*(1), 151–163.

Ibarra, H. (1992). Homophily and differential returns: Sex differences in network structure and access in an advertising firm. *Administrative Science Quarterly*, *37*(3), 422–447.

Independent Schools Council (2016). *Research*. Accessed 1 December 2016. Available at: www.isc.co.uk/research/

Johnson-Williams, E. (2014). *Imperial surveillance: The origins of power formation in Victorian music education*. Paper presented at the conference Classical Music: Critical Challenges, October 17th, King's College London.

Jones, D., & Pringle, J. K. (2015). Unmanageable inequalities: Sexism in the film industry. In B. Conor, R. Gill, & S. Taylor (Eds.), *Gender and creative labour* (pp. 37–49). Chichester: Wiley.

Klangzeitort (2014). *Statistiken*. Berlin: Institut für Neue Musik der Universität der Künste Berlin und der Hochschule für Musik Hanns Eisler Berlin. Accessed 1 December 2016. Available at: www.klangzeitort.de/uploads/text_discourse3/Statistiken.pdf

Kok, R.-M. (2006). Music for a postcolonial child: Theorizing Malaysian memories. In S. Boynton & R-M. Kok (Eds.), *Musical childhoods and the cultures of youth* (pp. 89–104). Middletown, CT: Wesleyan University Press.

Koppman, S. (2015). Different like me: Why cultural omnivores get creative jobs. *Administrative Science Quarterly*, *61*(2), 291–331.

League of American Orchestras (2016). *Racial/ethnic and gender diversity in the orchestra field: A report by the League of American Orchestras with research and data analysis by James Doeser, Ph.D*. New York: League of American Orchestras. Accessed 1 December 2016. Available at: www.ppv.issuelab.org/resources/25840/25840.pdf

Leberl, J., & Schulz, G. (2003). *Frauen in Kunst und Kultur II, 1995–2000*. Berlin: Deutscher Kulturrat. Accessed 1 December 2016. Available at: http://kulturrat.de/wp-content/uploads/altdocs/dokumente/studien/FraueninKunstundKultur2.pdf

Leppänen, T. (2014). The west and the rest of classical music: Asian musicians in the Finnish media coverage of the 1995 Jean Sibelius violin competition. *European Journal of Cultural Studies*, *18*(1), 1–16.

LSE (2012). The impact of three London conservatoires on the UK and London economies: A project for the Royal Academy of Music, the Guildhall School of Music & Drama and the Royal College of Music, with Universities UK. London: London School of Economics and Political Science. Accessed 1 December 2016. Available at: www.lse.ac.uk/geographyAndEnvironment/research/london/pdf/LSE-London-Conservatoires-Report-FINAL-July-2012.pdf

Macleod, B. A. (2001). *Women performing music: The emergence of American women as classical instrumentalists and conductors*. Jefferson, NC: McFarland.

Mäkinen, K. (2012). *Becoming valuable selves: Self-promotion, gender and individuality in late capitalism*. Unpublished PhD thesis, Tampere University.

McAndrew, S., & Everett, M. (2015). Symbolic versus commercial success among British female composers. In N. Crossley, S. McAndrew, & P. Widdop (Eds.), *Social networks and music worlds* (pp. 61–88). Abingdon, Oxon: Routledge.

McClure, B., Kokot, P., & Scharff, C. (2014). Demographic backgrounds of orchestral players and conservatoire teaching staff in the UK. In C. Scharff (Ed.), *Equality and diversity in the classical music profession.* Accessed 1 December 2016. Available at: http://blogs.kcl.ac.uk/young-female-and-entrepreneurial/files/2014/02/Equality-and-Diversity-in-the-Classical-Music-Profession.pdf

McCormick, L. (2009). Higher, faster, louder: Representations of the international music competition. *Cultural Sociology, 3*(1), 5–30.

McCormick, L. (2015). *Performing civility: International competitions in classical music.* Cambridge: Cambridge University Press.

McRobbie, A. (2009). *The aftermath of feminism: Gender, culture and social change.* London: Sage.

McRobbie, A. (2015). *Be creative: Making a living in the new culture industries.* Cambridge: Polity.

Mills, J. (2005). Addressing the concerns of conservatoire students about school music teaching. *British Journal of Music Education, 22*(1), 63–75.

Mills, J. (2007). Working in music: The violinist. *Music Performance Research, 1*(1), 76–89.

MIZ (2015a). *Studierende in Studiengängen für Musikerberufe – nach Frauen und Ausländern.* Bonn: Deutsches Musikinformationszentrum. Accessed 1 December 2016. Available at: www.miz.org/intern/uploads/statistik10.pdf

MIZ (2015b). *Bervorzugte Musikrichtung nach Geschlecht.* Bonn: Deutsches Musikinformationszentrum. Accessed 1 December 2016. Available at: www.miz.org/downloads/statistik/38/statistik38.pdf

MIZ (2016). *Freiberufliche Tätige in der Sparte Musik (Künstlersozialklasse) nach durchschnittlichem Jahreseinkommen und Tätigkeitsbereich.* Bonn: Deutsches Musikinformationszentrum. Accessed 1 December 2016. Available at: www.miz.org/downloads/statistik/85/85_Freiberuflich_Taetige_in_der_Sparte_Musik_nach_Taetigkeitsbereich_und_Durchschnittseinkommen_2016.pdf

Moss-Racusin, C. A., & Rudman, L. A. (2010). Disruptions in women's self-promotion: The backlash avoidance model. *Psychology of Women Quarterly, 34*(2), 186–202.

Musicians' Union (2012). *The working musician.* London: Musicians' Union. Accessed 1 December 2016. Available at: www.musiciansunion.org.uk/Files/Reports/Industry/The-Working-Musician-report

O'Brien, A. (2015). Producing television and reproducing gender. *Television & New Media, 16*(3), 259–274.

O'Brien, D., Laurison, D., Miles, A., & Friedman, S. (2016). Are the creative industries meritocratic? An analysis of the 2014 British Labour Force Survey. *Cultural Trends, 25*(2), 116–131.

O'Brien, D., & Oakley, K. (2015). *Cultural value and inequality: A critical literature review.* Swindon, Wiltshire: Arts and Humanities Research Council. Accessed 1 December 2016. Available at: www.ahrc.ac.uk/documents/project-reports-and-reviews/cultural-value-and-inequality-a-critical-literature-review/

Oakley, K., & O'Brien, D. (2016). Learning to labour unequally: Understanding the relationship between cultural production, cultural consumption and inequality. *Social Identities, 22*(5), 471–486.

Outshoorn, J. (Ed.). (2004). *The politics of prostitution: Women's movements, democratic states and the globalisation of sex commerce.* Cambridge: Cambridge University Press.

Paternoga, S. (2005). Orchestermusikerinnen: Frauenanteil an den Musikhochschulen und in den Kulturorchestern. *Das Orchester, 5*, 8–14.

Perrons, D. (2003). The new economy and the work – life balance: Conceptual explorations and a case study of new media. *Gender, Work & Organization, 10*(1), 65–93.

Pohlman, L. (1996). Creativity, gender and the family: A study of creative writers. *The Journal of Creative Behavior*, *30*(1), 1–24.

Potter, J., & Wetherell, M. (1987). *Discourse and social psychology: Beyond attitudes and behaviour*. London: Sage.

Proctor-Thomson, S. (2013). Feminist futures of cultural work: Creativity, gender and diversity in the digital media sector. In M. Banks, S. Taylor, & R. Gill (Eds.), *Theorizing cultural work: Labour, continuity and change in the creative industries* (pp. 137–148). London: Routledge.

PRS for Music Foundation (2016). *Background to women making music*. London: PRS for Music Foundation. Accessed 1 December 2016. Available at: www.prsformusicfounda tion.com/funding/women-make-music-2/background-to-women-make-music/

Rafnsdóttir, G. L., & Heijstra, T. M. (2013). Balancing work-family life in academia: The power of time. *Gender, Work & Organization*, *20*(3), 283–296.

Randle, K., Forson, C., & Calveley, M. (2015). Towards a Bourdieusian analysis of the social composition of the UK film and television workforce. *Work, Employment & Society*, *29*(4), 590–606.

Rudman, L. A. (1998). Self-promotion as a risk factor for women: The costs and benefits of counterstereotypical impression management. *Journal of Personality and Social Psychology*, *74*(3), 629–645.

Scharff, C. (2012). *Repudiating feminism: Young women in a neoliberal world*. Farnham: Ashgate.

Scharff, C. (2017). Inequalities in the classical music industry: The role of subjectivity in constructions of the 'ideal classical musician'. In C. Dromey & J. Haferkorn (Eds.), *The classical music industry*. London: Routledge.

Schmutz, V. (2009). Social and symbolic boundaries in newspaper coverage of music, 1955–2005: Gender and genre in the US, France, Germany, and the Netherlands. *Poetics*, *37*(4), 298–314.

Schulz, G. (2013a). Bestandsaufnahme zum Arbeitsmarkt Kultur. In G. Schulz, O. Zimmermann, & R. Hufnagel (Eds.), *Arbeitsmarkt Kultur: Zur wirtschaftlichen und sozialen Lage in Kulturberufen* (pp. 27–201). Berlin: Deutscher Kulturrat.

Schulz, G. (2013b). Arbeitsmarkt Kultur: Eine Analyse von KSK-Daten. In G. Schulz, O. Zimmermann & R. Hufnagel (Eds.), *Arbeitsmarkt Kultur: Zur wirtschaftlichen und sozialen Lage in Kulturberufen* (pp. 241–322). Berlin: Deutscher Kulturrat.

Schulz, G., Ries, C., & Zimmermann, O. (2016). *Frauen in Kultur und Medien: Ein Überblick über aktuelle Tendenzen, Entwicklungen und Lösungsvorschläge*. Berlin: Deutscher Kulturrat. Accessed 1 December 2016. Available at: www.kulturrat.de/publikationen/frauen-in-kultur-und-medien/

Skillset (2010). *Women in the creative media industries*. London: Skillset. Accessed 1 December 2016. Available at: www.ewawomen.com/uploads/files/surveyskillset.pdf

Steinpreis, R. E., Anders, K. A., & Ritzke, D. (1999). The impact of gender on the review of the curricula vitae of job applicants and tenure candidates: A national empirical study. *Sex Roles*, *41*(7/8), 509–528.

Storey, J., Salaman, G., & Platman, K. (2005). Living with enterprise in an enterprise economy: Freelance and contract workers in the media. *Human Relations*, *58*(8), 1033–1054.

Taking Part Survey (2015). *Taking part: Initial findings from the longitudinal survey*. London: Department for Culture, Media & Sport. Accessed 1 December 2016. Available at: www.gov.uk/government/uploads/system/uploads/attachment_data/file/447739/TP_ longitudinal_report.pdf

Taylor, S. (2011). Negotiating oppositions and uncertainties: Gendered conflicts in creative identity work. *Feminism & Psychology, 21*(3), 354–371.

Taylor, S., & Littleton, K. (2008). Art work or money: Conflicts in the construction of a creative identity. *The Sociological Review, 56*(2), 275–292.

Taylor, S., & Littleton, K. (2012). *Contemporary identities of creativity and creative work.* Farnham: Ashgate.

Thanki, A., & Jefferys, S. (2007). Who are the fairest? Ethnic segmentation in London's media production. *Work Organisation, Labour & Globalisation, 1*(1), 108–118.

Toynbee, J. (2013). How special? Cultural work, copyright, politics. In M. Banks, S. Taylor, & R. Gill (Eds.), *Theorizing cultural work: Labour, continuity and change in the creative industries* (pp. 85–98). London: Routledge.

UCAS Conservatoires (2015). *End of cycle report 2014.* Cheltenham: Universities and Colleges Admissions Service Conservatoires. Accessed 1 December 2016. Available at: www.ucas.com/sites/default/files/ucasconservatoires_eoc2014.pdf

Universities UK (2013). *Higher education in facts and figures 2013.* Accessed 1 December 2016. Available at: www.universitiesuk.ac.uk/facts-and-stats/data-and-analysis/Pages/higher-education-facts-and-figures-2013.aspx

Wagner, I. (2015). *Producing excellence: The making of virtuosos.* New Brunswick: Rutgers University Press.

Wang, G. (2009). Interlopers in the realm of high culture: "Music moms" and the performance of Asian and Asian American identities. *American Quarterly, 61*(4), 881–903.

Warwick Commission (2015). *Enriching Britain: Culture, creativity and growth.* Coventry: University of Warwick. Accessed 1 December 2016. Available at: www2.warwick.ac.uk/research/warwickcommission/futureculture/finalreport/warwick_commission_report_2015.pdf

Welsh, G., & Mason, B. (2014). *Advance network research.* Presentation at 'Taking Action', The Advance Network, London, City Hall, 10th February 2014 (no pagination).

Williams, C. L., Muller, C., & Kilanski, K. (2012). Gendered organizations in the new economy. *Gender and Society, 26*(4), 549–573.

Wimust (2013). *Final report.* Fiuggi Citta: Women in Music Uniting Strategies for Talent. Accessed 1 December 2016. Available at: www.donneinmusica.org/wimust/pdf/e-book-wimust/Ebook-WIMUST-FINAL-REPORT.pdf

Wing-Fai, L., Gill, R., & Randle, K. (2015). Getting in, getting on, getting out? Women as career scramblers in the UK film and television industries. In B. Conor, R. Gill, & S. Taylor (Eds.), *Gender and creative labour* (pp. 50–65). Chichester: Wiley.

Women in Music (2016). *BBC proms survey 2016.* Accessed 1 December 2016. Available at: www.womeninmusic.org.uk/proms-survey.htm

Wreyford, N. (2013). The real cost of childcare: Motherhood and flexible creative labour in the UK film industry. *Studies in the Maternal, 5*(2). Accessed 1 December 2016. Available at: www.mamsie.bbk.ac.uk/articles/abstract/2010.16995/sim.16926/

Wreyford, N. (2015a). *The gendered contexts of screenwriting work: Socialized recruitment and judgments of taste and talent in the UK film industry.* Unpublished PhD thesis, King's College London.

Wreyford, N. (2015b). Birds of a feather: Informal recruitment practices and gendered outcomes for screenwriting work in the UK film industry. In B. Conor, R. Gill, & S. Taylor (Eds.), *Gender and creative labour* (pp. 84–96). Chichester: Wiley.

Wright, F., & Scharff, C. (2014). *Demographic backgrounds of conservatoire teaching staff in Germany*. Unpublished.

Yang, M. (2007). East meets west in the concert hall: Asians and classical music in the century of imperialism, post-colonialism, and multiculturalism. *Asian Music*, *38*(1), 1–30.

Yoshihara, M. (2007). *Musicians from a different shore: Asians and Asian Americans in classical music*. Philadelphia, PA: Temple University Press.

Chapter 3

The silence that is not a rest

Negotiating hierarchies of class, race, and gender

Despite ongoing hierarchies, privileges, and exclusions in the classical music profession, inequalities were discussed ambivalently in the interviews. As this chapter demonstrates, the research participants openly talked about the middle-class culture of the classical music profession. However, they discussed power dynamics in relation to race, and particularly gender, in different ways. In fact, the research participants drew on several rhetorical tools to disavow gender inequalities, which ranged from normalisation and trivialisation to statements that women are now the advantaged sex. By analysing the research partici-pants' talk about class, race, and gender, this chapter explores the ways in which musicians negotiate the exclusions that characterise the classical music profession.

This chapter begins with a short overview of the patterns that I identified in the research participants' talk about inequalities. As my analysis shows, their views could shift over the course of a statement or an interview. It is therefore difficult to categorise the research participants' stances on existing exclusions and to provide a numerical account of how many openly talked about, or disa-vowed, inequalities. Instead, I found it more useful to focus on overarching patterns across all interviews. My analysis of these patterns shows that class inequalities were discussed openly, including the middle-class culture of the classical music sector but also the ways this affected those research partici-pants who did not come from a middle-class background. To be sure, talk about class was not entirely unproblematic; frequently, for example, middle-class privilege remained unacknowledged. Similarly, the research participants' discussion of racial hierarchies was marked by an absence of reflection on white privilege. Indeed, there were also disavowals of racial inequalities in the interviews and discussions of race were more ambiguous than reflections on class.

In comparison to talk about class and race, gender inequalities were dis-cussed most ambivalently. I draw on theories of individualisation (e.g. Bauman, 2001), the analytical framework of postfeminism (Gill, 2007; 2016; McRob-bie, 2009), as well as the positioning of young women as entrepreneurial subjects to make sense of frequent disavowals of gender inequalities. Consequently, this chapter devotes a considerable amount of attention to the ways in which gender inequalities were rendered unspeakable. As I argue, such an analysis of the unspeakability of inequalities (Gill, 2014) is important as it adds to our understanding of how gender inequalities in the cultural and creative industries remain unchallenged and may, in fact, be reproduced. If inequalities are unspeakable, it is difficult to address them and to implement change.

Class and classical music: "a luxury hobby for the better off"?

In the interviews, the research participants were asked about their views on inequalities in the classical music profession. One question, for example, was about their experience as a woman working in the sector, but I also invited them to talk about issues around race and class. As my analysis shows, some research participants spoke about the intersections of race and class, or race and gender. These statements reflected an intersectional perspective (Brah and Phoenix, 2004; Crenshaw, 1991; Nash, 2008; Lutz et al., 2011), which highlights the complex interplay between various axes of difference, such as race, class, and gender. Against this backdrop, it seems problematic to explore talk about gender, race, and class separately.

In conducting the interviews and in analysing the research participants' statements, however, I found that they negotiated issues around class differently from racial and gender inequalities. They seemed to be more open to discussing class inequalities and the ways they played out in the classical music profession (see also Randle et al., 2015; Wreyford, 2015). This may be related to several factors, including frequent associations of the classical music sector with 'high culture' and elitism (Bennett et al., 2009) and ongoing conversation in the industry about the cost of learning to play a musical instrument (ABRSM, 2014; for a critical discussion see Bull, 2015). There also seems to be an awareness of the link between private school education and classical music training. Peter Tregear et al. (2016: 280) have recently pointed to "the perceived nexus that exists in many countries (especially the United Kingdom and Australia) between classical music in particular and private secondary education – one commonly trumpeted as a point of difference in these schools' brochures". These discussions and perceptions may make class inequalities more visible and more easily detectable. In contrast, the research participants' negotiation of issues around race, and especially gender, was much more ambiguous. It is for this reason that I begin by analysing the ways in which class differences were discussed in the interviews. This analysis lays the groundwork for my subsequent argument where I contrast engagements with class differences with negotiations of racial and gender inequalities.

When I asked Ricarda about the class backgrounds of classical musicians, she stated:

> I don't know intimately the backgrounds of my colleagues but my instinct is – It would have been families that could afford the music lessons, could afford the instruments. Um, it's a shame [. . .] Unfortunately, I don't think it's going in the direction of having less to do with wealth. I think it's probably going in the direction of having to be even more wealthy to do it.

Echoing Ricarda's sense that classical musicians come from well-off families, Kristina said that most musicians she knew were "from higher, well-off backgrounds. Pretty much exclusively". She pointed out that many struggled to make a living but went on to say that they "simply come from good families, were introduced to music early". Indeed, Kristina ended her statement by describing classical music as "a luxury hobby for better-off people".

Sasha also observed that classical musicians were predominantly "middle-class". She felt that this had changed from previous times, at least in relation to brass players:

> I mean it used to be, with brass players that a lot came from a working-class background, so they came through brass bands. But I think less so now. And I think brass bands themselves are generally middle-class now, because all the pits have gone, so.

Kelly also found that the class background of musicians had changed:

> I am sure that when I was at [music] college, there was a lot more – there were many more people from different backgrounds, both foreign and from within the UK, but different demographics, different kind of poorer, richer backgrounds. Now, everybody I think looks the same, they all have this sort of very middle-class, privately schooled, kind of coiffed look, you know, and they are quite obviously from mostly wealthy backgrounds. And I find it a real shame. A real shame. But who can afford to send their kid to a music college when their chances of having a job at the end of the day is so slim, and the music fees have gone up massively. You can't come out of a music college owing 50 grand and hope to pay it back now, it's just impossible. So that's why, so it's becoming elitist again, despite all of our efforts to the contrary. It's a real shame.

As these statements illustrate, Ricarda, Kristina, Sasha, and Kelly openly talked about musicians' privileged socio-economic backgrounds and felt that the sector was becoming more, rather than less, exclusionary. Thus, they did not only discuss classed exclusions, but also challenged a narrative of progress that is often invoked in discussions about inequalities (Edley and Wetherell, 2001; see below). What these research participants did not point out, however, was their own socio-economic privilege and middle-class background. While some research participants highlighted their privileged class background at other stages in the interview (see chapter five), they did not do so in the context of discussing class differences in the classical music profession. This silence closed down avenues for exploring their own positioning in relation to existing inequalities.

In discussions about class and classical music, music education in particular was described as stratified. Sharing her experiences of teaching musical instruments at different schools in Berlin, Jette stated:

> I teach at a school in Berlin-Zehlendorf [known to be a wealthy area] where the children are sent to music lessons because this is part of a wider education. They then also have ballet, horseback riding, and swimming lessons and so on. Right? And then they have no time to play at home. So, um, and then I go to a primary school in Marzahn [a socio-economically deprived area] and, in a class of 30, there is somehow one child that has held a guitar. And they've never been to concerts and so on. So you are confronted with a different world there and they are obviously, somehow, the children from totally socially disadvantaged families and from very different strata.

Amanda established a similar contrast when she discussed her teaching experiences at a school in a "quite disadvantaged area in London":

> I really tried. I pushed so hard and I was entering them for festivals and for exams and and – but I just got nothing, and then I would call the parents and try to talk to them, and the parents would say: "But, you know, why? They have to do their homework, why should they practice an instrument as well? " And you are kind of thinking: "Well, okay." So there isn't that thing of – I mean from my experience they aren't being pushed in the same way, and I know with, you know, [a junior music college], when they are young, one of the parents has to be in the lesson so that they can go home and practice with the child.

Gudrun, too, reflected on the classed aspects of music education, stating:

> This sticking to it and constantly practicing and so on is for people who are not used to it, um, who do not experience this as a value for themselves and their own life, it is really difficult, also for the parents. And, I mean I don't know what it's like in London, but here it is, certain strata, for which classical music is totally distant, so to say. And even if you play pop music, it is always

this practicing and always this sticking to it and continuing and um. Really difficult, I think, for them. So it remains a bit of a privilege of certain people, certain families and that's obviously somehow sad, but it would simply have to be really, really well funded, so that they can afford it, also people who do not have any money.

Gudrun, Jette, and Amanda reflect on how class inequalities manifest themselves in music education. Jette and Amanda are setting up a strong contrast between children from middle-class families and those from less privileged socio-economic backgrounds. Amanda's statement in particular establishes distinctions (Bourdieu, 1984) and unwittingly sets up a problematic hierarchy between good, middle-class students and failing, working-class students.

Equally important, the statements do not question the underpinning, classed values of classical music education. As Anna Bull (2015; 2016; see chapter two) has shown, there is a strong link between classical music education and middle-class culture, which is for example evident in the long-term investment required for classical music. Interestingly, Gudrun discusses this long-term investment and the implications it has for class inequalities in music education. Indeed, she even uses the word "privilege" to talk about the fact that it is mainly children from middle-class families who do well in music education. There thus seems to be awareness in Gudrun's account that the reasons for class inequalities in music education are manifold and complex. However, she appears to take this back in her final statement about the need for more funding for music education. As afore-mentioned, this is a frequently made claim, but one that does not consider the continuities between middle-class culture and music education, thereby failing to acknowledge the important role this continuity plays in reproducing class inequal-ities (Bull, 2016). Similar to the absence of reflections on middle-class privilege in the context of discussions of class inequalities in the classical music sector, the research participants' statements demonstrate an awareness of and willingness to talk about issues around class. However, their insights do not contest middle-class values, such as investing in the long term, and the ways they affect inequalities in music education.

The research participants that I have quoted so far all came from middle-class backgrounds. They did not have any experiences of feeling like an outsider, at least not in terms of class. This was in contrast to some of the stories from research participants from lower middle-class or working-class backgrounds. Ashley was from a working-class background and got a music scholarship to attend a private school:

I felt like an outsider. I didn't actually get on well with that many people in school for many years because I had quite an accent. It's better now, but I had a bit of a rough accent when I was younger. And pocket money, things like that – and clothes. Yeah, definitely. All rich.

Lorraine had a similar experience when she got into the junior department of a prestigious conservatoire in the United States, where she had grown up:

> It was incredibly intimidating. Like now I realise what, 'cause a lot of these kids they just came from really, really wealthy families. Like incredibly wealthy. And they would go even, I know a girl she was a singer and she flew from Chicago to [city where conservatoire was based] every weekend [. . .] There was [the] incredibly wealthy and then there was the normal wealthy and then there was like, I don't know, me. I felt like my clothes were not cool enough you know, all these things, I put this like pressure on myself, like I felt I didn't fit in.

While Ashley and Lorraine spoke about past feelings of not 'fitting in', Mia and Lauren shared more recent experiences. Mia was still at music college and had become aware that other students received more financial support from their parents:

> The parents pay everything, the flat, the flute, the driver's licence. And then I think, "wow!" And if you yourself are from a very low-income background, like myself, then you notice this quickly and you think: "Wow, I want this too!"

Similar to Mia, Lauren indicated that she continued to be aware of differences between herself and her peers. Discussing chances for career success, she argued that a range of factors mattered, such as your playing, your background, your family name, or where you did your undergraduate degree:

> So, you know, for the renegades among us who have, you know, entered the country on a student visa from [Australasian country], who didn't attend [prestigious university], who didn't go and do their postgraduate accompanist course at [conservatoire], life has been different for me from how it is for some other people.

In these statements, the research participants position themselves as outsiders. They openly share feelings of exclusion, which they link to their less privileged socio-economic backgrounds.

This analysis demonstrates that several research participants – from various class backgrounds – discussed the middle-class culture prevalent in the classical music industry. In addition, many of the research participants who were from a lower middle-class or working-class background were not shy in sharing their experiences of not fitting in and thus disclosed how they felt class was affecting them. This is not to say that there were no occasions where class inequalities among musicians were obscured. Amy, for example, felt that the classical music audience was quite elitist but then went on to say: "But I think in sort of terms of the people actually performing, there is quite a big range, and people from different backgrounds and things." Also, I pointed out that middle-class privilege was rarely mentioned in the context of discussions about class inequalities in the classical music profession, and that the middle-class culture of music education was not acknowledged and questioned for its role in reproducing classed hierarchies and exclusions. On the whole, however, class inequalities in the classical music profession were addressed. As my subsequent analysis shows, the research participants discussed the existence and impact of racial and gender hierarchies, privileges, and exclusions more ambivalently.

Experiencing and disavowing racial prejudice and privilege

When I asked Holly about her views on diversity in the classical music profession, she told the following story:

> I went to a concert at the [name of concert venue] a few weeks ago, which is on [name of street], it's one of the most diverse areas of London. And I was still the only brown person at the concert, at this classical music concert in [one of the most diverse areas of London]! And it's ridiculous, and it's just, it's just such a shame, because you know classical music, you know can be, it should be for everyone. And, so yeah, so that definitely is an aspect as well. I have to say, you know, for [prestigious London orchestra], they are doing really, really important work in trying to change things. But yeah, of course, all of their musicians are the majority white middle-class people.

Holly was outspoken about the lack of diversity in the classical music profession and also adopted a more intersectional perspective at the end of her statement by talking about "white middle-class people". In a similar vein, Sasha described music colleges as "almost exclusively white, and almost exclusively middle-class" and Hope, in reflecting on her experiences of taking music lessons at school, stated: "When I was at school, when I started, there were only three or four of us in a class of 30 that weren't white middle-class." These statements illustrate that racial and class inequalities were not always talked about separately, but that a small number of research participants discussed them in tandem. In highlighting these incidents, I seek to demonstrate that issues of race, class, gender – and indeed, other axes of difference – do not have to be explored in isolation from each other. My analysis focuses on negotiations of class, racial, and gender inequalities separately because I found that they were negotiated differently in the interviews. As such, I do not make an ontological argument for the separateness of race, class, and gender, but I am unravelling these categories for analytical clarity.

Holly, Sasha, and Hope were not the only research participants who found there was a lack of racial diversity in the classical music profession. Lorraine observed that there was "not a single Asian violinist" in the prestigious orchestra in which she played. Esmeralda pointed out that "few black people" were represented in the classical music profession and Anke critically commented on hiring practices in her orchestra where some members said openly "they prefer to invite people [to auditions] who come from the region. Which I find pretty crass [. . .]. But this is talked about openly. It's also somehow known." Lorraine, Esmeralda, and Anke spoke about racial exclusions in their profession, but did so from a position of racial privilege (all of them were white) that they did not name or reflect upon (Ahmed, 2004). This parallels the pattern that I identified in relation to class where socio-economic privilege remained unaddressed in discussions about inequalities. Indeed, and as I point out again in the next chapter, 'privilege' as a term and concept was rarely evoked in the interviews. In the context of discussions about racial inequalities, this limited the emancipatory potential of well-intended statements about the lack of racial diversity in the classical music profession. The simple acknowledgement that black and minority ethnic musicians are underrepresented is not 'power-evasive', but also not power-strategic because it does not open up ways to reach towards a society that might move beyond racism (Frankenberg, 1993). It also does not increase awareness of how white people benefit from contexts that are marked by racial hierarchies (DiAngelo, 2012).

In the absence of discussions about white privilege, it is perhaps unsurprising that it was only black and minority ethnic research participants who discussed how the lack of racial diversity in the classical music profession affected them personally. Kim had attended the junior department of a conservatoire as a child and remembered that her and her mother's opinions (parents are obliged to attend lessons with their children in this context) were not taken seriously:

> We were not taken so seriously, because they always said: "Oh, but your family doesn't know anything about music". And also, I think, because I am half Indian and half English, and this idea of pedigree, or Western culture, so they felt, "well, how should you know?" Or I think they used to say to my mum: "How should you know this person is better or not, since you are not a musician and you are not from a Western culture?"

Kim's memory relates back to the argument I made in the previous chapter about some of the ways in which classical music as a genre is racialised and associated with European descent and whiteness. Indeed, Kim shared several stories about the different ways in which racial inequalities affected her personally. Since childhood, she had found herself dealing with a range of racial prejudices:

> You know, even just working in an orchestra, you can experience prejudice – how people interact with you. Just, you know, from your name and things like that. And also, I don't know, it might be, because I'm sort of a fiery player. That's sometimes put down to my ethnic origin, you know.

Kim stated that these experiences have "angered her", but also pointed out that "it is something that I have to live with, I mean it's something that even outside of the music situation one has to live with. So, it's something you work with." As I explore at the end of this chapter, Kim – along with other research participants – felt unable to bring these personal experiences of discrimination out into the open because she feared it would negatively affect her career. She only felt able to discuss them in the interview because I was an outsider and everything she said was kept anonymous.

Discussions of racial inequalities, and the ways they affected working lives, were more ambiguous among some of the other black and minority ethnic research participants. Susan told me she was "often the darkest person in the room, which is ridiculous. But it's tricky, it's really hard because you know – Afro-Caribbean people only make up one per cent of this country, one per cent."[1] Continuing to talk about her racial background, she went on to say: "I am hugely aware of it all the time. I wonder whether there is any sort of hindrance." Susan repeatedly stated that she found it "hard" to discern whether her racial background affected her career:

> It's really hard – it's a really hard situation. Because, at first when you are not getting jobs, you are thinking: "Oh, am I not getting jobs because I am, you know, sticking out too much?" And, I do stick out, you know, but am I sticking out for the wrong reasons? Or am I sticking out because I'm really good and people wanna watch me? So . . . it's really hard, it's a really hard one.

Susan's repeated emphasis on it being "hard" demonstrates that she is unsure whether her racial background has affected her working life. Indeed, towards the end of the interview, Susan confided that she was reluctant to think about it that way:

> I try to think about it less, because I don't want it to be an issue. I desperately don't want it to be an issue. I've been quite lucky in my life that I haven't faced too much in the way of racial trouble. But it would be a real shame if I really was a talented person but they didn't wanna hire me because of the colour of my skin. That would be a real shame.

In her statements, Susan goes back and forth between wondering whether her racial background may play a role and hoping that it does not. Her statements are marked by ambivalence: a sense that racial inequalities may affect her mixed with hopefulness and a certain degree of reluctance to explore these issues further.

In comparison to Susan, Faith was certain that her racial background had not impacted her career – at least not in ways that she was aware of. When I asked her about her experiences in relation to inequalities, Faith responded:

> If we were to talk about equality or anything like that, I would say I wouldn't have – even if it has had an effect on me, I haven't realised. I haven't actually had a conscious realisation that being Asian, small, or female has had any supposedly negative impact on me.

Foreshadowing a discursive trope that I discuss in more detail in the section on negotiations of gender inequalities, Faith underlines that her gender and racial background have not affected her. In making this statement, Faith acknowledges that racial and gender inequalities may exist, but at the same time weakens this acknowledgement by arguing they have not had a personal effect.

Indeed, Hope made a similar discursive move when discussing her views on, and experiences with, the lack of diversity in the classical music profession:

> There are few Asians and Indians and others working professionally. I don't think – I don't think I've ever felt I've not got work – particularly with orchestras – because I am different. I have never felt that there is any sort of racism issue. And, in fact, I think it probably now, because everyone is so concerned with being pc [politically correct] and ticking all the boxes, people are more like: "Oh, great, well we can tick that box if she is here!"

Hope openly acknowledges the underrepresentation of black and minority ethnic players, but distances herself from it by pointing out that it has not affected her personally. Similar to Faith, her statement is marked by an acknowledgement that racial inequalities exist but also by a simultaneous repudiation of the impact they may have on her professional life. Interestingly, Grace Wang (2009: 886) noted a similar pattern in her research on how Asian American musicians and their families understand their participation in classical music: "While asserting that they had never experienced outright discrimination, musicians nonetheless acknowledged the racialized terrain in which their music making takes place." In fact, and foreshadowing a further discursive trope that I discuss in relation to the negotiation of gender inequalities, Hope felt that it was perhaps even advantageous to be from a black and minority ethnic background. Similar to Susan and Faith, the engagement with and negotiation of racial inequalities is ambivalent in Hope's account.

Echoing Hope's sentiment, June stated that it was "sort of a bonus for being different coloured skin, in a way". This statement formed the end of a longer response to my question about ethnic and racial diversity in opera:

> I do know from some singer friends of mine who are of Caribbean descent that – that some of the companies, in order to get particular funding, they had to admit a certain quota of non-white British descent. So it's a shame – although I'm ha . . . – it's a very odd thing, in a way, I'm happy for them because – good on them, if they can take advantage. Someone's gonna benefit from something! Why not benefit from being employed. But, again, is it the right reason to employ someone, just because of that? Again, I always hoped it would be because they had the right skills set. They could do the job best, out of anyone else, you know, that's genuinely what you used to think one would be chosen for. But yeah, so no – ethnicity is – I was amazed and impressed with the range of ethnicities. You know, Indian, Pakistani, Eastern European, you know all, melting pot – potentially, probably a result of

London city itself. But all of them, there was no discrimination against – if anything it was for, that there was sort of a bonus for being different coloured skin, in a way.

By drawing on anecdotal evidence ("some singer friends of mine"), June positions herself as an insider and as somebody who has a racially diverse group of friends. On a rhetorical level, this gives her statement more credibility and also positions June as well meaning. June then contrasts the use of quotas with arguments that the person with the "right skills set" should be hired, who "could do the job best, out of anyone else". In making this argument, June seems to imply that "anyone else" is positioned equally, thereby discounting existing inequalities. Indeed, June makes this argument from a position of racial privilege, but this privilege remains unacknowledged. By stating that she is "happy for them", June sets herself apart from her black and minority ethnic peers. Her whiteness, however, remains unspoken, which in itself is a marker of white privilege. While she constructs ethnic diversity as something positive ("I was amazed and impressed with the range of ethnicities"), she also disavows the existence of discrimination and instead claims that it is an advantage to be from a black and minority ethnic background. Thus, June uses various rhetorical tools to disavow racial inequalities and her racial privilege.

June was not the only white research participant who disarticulated racial inequalities. When I asked Linda about her views on diversity in the classical music profession, she stated: "I don't think there is ever any kind of exclusion based on that [. . .] I have never noticed anything in particular as an issue, it is such an international place anyway that you sort of see all sorts of people." Linda's portrayal of the classical music sector as "international" resonates with common characterisations of the classical music profession as a "melting pot" (June), "very open" (Emilia), and where there is "one from each nation" (Sophie). Sometimes, these assertions were followed by a list of the countries represented, which were overwhelmingly white/European. References to the classical music profession's openness and internationalism seem to figure as cover terms that brush aside existing racial inequalities and as a further discursive trope through which racial privilege (all of these research participants where white) remains unacknowledged. Comparing the research participants' statements on racial and ethnic diversity with their claims about musicians' class backgrounds demonstrates that their engagements with racial hierarchies and exclusions was more ambivalent than their negotiation of class inequalities. Class issues were discussed more openly, whereas racial inequalities were sometimes talked about in depth or acknowledged, but also disavowed. Notably, class and racial privilege remained unnamed in both contexts.

"It's sexism. Pure and straight": acknowledging gender inequalities

On the whole, the research participants' talk about, and negotiation of, gender inequalities was highly ambivalent. However, there were some research participants who openly acknowledged sexism. Lauren, for example, was very outspoken about these issues. When discussing informal hiring practices, she pointed out that there was a preference for men (see also Carpos, 2014). When I asked her why this was the case, she said: "It's sexism. Pure and straight [. . .] It's there, it exists. As a woman, the most frequent comment I get is: 'Lauren, you play like a man'. [. . .] It's there, it's in the industry already, and it has been there for centuries."[2] Sasha also used the term sexism, stating:

> Sexism really gets me down [. . .] and plenty of my female colleagues would say: "Yes, it's there, but it doesn't necessarily affect them." But for me, I really struggle with that. I think because I wasn't prepared to compromise, so that would be a real low.

In a similar vein, Jane told me about a particular event where she was not taken seriously as a female conductor:

> I have never thought I'd experience any sort of sexism, really. Because, you know, my academic degree – very equal, and then we were all treated the same, even as a singer, you know. I don't think I experienced that at all, and it is the first time in my whole life I really feel I have experienced that.

Lauren, Sasha, and Jane use explicitly political language by evoking the term sexism and highlight the effect it has had on their professional lives. Gender inequalities are openly acknowledged in these statements.

Other research participants used different terms to pinpoint gender issues. Sonja, a brass player herself, told me "female brass players are definitely still totally underrepresented. And it's a total, it is still a men's club [Männerverein]." Holly used a similar metaphor by describing her field, composing, as "kind of a boys' club, which is quite difficult to penetrate" and Isabella referred to the classical music industry "as a man's world, whatever they say". In making these and similar statements, research participants highlighted a range of issues. Some observed that women were still "underrepresented" (Eve) and that they have to be better to get jobs in orchestras (Gudrun). Nora felt that men were "given better opportunities somehow or earlier opportunities or people take a risk on them more easily somehow". Others identified patterns of vertical segregation, either by noting that it was still "really difficult to be a woman conductor" (Lena) or that the profession was like a "pyramid" (Jasmin). According to Jasmin, piano was a "totally feminine subject, but um, at the very top, those who are on stage and those who really get the professorships, that's obviously much more the men". In addition, several research participants commented that women's looks mattered more than their playing. Having stated that the classical music world was a "man's world", Isabella said: "The women, when they look at the violinist, they think: 'Oh, she is so amazing', but when the men look they say: 'Wow, she is so pretty'. That is the first reaction." As these statements illustrate, gender inequalities were addressed in several interviews. They were thus not absent from the research participants' accounts and sometimes explicitly named and challenged.

Sometimes, research participants identified the existence of sexism, but discussed its effect on their professional life in ambivalent ways. Ashley told me about an experience where she was the only female playing in an all-male group:

> I think they used – they have one girl to sort of make sure the men don't eff and blind too much, so I sort of knew my place, I acted very much the lady, you know, when I was in there, because yeah, I think there was an element of slight sexism. But I don't come across it a lot, I must say.

Ashley continued her statement by reflecting on how work gets passed around, stating that "you try and get your friends in, and your friends are normally who you hang around with. I'm not saying that men and women and gays don't mix, but it's just, you know." She acknowledged that it wasn't always about "who is the very best person" but concluded her statement by saying: "But I haven't experienced a serious issue with being female, good or bad." At the beginning of her statement, Ashley describes one of her experiences as slightly sexist but subsequently emphasises that she "has not come across it a lot" and that she has "not experienced a serious issue with being female". Ashley's emphasis on not having had many personal experiences of sexism foreshadows a discursive trope that I encountered a lot in the interviews. As I demonstrate in the following section, the majority of the research participants disarticulated gender inequalities. While they were openly discussed in some interviews, gender imbalances were overwhelmingly disavowed and the trope of not having had any personal experiences of discrimination figured prominently in this context.

"I really have not had negative experiences": performing the empowered woman

Many research participants emphasised that they had not experienced any discrimination. Julianna stated, "in my career, I never had any bad feelings about being a woman. Only good. Only good. Only good." Astrid echoed these sentiments by pointing out that "she has never had a problem" as a woman and Angela said: "I have never had the feeling, or I don't know, that, um, that it played a role that, that I'm a woman [. . .] I have not noticed it." In a similar vein, Carolyn claimed that being female "is not actually something I've ever been bothered about. I don't really think it's important in any way. I don't think it makes my career stronger or weaker. It doesn't seem to impact." In these statements, the research participants frame experiences at work in individualistic terms; wider social forces, such as gender, are portrayed as not having an impact on their working lives.

This finding echoes existing research on negotiations of gender at work (Gill et al., 2016; Kelan, 2009; Kokot, 2014; 2015; O'Brien, 2014) and in the classical music profession (Yoshihara, 2007). Gender is represented as not having an effect on individual lives; in all these narratives, personal experiences become uncoupled from broader social dimensions, resonating with the wider trend of individualisation. As Zygmunt Bauman (2001: 9) has argued, personal experiences are increasingly told in a way that "excludes or suppresses (prevents from articulation) the possibility of tracking down the links connecting individual fate to the ways and means by which society as a whole operates". Angela McRobbie (2009) has developed these arguments in relation to young women. According to McRobbie (2009: 5), young women's narratives are characterised by an "aggressive individualism" that replaces consideration of wider social structures with a sustained focus on the individual. The accounts presented here, which reflect the viewpoints of young women, resonate with Bauman's and McRobbie's theories of individualisation.[3] Personal experiences are foregrounded in a way that disarticulates the links between one's background and wider social positioning.

Although the research participants emphasised they had not had any personal exposure to discrimination, their statements were frequently followed by a 'but'. When I asked Lena whether she had ever experienced any sexism, she responded:

> Not me personally, I don't think so. But I once had an issue with a conductor when I was at the conservatorium. And I went to our orchestral manager about it. I got a mark that I thought was very unfair. And she said to me: "I'll organise a meeting for you with the conductor. Make sure that you wear a low top because that will help."

Similarly, Anke told me that she "didn't spend a lot of time thinking about being a woman or a man. But I have, if I think about it now, most leading roles in orchestras, such as principal player or concert master, are mostly filled by men." Hope's statement followed a similar pattern. Having told me gender does not matter nowadays, she said:

> I certainly within orchestras don't feel marginalised in any way. But there is occasionally that thing of if I apply for a job now, I'm 36, are they going to look at me and think: "Oh, is she – has she had children, is she gonna have children, are we gonna have to pay?"

Rhetorically, Lena, Anke, and Hope's statements function as a disclaimer (Hewitt and Stokes, 1975). The first part of each statement indicates that gender is not an issue, but this is followed by an insight or incident that highlights ongoing inequalities. Such use of disclaimers enables the research participants to present themselves as individuals who have never experienced any form of discrimination, even though some of their experiences might be regarded in that way.

The rhetorical structure of the disclaimer was flexible and did not always involve the conjunction 'but'. When Stefanie talked about her experiences of being a female musician, she said:

> I really haven't had negative experiences. The only sort of – I mean, I was just playing in a quintet with all guys, and I got so many like, sexual harassment

comments. They were all kind of like joking, but eventually I got sick of it. I was like: "Guys, really, stop it." But other than that – no, I don't think so.

This rhetorical construction is meaningful for at least two reasons. First, even though there is an acknowledgement of gender issues – Stefanie even uses the term "sexual harassment" – the disclaimer and the phrase "other than that" rhetorically diminishes gender as a structuring force. Second, these disclaimers enable the research participants to present themselves as empowered individuals, who are not personally affected by wider inequalities.

In fact, these statements can be read as reflecting and reproducing wider neoliberal sentiments (Scharff, 2012; O'Brien, 2014; see chapters one and four). As Wendy Brown (2003: paragraph 15) has argued, "[neoliberalism] figures individuals as rational, calculating creatures whose moral autonomy is measured by their capacity for 'self-care'." By discussing instances of inequalities, and by simultaneously representing themselves as capably dealing with these experiences, the research participants demonstrate their ability to 'self-care'. Indeed, their stance on inequalities resonates with Catherine Rottenberg's (2014: 420) characterisation of the neoliberal feminist subject, who is

> distinctly aware of current inequalities between men and women. This same subject is, however, simultaneously neoliberal, not only because she disavows the social, cultural and economic forces producing this inequality, but also because she accepts full responsibility for her own well-being and self-care [. . .] The neoliberal feminist subject is thus mobilized to convert continued gender inequality from a structural problem into an individual affair.

While Rottenberg refers to neoliberal feminists, her insights also pertain to the rhetorical patterns discussed here. In negotiating gender inequalities, the research participants orient to neoliberal discourses of individual empowerment and self-care as well as their positioning as ideal entrepreneurial subjects (see chapter one; chapter four). Thus, their negotiation of inequalities is not only characterised by individualist rhetoric, but also by a neoliberal outlook.

The research participants also disavowed inequalities by attributing them to other countries. Kelly said that she was "not at all" aware of being a woman in the industry. However, she moved on to say "I'm aware of it outside the UK, certainly, and seeing some European orchestras come and play here, and the lack of women. But no, it has never affected me." Significantly, several research participants alluded to a sentiment that there are "very different sorts of attitudes towards women" in Germany, and other European countries (Hope). Referring to gender issues in London, Emilia said:

> It's been fine. It's definitely, in London, it's fine. I mean, obviously, Germany, it's still a bit . . . I mean I was thinking 'cause I wanted to do the audition for [German orchestra academy], and I was thinking "I wonder if it makes any difference that I am a woman."

Interestingly, however, research participants who were German or working in Germany considered yet another country, notably Italy, more sexist. Reflecting on the risk of sexual harassment, Alice pondered, "it depends what country you are working in. You know, different countries – like Germany – I would imagine would be fine, because the laws and regulations, but somewhere like Italy, where men are much more ruling. I don't know."

The comment that 'other' contexts or countries are sexist is a familiar trope in discussions about gender issues (Gill et al., 2016; Kelan, 2007; Scharff, 2012). By presenting themselves as working in contexts where discrimination is not an issue, the research participants disavow the relevance of inequalities to their personal lives. Importantly, the attribution of unequal power relations to 'other' countries stabilises their positioning as empowered and unaffected by gender issues. Inequalities are thus disarticulated in various ways, including the use of individualist claims and disclaimers, and the labelling of 'other' countries as less egalitarian. However, all of these rhetorical devices enable the research participants to adopt a neoliberal outlook by representing themselves as empowered and demonstrating their capacity for self-care.

"You just have to kind of be cool about it": a postfeminist sensibility

Inequalities were also disavowed through trivialisation and normalisation. Several musicians claimed that there was a culture of making dirty and sexist jokes, particularly among brass players. In this context, Annegret stated: "I know the dirtiest jokes and the most women-hostile jokes ever. But, I don't know, I'm not so sensitive, I can laugh along." Sophie had faced a similar working culture when she took up her orchestral post:

> I also somehow always got hit on, like a bit. But it was like a mutual sounding out, like testing what was possible. And, by now, it's sorted itself out. Yes, sometimes they make a crappy comment and then I simply say: "Well, I didn't hear this." And then this is dealt with. And sometimes, by now, I even find the jokes, even if they are stupid, funny. By now, it's sorted out. But it was an issue in the beginning.

Annegret and Sophie trivialise their experiences of sexist jokes and advances by male colleagues by emphasising that they "can laugh along" and that "it's sorted itself out". Their remarks indicate that there is a burden on women to laugh along (Kelan, 2014), leaving sexist jokes unchallenged.

Some research participants also used trivialising phrases when recounting experiences of sexual harassment by male teachers:

> It wasn't a big deal, or so, but it just went too far. He sent me text messages at night and then I went to the director and yes, this is how it's sorted

itself out. And now I'm a bit careful but – I mean I think that this happens to everybody.

(Gesche)

Starting her statement by saying that "it wasn't a big deal" and using the qualifier "just", Gesche trivialises the incident. She also normalises sexual harassment by arguing that it "happens to everybody". Indeed, her use of the word "everybody" gives sexual harassment a gender-neutral gloss. Kara also normalised an instance of sexual harassment that she told me about:

> I've been in a situation when one of my teachers tried something. I had an [specifics removed] exam and one was in the jury and the other had a concert at some residence and then we all met up in the bar, and all the time buying me whiskeys, and I was like, "I want a coke" and they gave me whiskey/ coke, like that, and they just wanted me to come home with them, and I was like: "Yeah sure, yeah sure", and then [laughter] and then we sit outside and I was like: "Okay, your house left, number [xx], that is your house." And then they were like: "Are you coming?" and I was like: "No, I'll go to my own house, thank you very much." And then I had a lesson the next day at 9:30 and that was the worst lesson of my life and I just thought because I was hung over and the teacher was hung over, but I talked to some people and they said . . . "You know, they are probably upset because they feel rejected." The student after me also had a rough lesson. I think it was probably more the hangover . . . you know this kind of thing [. . .] There it was normal. Many stories, not just – yeah.

Kara is unsure whether to attribute the bad lesson to the previous night's incident or to being hung-over. Her statement that "it was probably more the hangover" downplays the significance of her experience. Indeed, Kara ends her statement by pointing out that these experiences were "normal", which resonates with Gesche's normalisation of sexual harassment.

Apart from trivialisation and normalisation, there was an emphasis on being 'cool' about potentially sexist experiences. Discussing her working life as a woman, Emilia said:

> For example this gig that I told you I would do this weekend. The guy wants to have four hot girls, you know. So you can use it as well. And so I mean it does come up, I think. I don't know you just have to kind of be cool about it and uh, yeah. I haven't been in a situation where it was a problem.

Emilia's emphasis on being "cool" resonates with McRobbie's (2010) wider arguments about the ways in which cultural workers negotiate gender issues. According to McRobbie (2010: 74), advances in gender equality are "undermined by subtle forces of patriarchal retrenchment implemented through the seemingly harmless but in fact ruthless and tyrannical deployment of 'cool' as a disciplinary regime in work and leisure". By being "cool" about the fact that she was asked to work because she is a "hot girl", Emilia pre-empts critique of sexist work cultures and, quite literally, plays along.

Apart from doing 'coolness', Emilia's comment reflects a 'postfeminist sensibility' (Gill, 2007). According to Rosalind Gill (2007), postfeminism[4] is best conceived of as a 'sensibility', which is characterised by a range of recurrent features. These include, but are not limited to, the entanglement of feminist and anti-feminist ideas, the use of irony and knowingness in discussions about gender issues, and the view of femininity as primarily representing a bodily property. This postfeminist sensibility transpires through Emilia's account because of the entanglement of feminist and anti-feminist ideas. Feminist viewpoints are somewhat taken into account (being a woman "does come up"), but simultaneously disavowed through the statement that you "just have to kind of be cool about it".

Similar to Gill, McRobbie (2009) has emphasised that a postfeminist outlook is characterised by a 'double entanglement' where feminism has achieved the status of Gramscian common sense, but is represented as redundant at the same time. Reflecting the postfeminist view that feminism is a spent force, the research participants frequently located inequalities in the past (see also Gill et al., 2016; Kelan, 2007; 2014; Scharff, 2012). This rhetorical move enabled them to acknowledge the importance of gender equality (thereby evoking a feminist discourse), while putting forward the claim that gender was no longer a barrier (thereby rendering feminism redundant). When asked about her experiences as a woman working in classical music, Linda stated:

> I don't really think about it, to be honest. I don't think it is so much of an issue now as perhaps it was, so I mean I might be aware that a lot of the players in orchestras – At the moment, there are a lot more men than women, but I think that is sort of a leftover from a generation ago, when that was the norm. But as new players are coming in, I think women are, you know, accepted as valid musicians just as much, if that makes sense. So I don't feel that it is a barrier in any way, I suppose, at the moment.

The allocation of inequalities to the past often went hand in hand with a progress discourse where research participants emphasised that gender relations had changed, be it slowly or significantly (see also Wreyford, 2015):

> I think the time is changing. I think that generally it has been such a male-ish profession, earlier on, like everything else, like scientists as well, and it has been that the big jobs have been men's things and I think it is slowly starting to change.
>
> (Saaga)

I think within orchestras, particularly now, in a lot of the orchestras that I play for, it's almost swung the other way, there's almost more women than men. And not just in the string sections, in the violins or whatever. You go in and men are in the minority.

(Hope)

In these accounts, change is conceptualised as progressive. The possibility that things may change for the worse, which would indicate the persistence of sexism and intersecting inequalities, is not evoked. Indeed, male players were represented as being "marginalised" (Hope). Annegret, who was still a student, said: "My [male] classmates recently said 'We think we have to introduce a quota for men!' because there are more girls at the moment." While Annegret made this statement with a certain irony and knowingness, which Gill (2007) has also linked to the postfeminist sensibility, it is worth pointing out that her class comprised of 18 students and that only a third were female.

In the same way that the research participants were more at ease discussing men's rather than women's marginalisation, many readily stated that other women, and not men, were a hindrance to equal treatment. Reflecting on their experiences of orchestral playing, Elena, Judith, and Emilia stated:

I rather had the feeling that, as a young, pretty woman, you get more resentment from female colleagues than from men. Because they are suddenly no longer the ones – They were also once young and pretty and at some stage they are no longer that. It's rather that than the men. They are always very happy if a pretty woman sits there.

(Elena)

Being a young female going into an orchestra can have different effects. In one orchestra I went in and I felt very unwelcome, especially by the other females in the orchestra. And someone else had noticed that as well. It was sort of a general feeling of, I think, of the established women in the orchestra feeling threatened by new young women in the orchestra.

(Judith)

It's usually the other women that are more difficult and I've had like conversations about like women conductors and apparently it is often like the women sort of aged 40 or 50 who have a problem with the other women being in power or something.

(Emilia)

Elena, Judith, and Emilia's statements present other, older women as the problem. Indeed, research in the field of gender, work and organisation has used the term 'queen bee phenomenon' to describe "the general phenomenon that in particular women who have been individually successful in male-dominated environments are likely to oppose the women's movement" (Ellemers et al., 2004: 325). The queen bee phenomenon, and a related reluctance to support younger women, may be one explanation for the research participants' experiences and merits further analysis. In the context of my discussion of disavowals of gender inequalities and the ways they reflect a postfeminist sensibility, I am struck by Elena's reference to women's appearance and sexual attractiveness. This is noteworthy because it represents femininity as a bodily property, which is a further feature of the postfeminist sensibility (Gill, 2007). Femininity is not associated with particular forms of behaviour (being caring or nurturing, for example), but linked to particular looks and sexual attractiveness. This means that the research participants' accounts represent a postfeminist outlook in various ways: through the entanglement of feminist and anti-feminist ideas, the deployment of a 'cool' and ironic attitude, the allocation of inequalities to the past, and the representation of femininity as a bodily property. In the instances discussed here, the postfeminist outlook forecloses a discussion of sexism as a barrier that women may face.

"It's more of an advantage, that one is a woman": gender inequalities as unspeakable

Arguably, the individualist, neoliberal, and postfeminist outlook of the research participants' accounts laid the discursive groundwork for representations of women as the advantaged sex (see also Gill et al., 2016; Kelan, 2014; Wreyford, 2015). Jana answered the question about her experiences as a female musician in the following way:

> I have never detected a gender problem, let's put it that way. Um, I have actually also already heard that the pay is different for permanently employed music school teachers. I believe that men, I believe, also get more. Curiously! But I myself personally have somehow never experienced that or noticed it in relation to certain things or jobs. Not at all. I rather have the feeling, that it is sometimes even like, that they maybe prefer to have a female musician at the front of the stage, because she is maybe prettier than the guy. It's really like that. In that way, it's more of an advantage, that one is a woman.

Jana acknowledges that men get paid more as music school teachers, but subsequently renders this claim void by demonstrating an individualist outlook and stating that she has never experienced any inequalities. Significantly, she ends her statement by saying that it is now an advantage to be a woman. Against the backdrop of the disavowal of inequalities in the accounts of many research participants, the construction of women as advantaged becomes intelligible.

Conspicuously, female musicians' allegedly advantageous positioning was almost exclusively related to their physical appearance and sexual attractiveness. Amalia reiterated the feeling that she never felt being treated differently as a woman and continued by saying: "In Italy, yes. Because there, it's a bit more like, if you look good, if you are slim, if you dress in a certain way and so on, then it's easier to get gigs." TV work, in particular, was seen as privileging women:

> I think there are streams of work where women are used for an advantage, for example the kind of pop-backing stuff on TV, where they want the blond glamorous girlies with the short skirts. They are looking for a certain – it's a look they are going for, it's got nothing to do with playing an instrument, and in fact a lot of those things you are miming anyway, you are not actually being broadcast. So that is done purely on the fact that you're a woman, or that you have the particular look that they are going for. So I think now, nowadays, I think in some ways sometimes being a woman can be advantageous, and I know a lot of the guys feel marginalised because they don't get that type of TV work.
>
> (Hope)

> There are extra opportunities for ladies who are well presented for things like television and all that. You don't have to be, you know, a stunner, but you know, they like, sort of, you know, an attractive lady on the TV. Sometimes, that creates a bit of extra work.
>
> (Ashley)

In these statements, women are represented as the advantaged sex due to their alleged ability to obtain "extra work" on the basis of having a "particular look".

While the representation of women as advantaged seems to follow logically from disavowals of gender inequalities, it is worth highlighting what remains unsaid. First, the proposition that being a woman can be advantageous rests on the fact that "particular looks" are required. These looks are narrowly defined, relating to attractiveness, slimness, youth, and, apparently, whiteness ("blond glamorous girls"). The portrayal of women as advantaged thus overlooks that not all women fit these categories. Second, TV work is regarded as non-prestigious. As Ashley pointed out: "You know, the girls weren't brought in to do the proper work, and I personally wouldn't really want to mime." Reflecting on her personal experience of participating in such TV work, Kim similarly stated:

> I recently did some TV work, and that was horrifically different. That's where classical musicians often are called in to mime to their prerecorded music. And that's when they have to be pretty, that's the point [. . .] It was so sad that your playing did not count and it was about your looks only.

While TV work may give women access to slightly better-paid work, it does not add to their credibility as artists as it is not their playing, but only their looks, that count. In a context where women struggle to get recognition as artists (Bain, 2004; Taylor and Littleton, 2012; see chapter two), the pursuit of allegedly un-artistic work may further contribute to their marginalisation. Third, the construction of women as privileged disavows some of the disadvantages that are linked to being a woman in the classical music profession, such as sexual harassment (Baker, 2014; Gould, 2009; Hennekam and Bennett, 2017; Higgins, 2013; Lamb, 1993; Pidd, 2013; Tindall, 2005; Yoshihara, 2007). Ten out of 64 research participants shared stories of sexual harassment. Thus, the portrayal of women as advantaged does not only disavow wider gender inequalities, such as horizontal or vertical segregation; the representation of women as privileged also elides the very disadvantages that are related to the emphasis on their appearance and (hetero)sexual attractiveness.

Disavowals of gender inequalities did not only lay the discursive groundwork for the positioning of women as the advantaged sex, but also meant that many research participants seemed to find it difficult to name gender inequalities. At the beginning of this chapter, I cited Anke's observation that there were few female section leaders and principals. When I asked her why this was the case, she said: "I don't know. I have, I have no clue." In a similar vein, Eve had observed that there weren't many women brass players: "And, I guess you could say that women are really underrepresented as well, especially in areas I have been in. There is not a lot of promotion or hype around female artists. Why, I don't know." In these statements, sexism or gender inequalities are not put forward as explanations for the underrepresentation of women in leading roles or among brass players. Instead, Anke and Eve state that they "don't know" how to make sense of these phenomena. Interestingly, research on how key decision makers in the Irish film industry explain ongoing gender inequalities also found that

> [m]any accounts were interspersed with 'I don't know' to indicate that respondents often struggled to explain either the paucity of women screen-writers or writer/directors in the broader Irish film industry generally or as recipients of IFB [Irish Film Board] funding, specifically.
>
> (Liddy, 2016: 12)

To be sure, the statement "I don't know" can have different meanings in this context: it may be that the research participants do not know how to make sense of the lack of women in certain positions or that they seek to evade a discussion of gender imbalances. In both cases, however, gender inequalities are not made explicit.

Sexism also did not figure as an explanation in Judith's account about why there are more male professional flautists:

> Actually, flute players, a lot of professional flute players are men. I'd say you get a lot of [. . .] you get lots of little girls learning flute. But if you actually look at orchestras, there are as many men. Well, not mainly, it's equal, if not more men in the flute jobs. And we thought maybe that's because they've had, being a male they've had to compete with us very tight. And so it's made them driven and it's meant they had to succeed because they've known that's what they wanted to do and they'd fought past the stereotype. Whereas the

women perhaps can do it, and then if they're good enough they'll do it but they haven't had to fight the stereotype.

In trying to make sense of men's overrepresentation among professional flute players, Judith argues that their initial, marginalised position may have made them more driven and able to succeed. She does not mention sexism or vertical segregation. Judith also does not consider that a similar argument may apply to women in typically male segments of the profession (such as brass, percussion, composing, or conducting), but that women continue to be underrepresented in these parts of the industry. The accounts of Anke, Eve, and Judith resonate with other, existing research on the ways in which inequalities are negotiated in the cultural and creative industries. Apart from Susan Liddy's study on the Irish Film Board, Anne O'Brien (2014: 2) argued that "[c]ircumscribed by neo-liberal and postfeminist subjectivities, Irish women television workers do not articulate work inequalities in terms of gender". Cultural trends such as individualisation, neoliberalism, and postfeminism facilitate the disavowal of unequal gender power relations. Against this backdrop, many research participants did not draw on sexism as an explanation for some of the gender imbalances that they had observed. By claiming that they did not know how these imbalances came about, or by advancing different modes of explanation, these research participants rendered sexism and gender inequalities unspeakable.

As I have demonstrated earlier in the chapter, not all research participants disavowed gender inequalities and some addressed and discussed them openly in the interviews. These research participants did however feel that sexism was not openly discussed in the industry. Christine told me:

> I think sometimes decisions are made in a sexist way. No one would ever admit that it had been, because obviously they would be, you now, brought up on that, but I think there is sexism, but people are very closeted about it. I don't know why though, I don't know why.

Similarly, when I asked Sasha whether sexism was talked about, she replied:

> No, you can't really talk about it in any detail, because women are too – like with my quartet it's okay, because we all know each other, and we've all talked about it and come to terms with it, and recognised that everybody has had a different experience and a different way of dealing with it. But most girls are quite chippy about it. A lot pretend that it's not there because they don't want it to be there. No, it's not openly talked about, no.

Lauren also stated that sexism was not openly discussed in the industry. When I asked her why, she said:

> Because if we talked about it, it would be with men and they would just be: "What are you on about, love?" [. . .] I don't think it occurs to people. I think

if you are a woman, if you are the only woman in a band, it occurs to you. But I think the guys in the bands don't really notice it.

Holly echoed Lauren's sentiment. She told me that there was "no open discussion" of gender issues and said "because I don't feel as though I can speak about it with other men – it's not an issue for them".

June and Sasha, by contrast, felt that sexism was not talked about in the industry because it would reflect negatively on those who raised it as an issue. Sasha reiterated that sexism "is not something that people talk about that openly. And if you do, people tend to think you've got a chip on your shoulder, that's a really common expression." Similarly, June told me: "There is ageism and sexism, you know. It's very common. And no one has a leg to stand on, because of the nature of the beast, because of the way people are employed." When I asked her to expand, she said:

> Even if you are in an engaged contract, even when you are employed, that contract will come to an end, and you're then gonna be up against everyone, all of your colleagues, either again, or you know . . . So people, sadly, people still greatly feel guarded against sort of discussing these difficult topics. And these topics we should really be able to talk about openly, because that's how it's going to be resolved, that's how we'll be able to end it.

As these statements illustrate, many of the research participants who had talked about sexism openly in the interview felt that it remained largely unspoken in the industry, either because men were unaware or because complaints about sexism could damage one's reputation (see chapter two). This observation resonates with Brydie-Leigh Bartleet's (2008) research on female conductors who were "loath to create 'trouble'" by critiquing existing gender inequalities (for discussion of a similar trend in the Irish television industry, see O'Brien, 2014). Thus, the unspeakability of gender inequalities was not only a feature of many of the accounts of my research participants, but also seems to apply to the wider culture of the classical music profession. While several research participants acknowledged, named, and openly discussed gender hierarchies, they were also disavowed in numerous ways, suggesting that unspeakability constitutes a feature of engagements with gender inequalities.

Conclusion

In this chapter, I have traced the ways in which the research participants engaged with class, racial, and gender inequalities in the classical music profession. While I gestured towards the importance of adopting an intersectional framework, I discussed issues of class, race, and gender separately as they were negotiated differently in the interviews. As I have shown, class inequalities were openly discussed, both in terms of the middle-class culture of the classical music sector and the ways this affected research participants from lower middle-class or working-class backgrounds. What remained unaddressed in these conversations was the class privilege of many research participants and this foreshadowed a theme that I also identified in talk about race, namely the unspoken privilege of whiteness. In contrast to class inequalities, racial inequalities were discussed more ambivalently in the interviews. Some research participants talked about the effect their black and minority ethnic background had had on their education and professional lives, while others found it hard to discern if, and if so how, their status as a black and minority ethnic musician affected their working life. Crucially, racial inequalities were also disarticulated through the use of several discursive tropes, such that the classical music profession was 'international' and that it was an advantage to be from a black and minority ethnic background.

In comparison to racial and class inequalities, issues related to gender were discussed most ambivalently. Some research participants openly talked about sexism and the way it had affected their working lives, but most used a range of rhetorical tools to disavow gender inequalities in the classical music profession. They used individualist rhetoric and reiterated neoliberal discourses by representing themselves as empowered and seemingly unaffected by forms of discrimination. Gender inequalities were attributed to other contexts or countries, and thereby represented as not having an effect on personal lives. The research participants also exhibited a postfeminist sensibility by trivialising or normalising gender hierarchies, by locating them in the past, or by presenting other women as the problem. As the final section of my analysis has shown, women were sometimes portrayed as the advantaged sex and some research participants found it difficult to name sexism, even if they had identified gender imbalances. Several research participants pointed out that sexism was not discussed openly in the industry, adding to a sense that gender inequalities remain largely unspoken in the industry.

In summary, there were overarching patterns in the ways the research participants discussed class, race, and gender in classical music. Privilege, for example, remained unaddressed, thereby limiting the emancipatory potential of talk about inequalities. However, there were also marked differences in the ways that issues of class, race, and gender were talked about. Arguably, a range of factors, such as associations of classical music with high culture and repeated outcries about the cost of learning to play a musical instrument, have paved the way for a more open discussion of class inequalities in the classical music sector. By contrast, engagements with gender inequalities were much more ambivalent and I drew on theories of individualisation and postfeminism as well as the positioning of young women as entrepreneurial subjects to make sense of their frequent disavowal. As such, this chapter has traced in detail the ways in which inequalities were, or were not, spoken about in the interviews.

Open discussion of inequalities is a key step towards addressing them. Thus, the unspeakability of sexism is not a trivial issue, but one that potentially perpetuates existing gender inequalities and that therefore merits close examination. As such, this chapter has not only traced how research participants made sense of ongoing inequalities, but, by focusing on the unspeakability of inequalities, has further contributed to our understanding of why there has been relatively little change, especially in relation to gender. The next chapter shifts the attention away from negotiations of inequalities to explore how neoliberalism or, to put it more specifically, entrepreneurial subjectivity, is registered, negotiated, and lived out. It draws on the research participants' positioning as entrepreneurial subjects par excellence to map the contours of entrepreneurial subjectivity.

Notes

1 In making this comment, Susan refers to the United Kingdom.
2 In her study of international competitions in classical music, Lisa McCormick (2015: 154) also reports on portrayals of female musicians' playing as 'masculine'. She points out that they "indicate that the gendering of musical performance runs much deeper than physical appearance and bodily display".
3 For research on individualisation, gender and cultural work, see also Banks and Milestone, 2011.
4 Postfeminism is a contested concept that is understood in various ways. For a recent discussion of the history of the term, its various usages, and the ways it can be employed in the context of research on gender and work, see Gill, 2016; Gill et al., 2016; Lewis, 2014.

References

ABRSM (2014). *Making music: Teaching, learning and playing in the UK*. London: Associated Board of the Royal Schools of Music. Accessed 1 December 2016. Available at: http://gb.abrsm.org/fileadmin/user_upload/PDFs/makingMusic2014.pdf

Ahmed, S. (2004). Declarations of whiteness: The non-performativity of anti-racism. *Borderlands e-Journal*, *3*(2). Accessed 1 December 2016. Available at: www.borderlands. net.au/vol3no2_2004/ahmed_declarations.htm

Bain, A. L. (2004). Female artistic identity in place: The studio. *Social & Cultural Geography*, *5*(2), 171–193.

Baker, G. (2014). *El Sistema: Orchestrating Venezuela's youth*. New York: Oxford University Press.

Banks, M., & Milestone, K. (2011). Individualization, gender and cultural work. *Gender, Work & Organization*, *18*(1), 73–89.

Bartleet, B-L. (2008). Women conductors on the orchestral podium: Pedagogical and professional implications. *College Music Symposium*, *48*, 31–51.

Bauman, Z. (2001). *The individualized society*. Cambridge: Polity.

Bennett, T., Savage, M., Bortolaia Silva, E., Warde, A., Gayo-Cal, M., & Wright, D. (2009). *Culture, class, distinction*. Abingdon, Oxon; New York: Routledge.

Bourdieu, P. (1984). *Distinction: A social critique of the judgement of taste*. London: Routledge & Kegan Paul.

Brah, A., & Phoenix, A. (2004). "Ain't I a woman?" Revisiting intersectionality. *Journal of International Women's Studies*, *5*(3), 75–86.

Brown, W. (2003). Neo-liberalism and the end of liberal democracy. *Theory & Event*, *7*(1), 37–59.

Bull, A. (2015). *The musical body: How gender and class are reproduced among young people playing classical music in England*. Unpublished PhD thesis, Goldsmiths University of London.

Bull, A. (2016). El Sistema as a bourgeois social project: Class, gender, and Victorian values. *Action, Criticism, and Theory for Music Education, 15*(1), 120–153.

Carpos, F. (2014). *The London orchestra as a prestige economy*. Paper presented at the conference Classical Music as Contemporary Socio-cultural Practice, 23rd May 2014, King's College London.

Crenshaw, K. (1991). Mapping the margins: Intersectionality, identity politics, and violence against women of color. *Stanford Law Review, 43*(6), 1241–1299.

DiAngelo, R. (2012). *What does it mean to be white? Developing white racial literacy*. New York: Peter Lang.

Edley, N., & Wetherell, M. (2001). Jekyll and Hyde: Men's constructions of feminism and feminists. *Feminism and Psychology, 11*(4), 439–458.

Ellemers, N., van den Heuvel, H., de Gilder, D., Maass, A., & Bonvini, A. (2004). The underrepresentation of women in science: Differential commitment or the queen bee syndrome? *The British Journal of Social Psychology / The British Psychological Society, 43*(3), 315–338.

Frankenberg, R. (1993). *White women, race matters: The social construction of white women*. London: Routledge.

Gill, R. (2007). *Gender and the media*. Cambridge: Polity.

Gill, R. (2014). Unspeakable inequalities: Post feminism, entrepreneurial subjectivity, and the repudiation of sexism among cultural workers. *Social Politics: International Studies in Gender, State and Society, 21*(4), 509–528.

Gill, R. (2016). Postfeminism and the new cultural life of feminism. *Diffractions: Graduate Journal for the Study of Culture, 6*. Accessed 1 December 2016. Available at: https://lisbonconsortium.files.wordpress.com/2012/12/rosalind-gill_postfeminism-and-the-new-cultural-life-of-feminism.pdf

Gill, R., Kelan, E. K., & Scharff, C. (2016). A postfeminist sensibility at work. *Gender, Work & Organization, 24*(3), 226–244.

Gould, E. (2009). Disorientations of desire: Music education queer. In T. R. Regelski & T. Gates (Eds.), *Music education for changing times: Guiding visions for practice* (pp. 59–71). London: Springer.

Hennekam, S., & Bennett, D. (2017). Sexual harassment in the creative industries: Tolerance, culture and the need for change. *Gender, Work and Organization, 24*, 417–434.

Hewitt, J., & Stokes, R. (1975). Disclaimers. *American Sociological Review, 40*(6), 1–11.

Higgins, C. (2013). Call for blanket ban on teacher-student sex. *The Guardian*, 01.03.2013. Accessed 1 December 2016. Available at: www.theguardian.com/education/2013/mar/01/blanket-ban-teacher-student-sex

Kelan, E. K. (2007). 'I don't know why': Accounting for the scarcity of women in ICT work. *Women's Studies International Forum, 30*(6), 499–511.

Kelan, E. K. (2009). Gender fatigue: The ideological dilemma of gender neutrality and discrimination in organizations. *Canadian Journal of Administrative Sciences / Revue Canadienne des Sciences de l'Administration, 26*(3), 197–210.

Kelan, E. K. (2014). From biological clocks to unspeakable inequalities: The intersectional positioning of young professionals. *British Journal of Management, 25*(4), 790–804.

Kokot, P. (2014). Structures and relationships: Women partners' careers in Germany and the UK. *Accounting, Auditing & Accountability Journal, 27*(1), 48–72.

Kokot, P. (2015). Let's talk about sex(ism): Cross-national perspectives on women partners' narratives on equality and sexism at work in Germany and the UK. *Critical Perspectives on Accounting, 27*, 73–85.

Lamb, R. (1993). The possibilities of/for feminist music criticism in music education. *British Journal of Music Education*, *10*(3), 169–180.

Lewis, P. (2014). Postfeminism, femininities and organization studies: Exploring a new agenda. *Organization Studies*, *35*(12), 1845–1866.

Liddy, S. (2016). "Open to all and everybody"? The Irish Film Board: Accounting for the scarcity of women screenwriters. *Feminist Media Studies*, *16*(5), 901–917.

Lutz, H., Herrera Vivar, M. T., & Supik, L. (2011). *Framing intersectionality: Debates on a multi-faceted concept in gender studies*. Farnham: Ashgate.

McCormick, L. (2015). *Performing civility: International competitions in classical music*. Cambridge: Cambridge University Press.

McRobbie, A. (2009). *The aftermath of feminism: Gender, culture and social change*. London: Sage.

McRobbie, A. (2010). Reflections on feminism, immaterial labour and the post-Fordist regime. *New Formations*, (70), 60–76.

Nash, J. C. (2008). Re-thinking intersectionality. *Feminist Review*, *89*, 1–15.

O'Brien, A. (2014). Producing television and reproducing gender. *Television & New Media*, *16*(3), 259–274.

Pidd, H. (2013). 39 Manchester music school teachers face inquiry. *The Guardian*, 07.05.2013. Accessed 1 December 2016. Available at: www.theguardian.com/uk/2013/may/07/manchester-music-schools-teachers-investigation

Randle, K., Forson, C., & Calveley, M. (2015). Towards a Bourdieusian analysis of the social composition of the UK film and television workforce. *Work, Employment & Society*, *29*(4), 590–606.

Rottenberg, C. (2014). The rise of neoliberal feminism. *Cultural Studies*, *28*(3), 418–437.

Scharff, C. (2012). *Repudiating feminism: Young women in a neoliberal world*. Farnham: Ashgate.

Taylor, S., & Littleton, K. (2012). *Contemporary identities of creativity and creative work*. Farnham: Ashgate.

Tindall, B. (2005). *Mozart in the jungle: Sex, drugs, and classical music*. New York: Grove Press.

Tregear, P., Johansen, G., Jorgensen, H., Sloboda, J., Tulve, I., & Wistreich, R. (2016). Conservatoires in society: Institutional challenges and possibilities for change. *Arts and Humanities in Higher Education*, *15*(3–4), 276–292.

Wang, G. (2009). Interlopers in the realm of high culture: "Music moms" and the performance of Asian and Asian American identities. *American Quarterly*, *61*(4), 881–903.

Wreyford, N. (2015). *The gendered contexts of screenwriting work: Socialized recruitment and judgments of taste and talent in the UK film industry*. Unpublished PhD thesis, King's College London.

Yoshihara, M. (2007). *Musicians from a different shore: Asians and Asian Americans in classical music*. Philadelphia, PA: Temple University Press.

Chapter 4

Entrepreneurialism at work
Mapping the contours of entrepreneurial subjectivity

In this chapter, I draw on Foucauldian approaches to neoliberalism, which have shown that the neoliberal self is an entrepreneurial subject (Brown, 2003; Foucault, 2008; Lemke, 2001; Rose, 1992). More specifically, the chapter asks how entrepreneurial subjectivity is registered, negotiated, and lived out. In following this line of inquiry, I make use of the research participants' positioning as entrepreneurial subjects par excellence. As I have demonstrated in chapter one, public discourses have positioned young women (Baker, 2008; Gill and Scharff, 2011; Gonick, 2006; McRobbie, 2009; Ringrose and Walkerdine, 2008) and cultural workers (Gill and Pratt, 2008; McRobbie, 2002; 2015a; Ross, 2008) as ideal entrepreneurial subjects. By analysing my conversations with young, female, classical musicians, I draw on the accounts of individuals who, as cultural workers and young women, are twice positioned as entrepreneurial. This allows me to trace the contours of entrepreneurial subjectivity and to shed light on yet a different aspect of the interplay between gender, subjectivity, and cultural work in the classical music profession.

Following a review of the literature on neoliberalism, entrepreneurial subjectivity, and the ways it is lived out on a subjective level, the main part of this chapter is divided into ten sections. Each section sheds light on a distinct facet of entrepreneurial subjectivity. The sections show that entrepreneurial subjects relate to themselves as if they were a business, are active, embrace risks, capably manage difficulties, and hide injuries. Crucially, entrepreneurial rhetoric does not hold absolutely because individuals draw on a range of discourses in their talk. Some discourses, however, are also markedly absent, such as political perspectives that highlight the need for social change. Instead, desires for change are directed away from the socio-political sphere and turned inwards, thereby calling on the self to transform itself. Anxieties came to the fore in the interviews, but instead of arguing for one prevailing affect that characterises entrepreneurial subjectivity, I advance the notion of a multifaceted affective register. In line with existing arguments (Amable, 2011; Brown, 2015; Dardot and Laval, 2013; McNay, 2009; Mirowski, 2014), competition is a feature of entrepreneurial subjectivity. Yet, I argue that competition seems to be self-directed, suggesting that entrepreneurial subjects compete with the self, and not just with others. Last but not least, entrepreneurial subjects reject those who are not entrepreneurial. By drawing on theories of abjection, I argue that these repudiations are not side effects of entrepreneurial subjectivity, but that they are constitutive of it.

Neoliberalism, entrepreneurial subjectivity, and the ways it is lived out

In recent years, there has been a flurry of writings on neoliberalism (e.g. Brown, 2015; Crouch, 2011; Dardot and Laval, 2013; Gilbert, 2013; Mirowski, 2014; Mirowski and Phlewe, 2009; Springer et al., 2016; Stedman Jones, 2012). Most scholars tend to agree that neoliberalism involves the extension of market principles into all areas of life (e.g. Brown, 2015; Dardot and Laval, 2013; Mudge, 2008; Shamir, 2008; Springer et al., 2016), including subjectivity. And yet, neoliberalism continues to be a contested concept. It has been employed variously, not only across time (Thorsen and Lie, 2006) and space (Ong, 2006; Rofel, 2007), but also in different disciplinary contexts and orientations. Indeed, as Taylor Boas and Jordan Gans-Morse (2009) have shown, neoliberalism often remains undefined and is used to characterise a wide variety of phenomena.

A quick glance at some of the existing literature demonstrates that there are different interpretations of neoliberalism. Focusing on political economic practices, David Harvey (2005) has, for example, argued that neoliberalism is characterised by strong private property rights, free markets, and free trade, while other commentators have highlighted that neoliberalism extends beyond the economic and political spheres. Neoliberalism, in these writings, is a "political philosophy and ideology that affects every dimension of social life" (Giroux, 2004: 70), a strong discourse (Bourdieu, 1998), a political, economic *and* cultural force (Duggan, 2004), which is now common sense (Hall and O'Shea, 2013). Last but not least, writers in the Foucauldian tradition have traced how neoliberalism extends to the reconstitution of subjectivities (Brown, 2003; 2015; Foucault, 2008; Lemke, 2001; Rose, 1992).

The contested nature of the term neoliberalism has led some to map its meanings and interpretations (e.g. Hardin, 2014; Larner, 2000), while others have argued that the concept is no longer useful. John Clarke (2008), for example, suggests that neoliberalism has been stretched too far to be productive as a critical analytical tool (see also Garland and Harper, 2012). Other authors have instead called for analyses of neoliberalism that pay attention to its historically specific and internally contradictory aspects (Larner, 2000) and argued that neoliberalism should be understood as a "process, not an end-state"

(Peck and Tickell, 2002: 383). In a similar vein, anthropologists have insisted on understanding neoliberalism as situated and contingent, rather than a unified and coherent global trend (for a discussion, see Gershon, 2011). And recent historical research has attempted to revisit the origins of neoliberal thought (Gane, 2014a; b; Mirowski and Phlewe, 2009; Stedman Jones, 2012) in order to enhance our understanding of the specificities and heterogeneities of neoliberalism. In the following, I provide a detailed introduction to Foucauldian approaches to neoliberalism (for a brief discussion, see chapter one) in order to lay the theoretical groundwork for my subsequent mapping of the contours of entrepreneurial subjectivity.

As Michel Foucault (2008: 226; emphasis in original) has famously argued,

> the stake in all neoliberal analyses is the replacement every time of *homo oeconomicus* as partner of exchange with a *homo oeconomicus* as entrepreneur of himself, being for himself his own capital, being for himself his own producer, being for himself the source of [his] earnings.

Under neoliberalism, the enterprise form is extended "to *all* forms of conduct" (Burchell, 1993: 275; emphasis in original), including the conduct of individuals themselves. According to Wendy Brown (2003: paragraph 15), "neo-liberalism normatively constructs and interpellates individuals as entrepreneurial actors in every sphere of life" which means that the enterprise form encompasses subjectivity itself (McNay, 2009). In contrast to classical liberalism, neoliberalism does not assume that all forms of conduct automatically take on an entrepreneurial form; instead, neoliberal regimes develop institutional practices and rewards for enacting this vision (Brown, 2003; Gilbert, 2013; Lemke, 2001). Entrepreneurial forms of conduct are not, therefore, a historically recent phenomenon. Neoliberalism is distinct, however, in that it actively reconfigures subjects as entrepreneurial actors (Brown, 2003). This means that the neoliberal self is an entrepreneurial subject.[1]

Conducting its life as enterprise, the enterprising self is a "self that calculates *about* itself and that works *upon* itself in order to better itself" (Rose, 1992: 146; emphasis in original). Its conduct is bound by specific rules that emphasise "energy, initiative, ambition, calculation and personal responsibility" (Rose, 1996: 154). Entrepreneurial subjects are "active not passive, self-reliant, accountable and responsible for their actions" (du Gay, 1996: 134). Indeed, and as Ulrich Bröckling (2005: 12) has insightfully argued, the entrepreneurial self only ever exists in "the gerund as something being produced and optimized". Because the enterprising self is constantly called upon to change and self-improve, "[o]ne is not an enterprising self, but is rather becoming one" (12).

Importantly, the resources to become an entrepreneurial subject are unevenly distributed. As Jessica Ringrose and Valerie Walkerdine (2008) have argued, the subject of self-invention is predominantly middle-class. Research on education has suggested that neoliberal discourses are more accessible to students from a middle-class background (O'Flynn and Petersen, 2007) and that forms of self-making are not equally available to members of all social classes (Allen, 2014; see also Davies and Bansel, 2007). And while discourses of entrepreneurial self-help have appealed to members of black and migrant communities (Gilroy, 2013), the constitution of entrepreneurial subjectivities also produces its 'others' (Scharff, 2011). As Ruth Williams (2014) has demonstrated in her discussion of the neoliberal spiritual subject, new forms of colonialism are at play in contexts where 'white' people discover their spiritual selves through contact with 'brown' people.

Apart from race and class, the relationship between gender and entrepreneurial subjectivities has been discussed from various angles. Some authors have suggested that entrepreneurship is implicitly equated with the masculine (Bruni et al., 2004) because the supposed qualities of entrepreneurs, such as competitiveness, independence, and willingness to take risks, are associated with masculinity. As I have shown in chapter one, however, recent feminist research has made the opposite argument and demonstrated that women, and young women in particular, are increasingly positioned as entrepreneurial (Baker, 2008; Gill and Scharff, 2011; Gonick, 2006; McRobbie, 2009; Ringrose and Walkerdine, 2008). Rather than being the entrepreneur's other, this body of research suggests that young women are hailed as entrepreneurial subjects par excellence.

The neoliberal incitement to manage one's self as enterprise, and the way this cuts across gendered, racialised, and classed power dynamics, raises questions about the kinds of selves that are constructed in and through neoliberalism. What are the contours of entrepreneurial subjectivity and how is entrepreneurialism lived out? Psychoanalytic work has shown that the neoliberal emphasis on choice can increase anxieties because of fears of not making the ideal choice (Saleci, 2010). In addition, psychoanalytic perspectives have demonstrated that neoliberal subjects disavow vulnerability and instead manifest intensified forms of individualism (Layton, 2010). Denigrated aspects of the self, such as dependency, may be projected onto 'others', resulting in a decline of empathetic capacities (Layton, 2009) and the rigid drawing of boundaries between who is 'in' and who is 'out' (Layton, 2013a; b).

Apart from psychoanalysts, some social scientists and particularly Foucauldian thinkers have engaged with "the inner life of the neoliberal subject" (Binkley, 2009: 61). These authors have highlighted similar themes around the repudiation of dependencies (Binkley, 2011a), the creation of an illusion of autonomy (Davies, 2005), and the emphasis on personal responsibility and its depoliticising tendencies (McNay, 2009). More broadly, "feelings of insecurity, anxiety, stress and depression" (Hall and O'Shea, 2013: 6) have been linked to neoliberalism, with depression being evoked by several authors (Berardi, 2009; Bröckling, 2007; Dardot and Laval, 2013; Ehrenberg, 2010). Other researchers have shown that the difficulties of producing oneself as an entrepreneurial subject can lead to an increased need for therapeutic support, especially at work (Swan, 2008). Also discussing conditions of work, Richard Sennett (1998)[2] has famously argued that short-term capitalism threatens to corrode characters.

This literature makes a range of insightful and thought-provoking contributions, but is frequently theoretical in perspective (Berardi, 2009; Dardot and Laval, 2013; Davies, 2005; Hall and O'Shea, 2013; McNay, 2009) or rests on textual readings (Binkley, 2009; 2011a; Bröckling, 2007). Sennett's work (1998: 11) is also wider in focus, based loosely on mixed and informal sources, and an exploration of the "daily life around [him]". And although some of the psychoanalytic literature draws on vignettes from clinical work with patients (e.g. Layton, 2009; 2010), there is little systematic empirical research on the contours of entrepreneurial subjectivity. This chapter seeks to address this gap by exploring the accounts of individuals who, as cultural workers and young women, are twice positioned as entrepreneurial. More specifically related to the concerns addressed in this book, my analysis of the contours of entrepreneurial subjectivity allows me to shed light on a different dimension of the interplay between gender, subjectivity, and cultural work in the classical music profession. In line with my discourse analytic approach outlined in chapter one, the subsequent analysis presents and discusses patterns in how entrepreneurialism is registered, negotiated, and lived out.

The contours of entrepreneurial subjectivity: the self as business

Resonating with Lois McNay's (2009) argument about the economisation of subjectivity, the research participants frequently used business language to talk about themselves (see also Gershon, 2011; Storey et al., 2005). For example, they referred to themselves as a product or commodity:

> I look at myself as a business and a product [. . .] It's hard because it's such an emotional personal thing to be a singer, but it is business. Everything is a business. It may be, you know, all of the arts, the opera houses, are charity-run, but . . . You know, I'm a commodity.
>
> (Alice)

> What people want from you is for you to deliver a readily sellable product, you see how bad I actually call myself: a product. My God. But that's what it is. People want you to be a ready product that sells.
>
> (Isabella)

> I think it would not hurt to have some sort of information about how to run a business. How to run a freelance business, with yourself as the product, which is what we are.
>
> (Lauren)

These statements occurred in discussions about freelancing where participants emphasised the importance of "selling yourself as a product" (June) in order to get work (see chapter two). Indeed, various aspects of the self were commodified, including racial differences. Discussing her experiences as a black singer, Susan stated:

> Like I think: "Should I straighten my hair, should I, you know, blend in?" But then the idea isn't to blend in, it's to stand out, because there's so many singers that have got to have something – I suppose you'd call it a USP, wouldn't you – a unique selling point [laughs].

Susan makes this claim with more than a hint of irony as expressed by her laughter. Nevertheless, racial difference is presented as a potential selling point in a competitive market environment (see also Allen et al., 2013), which reflects wider trends where difference is commodified and diversity is primarily regarded as an economic value (Proctor-Thomson, 2013).

Along with the use of business language, research participants exhibited a calculative attitude (Bröckling, 2005; Rose, 1992). They said that they were well organised and liked to plan in advance: "My life is that I plan everything, that's the point" (Julianna). With regard to finances in particular, there was an emphasis on careful planning: "I just try and plan really meticulously and be really sensible, so sort of financially it's just – I work out my budget really carefully" (Linda; see also chapter five). The attention to planning and budgeting, as well as the use of business language to talk about the self, illustrates the shift to understanding the self as business.

According to Ilana Gershon (2011: 539), the view of oneself as a business designates a "move from the liberal vision of people owning themselves as though they were property to a neoliberal vision of people owning themselves as though they were a business". As part of this shift, one's relationship to oneself changes. As Nikolas Rose (1990: 240) puts it, "one becomes a subject for oneself". Thus, the shift from self as property to self as business does not only designate the economisation of subjectivity, but also a changed relationship with the self. By relating to itself as a business, the entrepreneurial subject establishes a distance to its self and can subsequently work on it.

The resulting work on the self took on various dimensions. Julianna stated: "I try to sleep well, eat well, exercise, meditate – basically work on myself." This work on the self could relate to the body, as expressed by Faith's statement that emphasised "how much we [musicians] have to take care of our bodies. Because of course when we are ill, we don't, we can't take sick leave." Mental and psychological aspects were also worked upon. Kim stated that "you have to take care of your mental health, and if you're down, you've got to just work through it and come back." Interestingly, work on the self was constructed as an ongoing activity. Resonating with Bröckling's (2005) argument that the entrepreneurial self is in a constant mode of becoming, Janine told me that there were "no limits" to self-improvement, while Jane emphasised that "you always want to improve and get better at what you do." These statements demonstrate that the self as business needs constant attention, and that various aspects of the self – physical, mental, and spiritual – are worked upon for optimisation.

The impetus to work on the self, and the view of the self as business, can further be understood in light of Michel Feher's (2009) argument about the rise of human capital as a dominant subjective form under neoliberalism. According to Feher (2009: 30–31), neoliberalism treats people "as entrepreneurs of themselves or, more precisely, as investors in themselves, as human capital that wishes to appreciate and to value itself and thus allocate its skills accordingly". All activities – whether they pertain to spiritual, physical, or psychological matters – contribute to the appreciation or depreciation of human capital. Indeed, Brown (2015: 33) has recently built on Feher's arguments and suggested that "the specific model for human capital and its spheres of activity is increasingly that of financial or investment capital, and not only productive or entrepreneurial capital." This means that a range of activities, behaviours, and conducts "are increasingly configured as strategic decisions and practices related to enhancing the self's future value" (34). In light of these arguments, the research participants' work on the self can be read as an investment in their own human capital (see also McRobbie, 2015a). As such, work on the self is not only indicative and constitutive of an entrepreneurial subjectivity, but more specifically points to the ways in which human beings are also figured as 'human capital' in neoliberalism.

Constantly active and still lacking time

According to Paul du Gay (1996: 182), "[t]here is a real sense in the world of enterprise that 'one is always at it'." This sense featured in the participants' accounts that emphasised the need to work hard, be active, and make the best use of time. As Alice stated, "I've always been a very hard worker. In my world, if I do something, I want to succeed." And even though some questioned whether hard work led to success, it was still deemed necessary:

> I had grown up believing, being taught, that if you work hard enough, if you worked hard enough, you would succeed. Simple equation, right? Work plus work plus work plus more work equals success. In music it's not like that. You have to do the work, there's no guarantee you will succeed.
>
> (Lauren)

Apart from hard work, research participants underlined the importance of being active:

> I am active in sending CVs, trying to do the odd audition, trying to do all that kind of networking side. I am not just sitting at home thinking: "The universe will take care of me!" [laughs] because I know it doesn't work like that.
>
> (Hope)

Being proactive meant taking opportunities as they come, but also creating them. As Lena pointed out:

> A lot of the things that people say is: "You just have to take the opportunities when they come." But not a lot of people say: "You have to create your own

opportunities", which I think is more the case. Because you can't wait around for someone to call you and say: "Can you please do this job?" Because it's not gonna happen, so you just really need to get out there and also make sure that you're really prepared for whatever does come along.

The emphasis on being active ties in with a neoliberal philosophy of time where being idle is to be avoided (O'Flynn and Petersen, 2007). Holly told me that she watched TV to relax, but said:

> I thought: "This is such a waste of time, I am just sitting here not doing any-thing, watching crappy TV!" So I started knitting these incredible, elaborate things, because if I am watching TV, at least I am getting something done. So basically, it is quite difficult to unwind. I can't really do that. So yeah, I feel as though I always have to be doing something.

The entrepreneurial self orients to time with a view to making the best use of it. The resulting constant activity means that there is also a feeling of a lack of time. As Julianna pointed out: "Seriously, the thing is: there is no time. There is no time for anything, you just need to grab and do. Time is very precious, very precious here." Since there are no limits to self-improvement, productive uses of time become paramount. And because self-optimisation applies to various spheres of life – professional, physical, mental, and spiritual – there is little scope for idle time and instead a sense of 'always being at it'.

At this stage, it is worth reminding the reader that I do not regard the research participants' accounts as reflections of 'reality', but as utterances that are doing things. As I have shown in my analysis of the gendered dynamics of self-promotion (see chapter two), I did not read the research participants' claims that they are 'naturally' modest as indicative of a 'feminine essence', but as performa-tively constituting femininity. In the present context, I do not aim to know whether Holly really does knit while watching TV. Instead, and in conjunction with my discursive approach, I regard the extracts presented here as enunciations in and through which entrepreneurial subjectivities are constructed. By using business language or by talking about productive uses of time, the research participants orient to entrepreneurial discourses, reiterate them, and, through these reiterative enunciations, performatively produce entrepreneurial subjectivity (Butler, 1993). By examining the accounts of the research participants, I therefore do not only trace the ways entrepreneurialism is lived out in the context of cultural work, but also provide insight into how entrepreneurial subjectivities are constituted in talk.

Embracing risks, learning from knock-backs, and staying positive

In line with the shift to the self as business, entrepreneurial subjects bear risks like companies (Neff, 2012). "According to the neoliberal perspective, to prosper, one must engage with risk" (Gershon, 2011: 540; see also Dardot and Laval, 2013; Mirowski, 2014). This attitude came to the fore in the research participants' talk. When speaking about the first CD she had recorded, which involved taking a financial risk, Isabella stated: "So it was a bit risky, but I believe in taking risks." Indeed, Amalia told me that she enjoyed taking risks: "I like it, because I like overcoming fears. And it's, it's not that I just like it, I love it!" Risks and fears were not to be avoided, but to be embraced and tackled. Indeed, the pressure that is associated with taking risks was presented in a positive light. Amanda told me: "I quite like pressure. I like the kind of buzz of: 'You have to do it'. I kind of like it because I'm very prepared to work really hard so that it will be good."

Similarly, knock-backs were not framed as discouraging, but as valuable learning experiences:

> If you get knocked back, do you go: "Oh, that means I am shit, and then I'm gonna give up", or do you go: "Oh well, I've got to learn something here so that it doesn't happen next time."
>
> (Lauren)

> You just have to keep going. And you get knock-back after knock-back after knock-back after knock-back. But that just makes you then stronger.
>
> (Kelly)

> My outlook on that is: "Well, I learned a lot from that." Okay, this isn't the way I would have chosen it, but I'm gonna make sure I gather all the knowledge I can from that experience and I'll move forward.
>
> (June)

Fears or worries that result from knock-backs were kept at bay and the participants adopted a positive attitude instead. In the face of difficulties or insecurities, they tried "not to worry too much" (Carolyn), to "stay positive", "steer away from negative people", and "to keep that sort of sunny and positive attitude, and not trying to get too bogged down in the future" (Christine). Resonating with a wider shift towards positive thinking and happiness which is "implicated in a more general logic of neoliberal subjectification" (Binkley, 2011b: 372), Elena told me that she weighted positive things more than negative things in order to be happy: "At the end of the day, I decide myself whether I'm happy."

This positive attitude had to be actively crafted. As Julianna reminded me: "You need to work on it, you know, to be positive." Energy was spent on maintaining a positive attitude out of fear that excessive worrying could interfere with one's work:

> I guess it is just reassuring yourself, like – trying not to think about just how difficult things are sometimes, because if you did, there would just be no energy left to do any work [laughs] – from worrying about things.
>
> (Eve; see also chapter five)

According to Barbara Ehrenreich (2009: 8), "positive thinking has made itself useful as an apology for the crueler aspects of the market economy". As I demonstrate in more detail below, some contours of entrepreneurial subjectivity, such as having a positive attitude, are depoliticising.[3] When positive attitudes are valued at the expense of anger or despair, critique and the impetus to change something other than the self have little use-value.

Surviving difficulties

Apart from responding to challenging circumstances by adopting a positive attitude, research participants talked about difficulties in their own lives as something that had happened previously and that had now been overcome. Difficulties, I noticed, were rarely in the here and now and mainly located in the past:

> Especially last year, I had a very difficult time last year just trying to just keep going. But this year I am getting more work, doing things with people and developing more contacts, so – it is always going in the right direction, so it's good.
>
> (Eve)

> I was in a little downward spiral maybe this time last year because I was teaching too much. And as much as I enjoy teaching and I enjoy, I like my pupils and everything, it's not what I want to do all the time. And I was feeling really, I was thinking: "How am I gonna get out of this? What am I gonna do?" And auditions weren't going very well, I wasn't getting anything, just rejections and just kept teaching, it was just rubbish and then finally an audition went well and then I played lots and then my confidence in playing went up and then auditions started to go well, like I got work and that – for me that's where I got out of my spiral.
>
> (Rose)

Some participants stated that it took them a long time to deal with difficulties and solve problems. Elena told me: "I started working on them in my early twenties. Now, I am 31 and I have the feeling that, for about a year, I've solved the biggest part. The penny has dropped. But it has taken ten years." And even when participants were in "a bit of a slump" at the time of interview, they emphasised "it's been mostly up, actually, since I started professionally so it hasn't been too much in the way of: 'Oh, this is awful'" (Susan).

The temporality of these statements is meaningful because it constructs the subjects in question as capable managers of their lives. Even though they encountered difficult times or downward spirals, they survived and transcended them. According to Katariina Mäkinen (2012: 113), who observed a similar temporal structure in her research on contemporary work cultures, "[t]he temporality here functions in such a way that they are ultimately narratives of survival and empowerment:

as the plot develops, the narrators achieve what they wanted, despite the odds." Examining the prevalence of such survivor discourses, Shani Orgad (2009: 151) has argued that this "formation is closely linked to the discourse of neoliberalism and its underpinning concept of the enterprising self". Stories about difficulties that were overcome (re-)constitute the entrepreneurial self because they demonstrate that the subject in question has the capacity to tackle and solve problems.

Indeed, and linking back to my earlier argument about the research participants' adopting a positive attitude and learning from knock-backs, difficult experiences in the past were often cast in a positive light by re-framing them as learning experiences. Reflecting on not getting into a prestigious conservatoire after she left school, Hope stated:

> When I didn't get into [prestigious conservatoire], the first time I applied, I was devastated. I was absolutely devastated. But I think, in many ways that was the best thing that could have happened to me, looking back, because I'd had that knock-back.

Equally, Janine told me about her difficulties at music college saying:

> I did have quite a lot of lows there, but it definitely made me much thicker skinned. It meant that I was really prepared for the world in that sense, and prepared for the fact that not everything would go my way, and this would be a very hard thing to make a living, and a very hard thing to do, and I would just have to dedicate a lot of time to it and be patient and work hard. And I wouldn't just get everything handed to me.

Along with the other statements that I discussed above, Hope and Janine openly talk about difficult experiences, but these difficulties are located in the past. Indeed, they are reframed in a positive light: Hope describes the rejection as "the best thing that could have happened" and Janine feels that the lows at music college made her "much thicker skinned". The link between the survivor discourse and entrepreneurialism comes strongly to the fore in Janine's statement, which drew on the tropes of hard work, dedication, and patience. Tellingly, the survivor discourse emphasises the individual's emergence from suffering, but not its root causes (Orgad, 2009), such as the lack of employment opportunities. Empowerment is thus framed as an individual endeavour and the wider socio-political causes of the difficulties that were encountered remain unaddressed.

Hiding injuries

The survivor discourse ties in with repudiations of vulnerability in neoliberalism. As Micki McGee (2005) has pointed out in her research on self-help culture, the emphasis on self-mastery goes hand in hand with a denial of vulnerabilities (see also Layton, 2010). "Not only is it the labor of others, and the value of labor itself, that must be denied by the masterful self, but also it is the vulnerabilities of our bodies" (McGee, 2005: 174). This denial of vulnerability came to the fore in the research participants' discussions of playing-related injuries (for a detailed analysis see Scharff, 2016). As I pointed out in chapter one, many musicians experience health problems from the high physical and psychological demands of their profession (Bennett, 2008; Help Musicians UK, 2014; Zaza et al., 1998). However, these injuries tend to be hidden (Alford and Szanto, 1996; Gembris and Heye, 2012). More than half of my research participants had suffered from a playing-related injury, ranging from hearing problems, postural issues, and repetitive strain injury to focal dystonia and more instrument-specific illnesses such as vocal problems among singers. And while they discussed these injuries in the interview, many pointed out they were not openly talked about among musicians.

When I asked Lauren whether she had ever had any injuries, she told me about her experiences and went on to say:

> Part of the problem with my industry – one of the problems of my industry – is that there is a massive stigma attached to injury, so people don't talk about it as much as they should. People will . . . musicians will keep on playing on injuries, rather than admit that they are having trouble, because they don't wanna lose their work or they don't wanna be seen to be unreliable.

Numerous research participants shared this sentiment. Kim told me that musicians did not discuss injuries openly and explained:

> It's because there's so many of us going for the same work. And there's always that competition, and you know, we all need money, and we can't just be dropped because of that. So yeah, you have to keep it under cover. And yet, you know, the strain of it creates injuries.

Injuries were covered up out of fear that others would think it develops into something chronic (Angela), that one would be seen as an unreliable player (Amanda), and, therefore, not asked to work (Linda). Summing up musicians' attitudes towards injuries, Susan stated that "they'll talk about how to look after yourself, but people don't really talk about their own problems, because it then shows weakness."

While research participants represented injuries as something that is best kept under cover, they also normalised them. According to Anke, "almost everybody has something" and Elena pointed out "there are specific things for every instrument which mean that it's unhealthy". Despite the acknowledgement that injuries were common, only a few research participants linked the prevalence of injuries to work conditions. In addition to her statement about injuries being the result of competition, cited above, Kim stated: "if you are playing in a very cold hall, that can cause injuries." Overwhelmingly, however, having an injury was seen as an individual failure, which "mostly shows that your technique is wrong" (Annegret).[4] Gesche told me that "actually, most musicians have back pain or something", but subsequently pointed out that it is basically "one's own fault" if one is or gets injured. This construction of injuries as personal failures reflects the widely discussed trend that failure is individualised in neoliberalism (Berardi, 2009; Bröckling, 2007; Burchell, 1993; Dardot and Laval, 2013; Layton, 2010; McRobbie, 2015a; Storey et al., 2005; Saleci, 2010). According to Mark Banks (2007: 63), "[f]aced with a multiplicity of discourses that reinforce the autonomy, and thus potential culpability, of the 'enterprising self', success and failure are understood as triumphs and tragedies of individual design". Responsible for managing opportunities and constraints independently, the entrepreneurial self only has itself to blame if something goes wrong. The impact of wider socio-economic forces, such as work conditions, remains unacknowledged and wellbeing is presented as achievable through appropriate self-management.

Negotiating competing discourses

Although the research participants preferred to hide their playing-related injuries, they openly discussed their emotional vulnerabilities as musicians. Ashley explained why it was terrible to get bad reviews of one's playing:

> If you are playing music, you are totally out there, you are totally stripped, you know. And so for someone to attack that, you are so vulnerable, because they are basically – I don't know what they called it, you know, but you are just basically saying you know, I didn't like your interpretation, I didn't like your soul very much.

Describing similar sentiments, Alice told me that being booed at after performances was "like somebody digging your heart out" and Amy stated: "I have read reviews that are bad, and you know, then I can be on stage thinking: 'Oh, but they think I'm terrible'. And things like that can be really quite upsetting." Also talking about receiving bad reviews, Janine told me "if you receive something really negative in that way, I think that can really knock you down and bring you down."

As opposed to their engagements with injuries, the participants did not hide their vulnerabilities in relation to negative feedback. This apparent paradox can be made sense of by recalling that entrepreneurial discourses do not hold absolutely, but that they "are received and interpreted in the particular and complex contexts that individuals move through in their everyday lives" (Halford and Leonard, 2006: 658; see also Crawshaw, 2012; Nairn and Higgins, 2007; Salmenniemi and Vorona; 2014; chapter one). Entrepreneurialism intersects with other discourses, such as discourses around artistic work. Jette explained that dealing with negative feedback was difficult because: "We obviously totally identify, on a very personal level, with what we do, somehow as artists, in the widest sense. And then you risk getting crushed by knock-backs." By discussing instances where they felt vulnerable, the research participants orient to their positioning as artists and evoke vulnerabilities as part of a wider discourse on artists' emotional investment in their work. Through this discursive move, the research participants draw on an alternative discourse and disrupt their performance of entrepreneurial subjectivity.

The research participants' engagements with vulnerabilities demonstrate that entrepreneurialism is negotiated in contexts that provide a range of discourses. While entrepreneurial rhetoric may be strongly represented (Bourdieu, 1998), it competes with other discourses and is taken up variously (Fenwick, 2002). This does not mean that alternative discourses are unproblematic. As I have shown in chapter two in my discussion of the gendered politics of self-promotion, discourses around artistic work, for example, have long relied on constructions of artists as men, thereby creating particular dilemmas for female artists (Taylor and Littleton, 2012). Indeed, the expressions of vulnerability could also be read as gendered discourses where women regard shameful experiences, such as negative feedback, as a reflection of a failed self (Seu, 2010). These various readings suggest that entrepreneurial discourses are not deterministic and that even those individuals, who are twice positioned as entrepreneurial, are not wholly subject to entrepreneurial rhetoric. Subjectivities are performed in various contexts and ways that may affirm, subvert, or resist entrepreneurial discourses.

Disarticulating structural constraints

While research participants drew on several competing discourses, some were markedly absent. As I have shown in the previous chapter, discourses that highlight structural constraints, and the ways that they affect individuals' abilities to master their own lives, were evoked occasionally, but overwhelmingly disarticulated. As Rosalind Gill (2014) has argued in relation to cultural work, sexism, racism, and other patterns of structural discrimination often remain unspeakable so as not to puncture neoliberal mythologies of individual achievement. For the entrepreneurial subject to be intelligible, structural patterns of discrimination and privilege have to be disarticulated. Arguably, entrepreneurial subjectivities are in part performed through a disarticulation of social structures.

The making invisible of structural constraints was achieved rhetorically in a variety of ways. In addition to the tools that I discussed in the previous chapter, many research participants employed the trope of 'luck' to account for their privileged position, especially in relation to class. In this context, research participants pointed out that they were 'lucky' that their parents could support their artistic lives (see also chapter five). Discussing the financial uncertainty of the profession, Amanda told me: "I'm probably quite lucky in that, you know, I know that if it was absolutely terrible, you know my parents would help me. I'm in a very fortunate position like that." Jana echoed this sentiment when she stated that she had never been in a financially precarious situation: "So, I've had enormous luck with my parents, who can finance a lot for me." Equally, Jane reflected on how hard it was to afford housing in London on a musician's income but said:

> I guess I'm luckier than most, in that I come from quite a reasonably well-off family, they could afford to send me to public school – yes, I got a scholarship, but actually, they – my dad was a lawyer and all the rest of it, so I have

been incredibly lucky, they basically lent me the money to buy a flat in central London.

Kristina also evoked the trope of luck when she told me how she was able to purchase her violin:

> And I had enormous luck, because my violin is not as expensive as violins can get. And my grandfather somehow saved a lot of money and he said he'd lend it to me for an indefinite period of time until I have a job. And that's simply, I mean, to find oneself in such a situation; not everybody has a rich grandfather.

In these statements, the research participants portray their financially secure background as a matter of "luck". They acknowledge that they are in a "fortunate position" (Amanda) and that "not everybody has a rich grandfather" (Kristina) and, through that, evoke the notion of privilege. And yet, by framing the certainty of financial support, the ability to purchase a property in Central London or a high-quality musical instrument as matters of 'luck', the research participants disarticulate their socio-economic privilege. Paralleling my argument about the disarticulation of structural inequalities (see chapter three), it is notable that privilege is not explicitly mentioned in these accounts.

In employing the trope of luck, the research participants elide the issue of the patterned nature of who is, and who is not, 'lucky'. As Donna Langston (1991: 146) has reminded us, it is not a coincidence "that the 'unlucky' come from certain race, gender and class backgrounds". The framing of privilege as a matter of personal luck also wards off potential criticism; in that sense, the trope of luck fulfils the rhetorical function of a disclaimer. Because: who can be held accountable for being lucky? Equally important, the narrative of personal luck is couched in an individualist framework where personal fates are disembedded from wider social structures because they are regarded as matters of luck. In the examples discussed here, 'luck' serves as another rhetorical tool, which disarticulates structural constraints and inequalities.[5]

The disavowal of structural constraints means that desires for change are directed away from the socio-political sphere and "turned inwards" (Mäkinen, 2012: 147), "transferring the site of activity from the public arena to each individual's psyche" (Rottenberg, 2014: 426). When structural constraints are rhetorically elided, the self, rather than the socio-political sphere, becomes the locus for change and "social critique is increasingly replaced by self-critique" (Saleci, 2010: 31). Anger and frustration are directed away from the broader context and turned inwards, resulting in an impetus to transform the self. Significantly, anger and frustration were almost absent from the interviews. Some musicians were frustrated or "pissed off" (Isabella) that they often had to work for free (see chapter five). On the whole, however, anger was rarely evoked. When structural patterns of privilege and inequality are discursively elided, and when change is directed inwards, anger is virtually absent.[6] This gives rise to the question of the affective register of entrepreneurial subjectivity, which I explore in the next section.

Anxiety as the prevailing affect?

According to Imogen Tyler (2013: 8), neoliberal democracies "function through the generation of consent via fear and anxiety". Anxieties came to the fore in the research participants' discussion of the uncertainty related to freelance work where "you just don't know what's gonna come" (Ashley; see chapter five). According to Kim, "most musicians would say it's very hard to project where we are going to be, what we are going to be doing", and "where your next pay-cheque is gonna come from" (Janine). These insecurities could give rise to anxieties. Ashley told me that she was living her ideal at the moment but that "there's this fear in the future that I just won't continue." Judith talked about the "fear of having no money and this being constantly on your mind" and Liz claimed "insecurities about my work and job are probably the single biggest thing that takes up my mental space". In a context where work is increasingly experienced as precarious, anxieties seem to be prevalent.

The observation that anxieties seem prevalent chimes with Plan C's (2014) claim that "[w]e are all very anxious." Arguing that each phase of capitalism has a particular affect that holds it together, Plan C suggests that anxiety characterises our current times and that this is intimately linked to precarity. They (2014) actually state that the "present dominant affect of anxiety is also known as precarity". However, and as I explore in detail in chapter five which looks at the research participants' responses to precarious work, anxiety was one affect that came to the fore, but not the only one. Feelings about precarious work seemed to differ, depending on the work context, the degree of freedom associated with particular forms of work, and the positioning of the research participants, especially in relation to class and the ability to fall back upon financial support. This insight cautions against positioning one affect as dominant, and instead invites us to think about the palette of emotions that were discussed in the interviews.[7]

Apart from anxiety, some research participants spoke about a growing sense of confidence when discussing the ups and downs of the classical music profession. Lorraine was aware of the need to constantly prove oneself in order to get work but said:

> It's like this constant "I put myself out there" and luckily, in my life, a good like 70 per cent of the time it works out. And the rest is like, yeah, it's hard but more and more I get the confidence that it will work out.

Similarly, Hope stated that she felt more confident: "I think certainly as I've got older I feel more confident, just generally. Because I know, I have a self-belief now that I know I can do the job." Among some research participants, there was thus a sense that past experience helped alleviate uncertainty because, to use Jane's words, "I deal with it better than I did at first."

In parallel with my argument that no one affect is prevalent, some research participants indicated that the opposite was the case by pointing to a sense of insecurity rather than confidence. According to Ashley, "everyone seems to be very insecure. Constantly worried and want assurance all the time that they are doing a good job and that they are playing alright." Many research participants made casual remarks about not being confident at all (Saaga), coming across as strong but being doubtful deep down (Isabella), or being "crap" in comparison to other musicians (Sasha). These references to self-doubt can be seen as performances of artistic identity through reiteration of the common trope that artists are never content with their work. They are another reminder that entrepreneurial rhetoric is not absolute, but also support my wider argument that the affective register of entrepreneurial subjects is multifaceted. Crucially, and as I have discussed in the previous section, some affects, such as anger, were markedly absent and this absence has a depoliticising effect. To state that multiple affects are present is thus not to forego a critical analysis, but is indicative of an attempt to acknowledge the range of affects associated with entrepreneurial subjectivity.

Competing with the self

Many commentators have pointed out that the entrepreneurial subject is competitive and that it "relates to others as competitors" (McNay, 2009: 63; see also Amable, 2011; Brown, 2015; Mirowski, 2014). According to Pierre Dardot and Christian Laval (2013: 4), "[n]eo-liberalism can be defined as the set of discourses, practices and apparatuses that determine a new mode of government of human beings in accordance with the universal principle of competition." Resonating with these claims, the research participants described the classical music sector as "very competitive" (Kerry) and June referred to it as "quite a competitive industry". Many participants described music college as particularly competitive. Competition, according to Sasha, "is rife at music colleges. Absolutely rife". While acknowledging the competitive nature of the industry and music education, research participants emphasised their dislike for competition. Holly said that the profession "can be quite competitive. And I don't like that and I try to remove myself from that as much as possible." Like Holly, Saaga claimed she did not "see the point" of competition and Judith felt that musicians should "support each other" instead. Rather than engage in competition, research participants emphasised that they "fended it off" (Jasmin).

In distancing themselves from competition, some research participants drew on an artistic discourse and claimed that competition was "uncreative" (Sonja). According to Clarissa, "this pressure to compete, this everybody-against-each-other. I find, for me, this is incompatible with music." Saaga echoed these sentiments feeling that "it's important that the music is what matters and not the kind of, how strong you are". In addition, some research participants rejected competition by describing themselves as "unpushy" (Jane) or avoiding aggression. In telling me how she dealt with competition, Esther told me "I just try to withdraw if someone is aggressive [. . .] just trying to work with people and not against people, and I think that is my motto." Similarly, Judith distanced herself from competition by saying: "Why make life harder? Let's just all get on." Resonating with my arguments in chapter two, this rejection of competitiveness can be read as a performance of femininity. By distancing themselves from competitive behaviour, the research participants orient to social norms that women take into account "the requirements and preferences of other people" (Taylor, 2011: 366). This is a further instance where entrepreneurial rhetoric intersects with other discourses. Indeed, the research participants' reluctance to engage in competition seems to break with the entrepreneurial logic of constant competition and suggests a rupture in the performance of entrepreneurial subjectivity.

While this represents one possible interpretation, I want to offer an additional reading by suggesting that competition may also be self-directed under neoliberalism. As Eva Bendix Petersen and Gabrielle O'Flynn (2007: 205) have argued in relation to neoliberal subjectification, "[t]he only person with whom one competes is oneself"; "[t]he voluntary 'competition with oneself' is the only fuel needed for the fully entrepreneurial subject." This 'competition with oneself' came to the fore in Nora's statement:

> It's nice to recognise your individuality as well, rather than kind of thinking: "Well, I want to be doing better than that person, or I want to be at the top of my field" or that sort of thing. Just thinking: "Well, aren't we all doing very different things."

Instead of engaging in competition with others, Nora emphasises her individuality. Crucially, competition is not absent from Nora's account; she explicitly orients to it by referring to thoughts such as "I want to be better than that person." However, Nora rejects these thoughts and instead attempts to recognise her individuality. Similarly, Carolyn told me in relation to competition that "you have to try and be really grounded, and realise that you are all on your own routes." In both statements, competition seems to be directed towards the self through the emphasis on "individuality" or being "on your own routes". Accordingly, Julianne emphasised that her life as a musician was a "life of competition. A life of, you know, being better and better." Similar to Nora's and Carolyn's statement, competition is not framed in terms of being better than others, but in terms of self-transformation.

Along with other authors, I maintain that competition with others continues to exist under neoliberalism. By offering a reading that shows that the entrepreneurial subject also competes with the self, my aim is to expand our understanding of the different ways in which competition may manifest itself. In parallel with my observation that desires for change are internalised, competition may also be turned inwards in neoliberalism, especially for young women (McRobbie, 2015b). As Gill (2007) has argued in relation to the shift from sexual objectification to sexual subjectification, internalisation can denote a 'deeper' form of exploitation. The entrepreneurial subject's reluctance to engage in open competition with others may be indicative of power dynamics working on a 'deeper' level where competition is not only directed at others, but also at the self.

Establishing boundaries and blaming 'others'

In talking about their feelings towards other musicians, the research participants also established boundaries between different kinds of individuals by, for example, presenting themselves as more determined or organised than others. Christine explained why some of her peers from university had left the profession and stated: "People get to the end of their degree and they think: 'Oh, I just couldn't do this as a living' [. . .] But I was determined, absolutely determined." Similarly, Jana drew a boundary between herself and other musicians by emphasising her organisational skills:

> I'm finding it easy to organise things and to structure things, in terms of, that I simply have a plan in my head and I'm not totally disorganised, as in not being able to manage anything and, somehow, forgetting that I have a concert next week because I'm so immersed in practicing my instrument. That's never happened to me. There. I mean, there are musicians like that. That's why. I mean, I really know many who, who are like that and who, apart from their instrument, do not think and who can't organise and who also can't organise their everyday life. I mean, I'm really very structured in this respect.

By portraying themselves as "absolutely determined" and "very structured", and underlining how they differ in that respect from other musicians, Christine and Jana draw distinctions and set themselves apart from others.

Frequently, the research participants established boundaries between "lazy" and "hard working" people:

> We have this kind of stigma about civil servants [. . .] "I have a cold so I'm gonna take at least a week off and get paid by the tax payer, thanks very much." You know – musicians aren't like that. We wanna work. We really want to work.
>
> (Lauren)

In telling me that she had successfully secured funding for her training as a singer, Alice expressed a similar disdain for laziness:

> I put my head down and I did the applications. Nothing happens by accident. It really doesn't. And there are so many lazy singers, and I don't have any time – I don't have any – I don't have any pity for them if they are in that situation, because they are just lazy.

Kira also showed little understanding for musicians she considered lazy. She told me she proactively pursued employment opportunities, even though she was not a native speaker of German:

> But still, I try [to talk to people] so that I get to play a bit. And I know so many German pianists who don't do anything, for example. Or who have already given up. Okay, it's not easy and it's so tedious. But if you don't do it, who does it for you? And then you complain that you don't get to play. But it's kinda your fault.

Resonating with the findings of psychoanalytic research on neoliberal subjectivity (e.g. Layton, 2009; 2013b), the research participants showed little empathy for the hardships of others.

Rather than regard the lack of empathy as an *effect* of neoliberalism (Layton, 2013a), the drawing of boundaries and disdain for laziness can be seen as *constitutive* of entrepreneurial subjectivity. Tyler (2013), as well as Ringrose and Walkerdine (2008), have used the wider theoretical framework of abjection to show that neoliberal subjectivities are constituted through exclusionary dynamics. While the processes described here are more akin to repudiation than abjection, the theoretical tool of abjection suggests that the entrepreneurial subject configures itself through the rejection of that which it is not. By presenting themselves as hard working, the research participants construct themselves as entrepreneurial. This construction simultaneously involves the repudiation of those who do not work hard and a lack of empathy if they do not achieve. Accordingly, the drawing of boundaries between "hard working" and "lazy" people may not simply be an effect or outcome of neoliberal governmentality, but "a core organ" (Tyler, 2013: 212). Arguably, this link between repudiations of laziness and the construction of entrepreneurial subjectivity comes to the fore in Susan's statement: "I'm not the sort of person who will mope around for weeks on end [. . .] I'm pretty motivated and quite driven as a person." By distinguishing herself from others who "mope around", she constructs herself as "quite driven".

Crucially, and as Tyler (2013) and Ringrose and Walkerdine (2008) have shown, racialised and classed subjects tend to be positioned as the 'other'. In my previous research on engagements with feminism among a diverse group of young women, I had also found that neoliberal femininities were constructed in and through racialised processes of othering (Scharff, 2011). Thus, the exclusionary dynamics of entrepreneurial subjectivity do not only extend to the positionalities required to become an entrepreneurial subject, but also to the kinds of subjects that are othered in this process of becoming. This observation adds to the existing literature on the exclusions of entrepreneurial subjectivity, which I discussed at the beginning of this chapter. Following this line of argument, exclusions under neoliberalism do not only relate to the kinds of subjects that do not have the resources to become entrepreneurial. If the constitution of entrepreneurial subjectivities involves othering, exclusionary processes may lie at the heart of neoliberalism.

Conclusion

This chapter has homed in on the research participants' positioning as entrepreneurial subjects par excellence in order to explore how entrepreneurialism is registered, negotiated, and lived out. My analysis highlighted various aspects, such as the construction of the self as business, which needs constant work, thrives on risks and knock-backs, stays positive, survives difficulties, and hides injuries. Throughout my analysis, I have highlighted that entrepreneurial rhetoric does not hold absolutely because individuals draw on a range of available discourses in their talk. Some discourses, such as an acknowledgement of structural constraints were however rarely evoked and 'luck' was instead advanced as an explanation for why some make it and others do not. When structural constraints are disavowed, desires for change are directed at the self, inciting individuals to self-transform. Anxieties were present, but I cautioned against positioning anxiety as a prevailing affect and instead showed that a palette of emotions marked the interviews. Lastly, I suggested that competition is not only other-directed, but also self-directed and that exclusionary processes play a key role in the constitution of entrepreneurial subjectivity.

Significantly, my analysis has not foregrounded all the possible contours of entrepreneurial subjectivity. Some aspects of entrepreneurial subjectivity need more investigation. Talk about consumption, for example, was relatively absent from my research participants' accounts. And yet, consumption may be another practice through which the entrepreneurial subject constitutes itself. In this vein, I hope that my analysis represents the beginning of a larger conversation about the contours of entrepreneurial subjectivity in the context of cultural work, and beyond.

On the whole, my analysis resonates with the wider literature in many ways, specifically with regard to the characterisation of entrepreneurial subjects as responsibilised, risk-taking, and depoliticised. And yet, I also reframed existing accounts. First, I argued that competition is not only other directed, but also directed at the self. This argument suggests that power may be working at a 'deeper' level, but also expands our understanding of the different ways in which competition may manifest itself in neoliberalism. Second, my argument that othering processes are constitutive of entrepreneurial subjectivity has added to existing debates on the exclusionary dynamics of neoliberalism by demonstrating that exclusionary processes are not a side-product of entrepreneurial subjectivity, but that they lie at the heart of its production. Third, my findings call into question existing claims (including claims I have made previously) that anxiety is a prevailing affect. Anxieties were present in the interviews and openly discussed, but I also detected a range of other emotions, especially in relation to the negotiation of precarious work, which is the subject of the following chapter. After a discussion of the wider literature on precarity, the next chapter discusses the subjective experiences of precarious work. In doing so, it sheds light on several dimensions, relating to the reshaping of time under precarity, the research participants' feelings towards and responses to precarious work, and the ways in which positive and negative aspects of precarious, cultural work are inextricably intertwined.

Notes

1 While I prefer the term 'entrepreneurial subject', I use the expression 'neoliberal subject' when citing literature that employs this terminology.
2 While Sennett does not explicitly use the terms neoliberalism or entrepreneurialism, his research is frequently cited in discussions of the ways in which neoliberalism is lived out and therefore discussed here.
3 For a more general argument about the depoliticising effects of neoliberalism, see Wendy Brown's (2015) recent book *Undoing the Demos: Neoliberalism's Stealth Revolution*.
4 As Henry Kingsbury (1988: 133) has pointed out, "although an improper technique is unquestionably liable to be a factor leading toward just this sort of physical injury, it cannot meaningfully be said that injuries to musical performers are caused only by faulty technique". According to Kingsbury, this is because the proper technique for one person may not be optimal for another person due, for example, to physical differences. More generally, long hours of work tend "to bring the risk of injury to even the most skilled of performers" (133).
5 Other studies (e.g. Atkinson, 2006; Hoskins, 2012; Huhtala, 2014; Wagner and Wodak, 2006) have also documented that the notion of luck is drawn on in career narratives. Crucially, 'luck' can be evoked to fulfil a range of rhetorical functions, such as accounting for success (Wagner and Wodak, 2006). My argument that accounts of personal luck disavow structural constraints is thus contextually specific.
6 The absence of anger should also be placed in a wider postfeminist context where, as Gill (2016) has argued, emotions such as anger and rage are increasingly disallowed or rendered toxic states for women (see also, Gill and Orgad, forthcoming).
7 Here, I depart from a previous argument where I suggested that anxiety was prevailing in neoliberalism (Scharff, 2015).

References

Alford, R. R., & Szanto, A. (1996). Orpheus wounded: The experience of pain in the professional worlds of the piano. *Theory and Society, 25*(1), 1–44.

Allen, K. (2014). 'Blair's children': Young women as 'aspirational subjects' in the psychic landscape of class. *Sociological Review, 62*(4), 760–779.

Allen, K., Quinn, J., Hollingworth, S., & Rose, A. (2013). Becoming employable students and 'ideal' creative workers: Exclusion and inequality in higher education work placements. *British Journal of Sociology of Education, 34*(3), 431–452.

Amable, B. (2011). Morals and politics in the ideology of neo-liberalism. *Socio-Economic Review, 9*(1), 3–30.

Atkinson, P. (2006). *Everyday arias: An operatic ethnography*. Lanham, MD: AltaMira Press.

Baker, J. (2008). The ideology of choice. Overstating progress and hiding injustice in the lives of young women: Findings from a study in North Queensland, Australia. *Women's Studies International Forum, 31*(1), 53–64.

Banks, M. (2007). *The politics of cultural work*. Basingstoke: Palgrave Macmillan.

Bennett, D. (2008). *Understanding the classical music profession: The past, the present and strategies for the future*. Farnham: Ashgate.

Berardi, F. (2009). *The soul at work*. Cambridge, MA: MIT Press.

Binkley, S. (2009). The work of neoliberal governmentality: Temporality and ethical substance in the tale of two dads. *Foucault Studies*, *6*(February), 60–78.

Binkley, S. (2011a). Psychological life as enterprise: Social practice and the government of neo-liberal interiority. *History of the Human Sciences*, *24*(2), 83–102.

Binkley, S. (2011b). Happiness, positive psychology and the program of neoliberal governmentality. *Subjectivity*, *4*(4), 371–394.

Boas, T. C., & Gans-Morse, J. (2009). Neoliberalism: From new liberal philosophy to anti-liberal slogan. *Studies in Comparative International Development*, *44*(2), 137–161.

Bourdieu, P. (1998). The essence of neoliberalism. *Le Monde Diplomatique December 8 (English edition)*. Accessed 1 December 2016. Available at: http://mondediplo.com/1998/12/08bourdieu

Bröckling, U. (2005). Gendering the enterprising self: Subjectification programs and gender differences in guides to success. *Distinktion: Scandinavian Journal of Social Theory*, *6*(2), 7–25.

Bröckling, U. (2007). *Das unternehmerische Selbst: Soziologie einer Subjektivierungsform*. Berlin: Suhrkamp.

Brown, W. (2003). Neo-liberalism and the end of liberal democracy. *Theory & Event*, *7*(1), 37–59.

Brown, W. (2015). *Undoing the demos: Neoliberalism's stealth revolution*. New York: Zone Books.

Bruni, A., Gherardi, S., & Poggio, B. (2004). Doing gender, doing entrepreneurship: An ethnographic account of intertwined practices. *Gender, Work & Organization*, *11*(4), 406–429.

Burchell, G. (1993). Liberal government and techniques of the self. *Economy and Society*, *22*(3), 267–282.

Butler, J. (1993). *Bodies that matter: On the discursive limits of "sex"*. London; New York: Routledge.

Clarke, J. (2008). Living with/in and without neo-liberalism. *Focaal*, *51*, 135–147.

Crawshaw, P. (2012). Governing at a distance: Social marketing and the (bio) politics of responsibility. *Social Science Medical*, *75*(1), 200–207.

Crouch, C. (2011). *The strange non-death of neo-liberalism*. London: Polity.

Dardot, P., & Laval, C. (2013). *The new way of the world: On neoliberal society*. London: Verso.

Davies, B. (2005). The (im)possibility of intellectual work in neoliberal regimes. *Discourse: Studies in the Cultural Politics of Education*, *26*(1), 1–14.

Davies, B., & Bansel, P. (2007). Neoliberalism and education. *International Journal of Qualitative Studies in Education*, *20*(3), 247–259.

du Gay, P. (1996). *Consumption and identity at work*. London: Sage.

Duggan, L. (2004). *The twilight of equality? Neoliberalism, cultural politics, and the attack on democracy*. Boston, MA: Beacon Press.

Ehrenberg, A. (2010). *The weariness of the self: Diagnosing the history of depression in the contemporary age*. Quebec: McGill-Queen's University Press.

Ehrenreich, B. (2009). *Smile or die: How positive thinking fooled America and the world*. London: Granta.

Feher, M. (2009). Self-Appreciation, or, the aspirations of human capital. *Public Culture*, *21*(1), 21–41.

Fenwick, T. J. (2002). Transgressive desires: New enterprising selves in the new capitalism. *Work, Employment & Society*, *16*(4), 703–723.

Foucault, M. (2008). *The birth of biopolitics: Lectures at the Collège de France, 1978–79* (M. Senellart, Ed.). Basingstoke: Palgrave Macmillan.

Gane, N. (2014a). The emergence of neoliberalism: Thinking through and beyond Michel Foucault's lectures on biopolitics. *Theory, Culture & Society, 31*(4), 3–24.

Gane, N. (2014b). Thinking historically about neoliberalism: A response to William Davies. *Theory, Culture & Society, 31*(7–8), 303–307.

Garland, C., & Harper, S. (2012). Did somebody say neoliberalism? On the uses and limitations of a critical concept in media and communication studies. *TripleC, 10*(2), 413–424.

Gembris, H., & Heye, A. (2012). *Älter werden im Orchester: Eine empirische Studie zu Erfahrungen, Einstellungen, Performanz und Lebensperspektiven von professionellen Orchestermusikern.* Paper presented at the symposium Musikalische Begabung und Alter(n), 21st and 22nd September 2012, Institut für Begabungsforschung in der Musik, Paderborn.

Gershon, I. (2011). Neoliberal agency. *Current Anthropology, 52*(4), 537–555.

Gilbert, J. (2013). *Common ground: Democracy and collectivity in an age of individualism.* London: Pluto Press.

Gill, R. (2007). *Gender and the media.* Cambridge: Polity.

Gill, R. (2014). Unspeakable inequalities: Post feminism, entrepreneurial subjectivity, and the repudiation of sexism among cultural workers. *Social Politics: International Studies in Gender, State and Society, 21*(4), 509–528.

Gill, R. (2016). Postfeminism and the new cultural life of feminism. *Diffractions: Graduate Journal for the Study of Culture, 6*. Accessed 1 December 2016. Available at: https:// lisbonconsortium.files.wordpress.com/2012/2012/rosalind-gill_postfeminism-and-the-new-cultural-life-of-feminism.pdf

Gill, R., & Orgad, S. (forthcoming). Confidence culture and the remaking of feminism. *New Formations.*

Gill, R., & Pratt, A. C. (2008). In the social factory? Immaterial labour, precariousness and cultural work. *Theory, Culture & Society, 25*(7–8), 1–30.

Gill, R., & Scharff, C. (Eds.). (2011). *New femininities: Postfeminism, neoliberalism and subjectivity.* Basingstoke: Palgrave Macmillan.

Gilroy, P. (2013). '. . . We got to get over before we go under. . . ' fragments for a history of black vernacular neoliberalism. *New Formations, 80–81*, 23–38.

Giroux, H. A. (2004). *Proto-fascism in America: Neoliberalism and the demise of democracy.* Bloomington, IN: Phi Delta Kappa Educational Foundation.

Gonick, M. (2006). Between "girl power" and "reviving ophelia": Constituting the neoliberal girl subject. *NWSA Journal, 18*(2), 1–23.

Halford, S., & Leonard, P. (2006). Place, space and time: Contextualising work-place subjectivities. *Organisation Studies, 27*(5), 657–676.

Hall, S., & O'Shea, A. (2013). Common-sense neoliberalism. *Soundings: A Journal of Politics and Culture, Special Issue: After neoliberalism? The Kilburn manifesto* (S. Hall, D. Massey, & M. Rustin, Eds.), 1–16. Accessed 1 December 2016. Available at: www. lwbooks.co.uk/sites/default/files/03_commonsenseneoliberalism.pdf

Hardin, C. (2014). Finding the 'neo' in neoliberalism. *Cultural Studies, 28*(2), 199–221.

Harvey, D. (2005). *A brief history of neoliberalism.* Oxford; New York: Oxford University Press.

Help Musicians UK (2014). *Professional music in the UK: Health and wellbeing survey.* London: Help Musicians UK. Accessed 1 December 2016. Available at: https://issuu.com/ helpmusiciansuk/docs/help_musicians_uk_health_and_wellbe?e=10405134/8971874

Hoskins, K. (2012). *Women and success: Professors in the UK academy*. London: Trentham Books.

Huhtala, A. (2014). Creating oneself through narratives: Agency in first-semester university students' career plans. *Apples – Journal of Applied Language Studies, 8*(1), 29–45.

Kingsbury, H. (1988). *Music, talent, and performance: A conservatory cultural system*. Philadelphia, PA: Temple University Press.

Langston, D. (1991). Tired of playing monopoly? In J. Whitehorse Cochran, D. Langston, & C. Woodward (Eds.), *Changing our power: An introduction to Women Studies*. Dubuque, IA: Kendall Hunt.

Larner, W. (2000). Neo-liberalism: Policy, ideology, governmentality. *Studies in Political Economy, 63*, 5–25.

Layton, L. (2009). Who's responsible? Our mutual implication in each other's suffering. *Psychoanalytic Dialogues, 19*(2), 105–120.

Layton, L. (2010). Irrational exuberance: Neoliberal subjectivity and the perversion of truth. *Subjectivity, 3*(3), 303–322.

Layton, L. (2013a). Editor's introduction to special section on the psychosocial effects of neoliberalism. *Psychoanalysis, Culture & Society, 19*(1), 1–4.

Layton, L. (2013b). Psychoanalysis and politics: Historicising subjectivity. *Mens Sana Monographs, 11*(1), 68–81.

Lemke, T. (2001). 'The birth of bio-politics': Michel Foucault's lecture at the Collège de France on neo-liberal governmentality. *Economy and Society, 30*(2), 190–207.

Mäkinen, K. (2012). *Becoming valuable selves: Self-promotion, gender and individuality in late capitalism*. Unpublished PhD thesis, Tampere University.

McGee, M. (2005). *Self-help, Inc.: Makeover culture in American life*. Oxford: Oxford University Press.

McNay, L. (2009). Self as enterprise: Dilemmas of control and resistance in Foucault's The Birth of Biopolitics. *Theory, Culture & Society, 26*(6), 55–77.

McRobbie, A. (2002). Clubs to companies: Notes on the decline of political culture in speeded up creative worlds. *Cultural Studies, 16*(4), 516–531.

McRobbie, A. (2009). *The aftermath of feminism: Gender, culture and social change*. London: Sage.

McRobbie, A. (2015a). *Be creative: Making a living in the new culture industries*. Cambridge: Polity.

McRobbie, A. (2015b). Notes on the perfect. *Australian Feminist Studies, 30*(83), 3–20.

Mirowski, P. (2014). *Never let a serious crisis go to waste: How neoliberalism survived the financial meltdown*. London: Verso.

Mirowski, P., & Phlewe, D. (2009). *The road from Mont Pelerin: The making of the neoliberal thought collective*. Cambridge, MA: Harvard University Press.

Mudge, S. L. (2008). What is neo-liberalism? *Socio-Economic Review, 6*(4), 703–731.

Nairn, K., & Higgins, J. (2007). New Zealand's neoliberal generation: Tracing discourses of economic (ir)rationality. *International Journal of Qualitative Studies in Education, 20*(3), 261–281.

Neff, G. (2012). *Venture labor: Work and the burden of risk in innovative industries*. Cambridge, MA; London: MIT Press.

O'Flynn, G., & Petersen, E. B. (2007). The 'good life' and the 'rich portfolio': Young women, schooling and neoliberal subjectification. *British Journal of Sociology of Education, 28*(4), 459–472.

Ong, A. (2006). *Neoliberalism as exception: Mutations in citizenship and sovereignty.* London: Duke University Press.

Orgad, S. (2009). The survivor in contemporary culture and public discourse: A genealogy. *The Communication Review, 12*(2), 132–161.

Peck, J., & Tickell, A. (2002). Neoliberalizing space. *Antipode, 34*(3), 380–404.

Petersen, E. B., & O'Flynn, G. (2007). Neoliberal technologies of subject formation: A case study of the Duke of Edinburgh's Award scheme. *Critical Studies in Education, 48*(2), 197.

Plan C. (2014). *We are all very anxious.* Accessed 1 December 2016. Available at: www.weareplanc.org/blog/we-are-all-very-anxious/

Proctor-Thomson, S. (2013). Feminist futures of cultural work: Creativity, gender and diversity in the digital media sector. In M. Banks, S. Taylor, & R. Gill (Eds.), *Theorizing cultural work: Labour, continuity and change in the creative industries* (pp. 137–148). London: Routledge.

Ringrose, J., & Walkerdine, V. (2008). Regulating the abject: The TV make-over as site of neo-liberal reinvention toward bourgeois femininity. *Feminist Media Studies, 8*(3), 227–246.

Rofel, L. (2007). *Desiring China: Experiments in neoliberalism, sexuality, and public culture.* Durham, NC; London: Duke University Press.

Rose, N. (1990). *Governing the soul: The shaping of the private self.* London: Routledge.

Rose, N. (1992). Governing the enterprising self. In P. Heelas & P. Morris (Eds.), *The values of the enterprise culture: The moral debate.* London: Routledge.

Rose, N. (1996). *Inventing our selves: Psychology, power, and personhood.* Cambridge: Cambridge University Press.

Ross, A. (2008). The new geography of work: Power to the precarious? *Theory, Culture & Society, 25*(7–8), 31–49.

Rottenberg, C. (2014). The rise of neoliberal feminism. *Cultural Studies, 28*(3), 418–437.

Saleci, R. (2010). *The tyranny of choice.* London: Profile Books.

Salmenniemi, S., & Vorona, M. (2014). Reading self-help literature in Russia: Governmentality, psychology and subjectivity. *British Journal of Sociology, 65*(1), 43–62.

Scharff, C. (2011). Disarticulating feminism: Individualization, neoliberalism and the othering of 'Muslim women'. *European Journal of Women's Studies, 18*(2), 119–134.

Scharff, C. (2015). The psychic life of neoliberalism: Mapping the contours of entrepreneurial subjectivity. *Theory, Culture & Society, 33*(6), 107–122.

Scharff, C. (2016). Gender and neoliberalism: Young women as ideal neoliberal subjects. In S. Springer, K. Birch, & J. MacLeavy (Eds.), *The handbook of neoliberalism* (pp. 217–226). Abingdon, Oxon; New York Routledge.

Sennett, R. (1998). *The corrosion of character: The personal consequences of work in the new capitalism.* New York: Norton.

Seu, B. (2010). Shameful silences: Self-protective secrets and theoretical omissions. In R. Gill & R. Ryan-Flood (Eds.), *Secrets and silences in the research process: Feminist reflections* (pp. 257–272). Abingdon, Oxon; New York: Routledge.

Shamir, R. (2008). The age of responsibilization: On market-embedded morality. *Economy and Society, 37*(1), 1–19.

Springer, S., Birch, K., & MacLeavy, J. (Eds.). (2016). *The handbook of neoliberalism.* New York: Routledge.

Stedman Jones, D. (2012). *Masters of the universe: Hayek, Friedman, and the birth of neoliberal politics.* Princeton, NJ; Woodstock: Princeton University Press.

Storey, J., Salaman, G., & Platman, K. (2005). Living with enterprise in an enterprise economy: Freelance and contract workers in the media. *Human Relations, 58*(8), 1033–1054.

Swan, E. (2008). 'You make me feel like a woman': Therapeutic cultures and the contagion of femininity. *Gender, Work & Organization, 15*(1), 88–107.

Taylor, S. (2011). Negotiating oppositions and uncertainties: Gendered conflicts in creative identity work. *Feminism & Psychology, 21*(3), 354–371.

Taylor, S., & Littleton, K. (2012). *Contemporary identities of creativity and creative work.* Farnham: Ashgate.

Thorsen, D. E., & Lie, A. (2006). *What is neoliberalism?* University of Oslo, Department of Political Science, Manuscript.

Tyler, I. (2013). *Revolting subjects.* London: Zed.

Wagner, I., & Wodak, R. (2006). Performing success: Identifying strategies of self-presentation in women's biographical narratives. *Discourse & Society, 17*(3), 385–411.

Williams, R. (2014). "Eat, pray, love": Producing the female neoliberal spiritual subject. *Journal of Popular Culture, 47*(3), 613–633.

Zaza, C., Charles, C., & Muszynski, A. (1998). The meaning of playing-related musculo-skeletal disorders to classical musicians. *Social Science & Medicine, 47*(12), 2013–2023.

Chapter 5

"Difficult, fickle, tumultuous" and yet "the best job in the world"

Analysing subjective experiences of precarious work

In recent years, public and academic debates have drawn attention to the issue of precarious work, understood here as "work for remuneration characterized by uncertainty, low income, and limited social benefits and statutory entitlements" (Vosco, 2009: 2). In relation to musicians, cultural sector reports (Bossen, 2012; Help Musicians UK, 2014; Musicians' Union, 2012; Schulz et al., 2013) have documented high degrees of insecurity, low pay, and limited benefits. Equally, precarious work has become the focus of academic debates (e.g. Brophy and de Peuter, 2007; Ettlinger, 2007; Waite, 2009) and research on the working lives of cultural workers (e.g. de Peuter, 2014; Gill and Pratt, 2008; Neilson and Rossiter, 2008). Indeed, it has been argued that while insecurity is a feature of a great deal of working life, it is worse in the cultural and creative industries "because of the uncertain and short-term nature of many cultural-industry job contracts, and the high level of subjective investment that many creative workers have in what they do" (Hesmondhalgh and Baker, 2011: 113, see also Toynbee, 2013). This portrayal of cultural work raises the question of how cultural workers describe, experience, and negotiate precarious work. Against this backdrop, this chapter explores how precarious work is lived out on the subjective level, thereby adding to a growing body of literature on the interplay between subjectivity and precarity in the cultural and creative industries (e.g. Armano and Murgia, 2013; Hennekam and Bennett, 2017; Hesmondhalgh and Baker, 2011; Kennedy, 2012; Morgan et al., 2013; Ross, 2003; Rowlands and Handy, 2012; Taylor and Littleton, 2012).

The chapter begins with a review of the existing literature on precarity, which has explored various aspects, such as the meaning of precarity, whether it is a novel phenomenon and whether it bears the potential for political mobilisation, particularly in the context of cultural work. The main part of the chapter, however, focuses on subjective experiences of precarious work. As the first analytical section shows, many research participants reported they constantly looked for work, making it difficult to take time off. Time was reshaped in crucial ways under precarious work, relating both to the blurring of boundaries between work and leisure as well as the inability to predict the future. The feelings associated with precarious work, which are the subject of the second analytical section, were changeable over time, and ranged from fear and anxiety to excitement. Far from being homogenous, feelings about precarious work seem to fluctuate and depend on the degree of freedom associated with particular forms of work, and the wider positioning of the worker. For example, being from a middle-class background and, more specifically, having the ability to depend on one's parents' support can act as a buffer against some of the insecurities and anxieties related to precarious work.

As the third analytical section shows, the precarious nature of work in the classical music profession was often silenced, leading to a situation where research participants individualised the difficulties associated with insecurity and low incomes. Instead of discussing the highs and lows of precarious work openly with colleagues, the research participants tried not to worry too much about the uncertainties characterising their working lives or accepted precarious work as a given. Their attitudes were depoliticised which cannot, however, be equated with passivity. Instead, and as I discuss in the fourth analytical section, the research participants exhibited an entrepreneurial attitude towards precarious work by emphasising their flexibility, ability to plan financially, and willingness to take risks.

This entrepreneurial response to precarious work took place in the wider context of an ambivalent relationship with work in the classical music profession, where the research participants discussed its negative components at the same time as highlighting the immense pleasure they derived from it. As the two final analytical sections demonstrate, the research participants spoke with great passion about their love for playing music, the satisfaction they derived from moments of 'being in the zone' (Jordan et al., 2017), and the joys associated with being given a platform for self-expression. Crucially, the research participants' accounts of their motivations for working as musicians also constituted moments of rupture. Being in the zone, for example, did not only give rise to great highs, but also provided an opportunity to connect with the audience, which broke with the individualism that otherwise characterised many accounts. More broadly, the final sections of the chapter argue that the positive and negative aspects of precarious, cultural work are deeply intertwined, and that neither can be dismissed in analyses of the subjective experiences of cultural workers.

Debating precarity

Given different histories and usages of the term precarity, there have been lively debates about its meaning. According to Louise Waite (2009), some authors regard precarity as specifically linked to neoliberal labour markets (e.g. Bourdieu, 1999; Brophy and de Peuter, 2007) while others think of it as a wider condition of vulnerability that is not limited to the world of work (e.g. Butler, 2004; Ettlinger, 2007;

Neilson and Rossiter, 2008; Precarias a la deriva, 2004). Furthermore, several authors have highlighted that the concept of precarity is "constitutively double-edged" (Rossiter and Neilson, 2005: 2), referring both to experiences of material and existential uncertainty *and* to the potential for political mobilisation. According to Rosalind Gill and Andy Pratt (2008: 3), "precarity signifies both the multiplication of precarious, unstable, insecure forms of living and, simultaneously, new forms of political struggle and solidarity that reach beyond the traditional models of the political party or trade union" (see also Murgia and Selmi, 2012; Lorey, 2015).

Apart from discussions about the meaning of precarity, researchers have debated the novelty of the phenomenon. The recent era of precarious work in Western societies is often linked to neoliberal globalisation (Kalleberg, 2009), which saw increased global competition, technological changes, as well as institutional, political, and ideological transformations that led to greater labour market flexibility (see also Standing, 2011). These changes have produced an apparently novel situation where more and more workers in affluent societies are engaged in unpredictable and uncertain work. However, and as numerous commentators have pointed out, if we widen our perspective both geographically and historically, precarity becomes the norm (Waite, 2009; see also Brophy and de Peuter, 2007; Ettlinger, 2007; Luckman, 2013; Mitropoulos, 2005; Neilson and Rossiter, 2008). As Michael Quinlan's (2012: 19) historical research on Britain and Australia has shown, "from the early nineteenth century until the 1930s, the term precarious employment was not only in regular use, but its use by policy makers and the press was similar – if not identical – to current understandings of the term." Precarity, then, is not a new phenomenon. Even during the Fordist era, precarity underscored the lives of countless workers, especially migrants and women (Waite, 2009). Equally relevant, musicians' working lives have been precarious historically. As Dawn Bennett (2008) has argued, multiple employments have characterised musicians' working lives from the Middle Ages to the present day.

A further set of issues in debates about precarity relates to the workers who can be subsumed under the heading precarious. According to Waite (2009: 426), "[p]recarious subjectivities do not constitute a unified social actor [. . .] as precarity is lived very differently by workers in various contexts." To draw on an example provided by Precarias a la deriva (2004), a freelance designer and a sex worker have certain commonalities, such as the unpredictability of work, but differences in social recognition and degrees of vulnerability are also pronounced. Vulnerability to precarious work depends on a range of factors, such as gender, race, and class, but also levels and kinds of education, age, family responsibilities, etc. (Kalleberg, 2009). "Precarity then, does not have its model worker" (Rossiter and Neilson, 2005: 4) but "strays across any number of labour practices, rendering their relations precisely precarious" (4). Studies of precarious work therefore have to incorporate the insight that precarious workers are a heterogeneous group. Even within the same professional group, such as the female musicians interviewed for this study, differences exist in terms of the workers' positioning which in turn affect experiences of precarious work.

Lastly, research has attempted to explore the consequences of precarious work for individuals and has variously positioned precarious workers on the continuum of structure and agency. Discussing the working lives of precariously employed cultural workers, Isabell Lorey (2011: 87) presents them as "easily exploited" subjects, who "seem able to tolerate their living and working conditions with infinite patience because of the belief in their own freedoms and autonomies, and because of the fantasies of self-realization" (see also Rowlands and Handy, 2012; Sennett, 1998).[1] Andrew Ross (2008), by contrast, cautions against conflating the appeal of flexible work and self-employment with the neoliberal ethos of the self-absorbed entrepreneur. Similarly, George Morgan et al. (2013: 406) emphasise the agency of young Australian precarious workers and argue against positioning them as victims of "an unstoppable and wholly negative set of historical and social evolutions" (see also de Peuter, 2014; Rogaly, 2008; Waite, 2009).

Indeed, debates about the agency of precarious workers have been particularly lively in research on cultural work with various authors calling for the need to take seriously workers' personal accounts of creative fulfilment, pleasure, and freedom while not losing sight of the often-precarious nature of this work. Indeed, several studies of cultural work have critiqued analyses influenced by "neo-Foucauldian governmentality theory" (Hesmondhalgh and Baker, 2011: 8) as understanding the positive features of cultural work to be the basis of alienation and self-exploitation and as failing to address "all of the meanings and attractions which creative careers" can offer (Taylor and Littleton, 2012: 45; see also Kennedy, 2012). As I adopt a Foucauldian perspective in this book, there is thus a risk to present an overly critical reading, which downplays the positive aspects of being a musician and represents the research participants as unaware of the precarious nature of the classical music profession as well as "deluded" in their career motivations (Taylor and Littleton, 2012: 45). I hope that my analysis does not fall into this trap and instead I aim to analyse the interplay between the negative and positive aspects of being a musician as they are discussed in the research participants' reflections on precarious work. As such, I attempt to follow Mark Bankset et al.'s (2013: 7) call for analyses that "avoid the various caricatures of either the cultural dupe or the rational maximiser of information or (economic) benefits, in order to develop a fuller notion of the creative worker". My interest, then, is less in a theoretical argument than in the need to take seriously musicians' subjective experiences.

Musicians as precarious workers

Resonating with the literature discussed so far, the working lives of musicians are precarious. Musicians frequently encounter money problems and work insecurity (Help Musicians UK, 2014). As a report by the Musicians' Union (2012) has demonstrated, many musicians have portfolio careers, which are marked by low incomes (less than £20, 000 a year for 56 per cent of those surveyed), uncertainty, and lack of workplace benefits such as pensions (see also Banks et al., 2014). Sixty-five per cent of surveyed musicians had no independent pension provision and over 60 per cent reported working for free in the last 12 months (see also Help

Musicians UK, 2014). Only 10 per cent were full-time salaried employees, half reported not having any regular employment whatsoever, and the vast majority of musicians (94 per cent) work freelance for all or part of their income. According to the study, around a third (34 per cent) worked additional jobs not connected to their music careers in order to maintain an income (see also Bennett, 2016).

An analysis of freelance cultural work in Germany has documented similar trends (Schulz, 2013a). This study demonstrated that the average annual income was just over €13, 000 in 2009, which amounts to an average monthly income of €1, 092. Musicians' incomes are below this average figure for freelance cultural workers and, as mentioned in chapter two, also affected by a gender pay gap. In 2009, the annual income was €12, 179 and €9, 539 for male and female musicians, respectively. Notably, cultural workers earn less than other freelancers with comparable educational credentials (Schulz, 2013b) and reports on the German orchestral landscape (DOV, 2014) and music school teaching (Bossen, 2012) have highlighted that salaried positions are on the decline. In Berlin, only 0.9 per cent of music school teachers had a full-time position in 2012 and 94.2 per cent were employed on a freelance basis. Many music school teachers juggle multiple freelance jobs in order to earn a living, even though they would prefer to be in permanent full-time or part-time employment (see chapter two). These precarious forms of employment have negative consequences for pensions, health insurance, and other benefits, such as maternity leave.

In line with the findings on the working lives of musicians in Germany and the United Kingdom, most of my research participants were self-employed. Some were still in the final year of their studies and only a handful had permanent positions in orchestras or at teaching institutions. Almost all of the research participants held multiple jobs, ranging from teaching and freelancing with orchestras or ensembles, to jobs unrelated to performing. Several research participants worked in fields relevant to their training, such as work in music therapy, while others supplemented their income by working outside the music industry as temps, waitresses, or sales staff. Apart from a few exceptions, such as the research participants who held permanent posts, their reported earnings were in line with existing data on musicians' remuneration in Germany and the United Kingdom. In many ways, then, the research participants' working lives were precarious, raising the question of how they experienced uncertainty, low incomes, and limited benefits in their work as musicians.

The temporal dimensions of precarious work

In discussing their experiences of precarious work, many research participants felt there was a relentless need to prove themselves, particularly in order to get work. Hope observed:

> There is very much a thing of – particularly if you play for a particular orchestra regularly or semi-regularly – of always having to be on the top of your game, because if you are not, they may not ask you anymore.

Hope's impression that a good performance was necessary in order to be asked back resonates with the sense that "you're only as good as your last job", documented elsewhere in the cultural and creative industries (Blair, 2001; see chapter one). Indeed, Lauren used this phrase when describing the need to prove herself:

> I get all my work by word of mouth, all of it. I don't advertise, ever. So that's what I mean when I said you are as good as your last job, because if you screw it up, then you won't be recommended for the next one.

Echoing Hope's and Lauren's concerns, but linking them to fears about her livelihood, Liz told me: "I feel that if you are not at the top then you're in danger of losing your livelihood." Similar to her peers' statements, I read Liz's remark as pointing to the need to be "at the top" of one's game and to do the best job one can in order to secure work.

The relentless need to prove oneself also related to a widespread sense of not being able to say 'no' to work. Eve told me that getting work is about knowing the right people:

> So turning down anything would mean losing a contact with someone who might direct you to something else, or you might meet someone else through that who says: "Hey, I've got thirty thousand pounds to fund an opera, do you want to write it?"

As Bridget Anderson (2007: 5) has pointed out, "[t]emporary workers may feel that they cannot refuse certain jobs for example, or join a trades union, because they may lose the opportunity to work in the future." Eve's reluctance to turn down work for fear of losing out on future opportunities resonates with the concept of 'hope labour' (Kuehn and Corrigan, 2013) and 'the big break narrative' (Taylor and Littleton, 2012). Kathleen Kuehn and Thomas F. Corrigan (2013: 10) describe 'hope labour' as "un- or under-compensated work carried out in the present, often for experience or exposure, in the hope that future employment opportunities may follow". This future orientation is also present in the 'big break narrative', which rests on the assumption that an individual may work "without acknowledgment and reward, possibly for many years, until suddenly they achieve exceptional success, including creative and monetary recognition" (Taylor and Littleton, 2012: 68). While Eve is not talking about un- or undercompensated work, the sense of not wanting to turn down work because something may happen in the future resonates with the 'big break narrative' and the motivations underpinning hope labour, primarily through the future orientation that is evident in her statement. Eve hopes that if she keeps working in the here and now, she may one day meet someone who has "got thirty thousand pounds to fund an opera", enabling her big break which, in this case, is cast in monetary terms.

Linked to the feeling that it was difficult to turn down work, many research participants felt "you can never relax" (Emilia). Alice told me, "I've always got this guilt that I should be working all day every day." Eve similarly reported:

> I don't think I ever switch off – I don't remember the last time I went on holidays. When I have any time off that is more than a few days, I go and see my family . . . But I'm always, I take my computer with me everywhere I go, and I have them on my phone as well – emails. It's bad.

Notably, several research participants felt that social media and smart phones made it more difficult to disengage from work. Although Jane did not take any time off during work weeks because, as she put it "I'm constantly working, really", she went on an annual holiday and described how she and her partner attempted to limit the use of mobile phones and computers:

> We do listen to messages, yeah. And, but try and restrict it to keeping it off most of the day and maybe checking, maybe once in the evening or something. And these days, because it is such a fast-moving technology, people get annoyed if you haven't replied quickly. Sometimes you may be somewhere with no signal and not be able to reply, but people are, the work can often have gone . . . so life is faster, I suppose, with modern technology that people expect a very quick response.

Similarly, Janine told me about her difficulties with taking time off:

> It's harder when you have got a career like that and you have so many strings to it, and you are also trying to network via social media all the time, you don't want to miss anything or miss a new composer's piece or something like that, and it's harder to switch off.

Eve's, Jane's, and Janine's statements resonate with Melissa Gregg's (2011; 2013) research on technology's impact on work: "If work in creative industries has often involved a degree of flexibility and availability – as jobs appear in unpredictable patterns, with little ongoing security – the added component in today's work context is how always-on connectivity accelerates these features" (2013: 122). Arguably, new media technology exacerbates existing tendencies to put work at the heart of daily concerns.

Several research participants reported a blurring of boundaries between work and leisure time. Judith told me, "there is so much outside of the working hours. So there's never really, it sort of blurs between leisure and work time because you're constantly having to do outside preparation and practice." According to Vassilis Tsianos and Dimitris Papadopoulos (2006: unpaginated), "precarity is a form of exploitation which operates primarily on the level of time." Placing precarity in the wider context of post-Fordism, Tsianos and Papadopoulos argue that anticipated periods of non-productivity have disappeared, meaning that all time can potentially be made available to work. The research participants' claims about their difficulties to take time off resonate with this observation.

Equally, Tsianos and Papadopoulos (2006) argue that precarity further shapes time due to the unpredictability of the future. This second, temporal dimension of precarity also came to the fore in the research participants' accounts. Many claimed that they were unable to plan their lives due to the last-minute nature of work. Holly, who was based in London, explained: "There's one orchestra in Ireland that I've gone over quite regularly now the last couple of months, and he literally calls on a Sunday night and says: 'Can you be here at 10 o'clock tomorrow morning?'" Lauren echoed these sentiments by telling me "it's hard for me to plan ahead, because a lot of my work is last minute. You know, I get called a day before if I'm lucky, sometimes on the day to do a show." The inability to plan makes it more difficult to secure a stable and reliable income (Rowlands and Handy, 2012), but also means that 'bulimic patterns of working' (Gill and Pratt, 2008: 14) are common among musicians. According to Kelly, "there will be times when you have a week off, and then three people phone you up for the same date the next week." Indeed, several research participants felt that there were periods with too much work, such as the run-up to Christmas, or times with too little work, especially during the summer when there was no teaching (see also Ikonen, 2013). Based on the research participants' accounts, time is reshaped in at least two dimensions under precarity. A lot of work is last minute, making it difficult to predict the future. This unpredictability, and the consequent inability to plan ahead also means that it is hard to take time off, particularly in the context of new media technology, 'hope labour', and 'the big break narrative'.

Insecure but free? The ups and downs of precarious work

Apart from highlighting the temporal dimensions of precarious work, the research participants portrayed insecurity as a key characteristic. In the previous chapter, I discussed the research participants' anxieties and cited Ashley's statement, "you just don't know what's going to come." Jette used almost identical phrasing when claiming "this job is simply so insecure. You just never know what's going to come." This insecurity related to the uncertainty of what the future would hold, but also referred to the lack of financial security and other benefits, such as sick pay. Several participants pointed out that musicians earn "incredibly little" (Carla), recounted that their income was irregular, and remarked that they would have difficulties getting a mortgage. Equally important, and as Amy pointed out, "there is no insurance. You can't just have a sick day, if you are freelance." Against the backdrop of high rates of playing-related injuries among musicians (see chapter four; Scharff, 2016), the absence of sick pay is significant. According to Christine,

> It is a worry, being freelance. If you ever did get ill, how would you pay the rent, you know, because there is only a certain amount of benefits that you could get, it wouldn't be anywhere near what you would actually earn, and that is a real worry.

As I have mentioned in the previous chapter, over half of the research participants had struggled with injuries, which, in some cases, meant that they could not play their instruments for several months. The risk of injury thus added to a sense of insecurity.[2]

Crucially, the sense of insecurity was constructed differently. Some research participants portrayed it as a burden, such as Liz, who I also cited in the previous chapter:

> Insecurities about my work and job are probably the single biggest thing that takes up my mental space. I really enjoy most of the work I do when I am actually there, but it can almost get to the point where that employment is overshadowed by all the worries.

Others, by contrast, regarded the insecurity as a necessary trade-off for the increased freedom they associated with their work. Amy, an opera singer, had turned down a permanent contract abroad and stated:

> In one way it's good, because you don't have to do things that you think don't suit you, like roles that are either too big for you or wrong vocally, that you might have to do if you are on a permanent contract. At the same time, there is no security financially, and yeah, that can be quite stressful.

Similarly, Holly told me she much preferred "the freedom" of being a freelancer to having a regular job, which supports David Hesmondhalgh and Sarah Baker's (2010: 12) finding that cultural workers "set these worries about money and employment against the relative freedom that freelancing provided them" (see also Taylor and Littleton, 2012).

This freedom, however, was not always experienced as a blessing. Jana described it as difficult and when I asked her why, she said: "Well, nobody can make the decision for you, what you want. The decision and also the, the responsibility, nobody takes that for you." Equally, Kathrin pondered whether freelancers had more freedom "because you are under pressure to do a lot and to produce, otherwise the money does not come in". Kathrin thus suggested that the freedom of freelance work is compromised by the need to work hard in order to make a living. Sophie, who was one of the few research participants to have a permanent post, went as far as to say:

> I also know many freelancers who always emphasise how important their freedom is to them. But I have to say, for me this would not be freedom. For me, the freedom is that I have a permanent post.

As these extracts demonstrate, insecurity related to precarious work is constructed differently, depending on the research participants' perspectives on the degree of freedom afforded by their freelancing careers. Amy had turned down a permanent contract in favour of professional freedom, while Jana, Kathrin, and Sophie linked this same freedom to an increased sense of responsibility, pressure to produce, or – in Sophie's case – portrayed it as the opposite of freedom. Insecurity was perceived as a key feature of musicians' working lives, but whether this was seen as positive, negative, or a necessary trade-off depended on the degree of freedom associated with freelance work. These conflicting perspectives illustrate that negotiations of insecurity are not unanimous and caution against overly generalised accounts of the experiences of precarious work.

Similar to the research participants' varying stances on insecurity, the feelings associated with precarious work differed. Several research participants reported feelings of anxiety, particularly in relation to the uncertainty of their working lives. As I mentioned in the previous chapter, Ashley told me "I'm living my ideal at the moment. I just – there's that fear in the future that it just won't continue, you know." Reflecting on her experiences of being on fixed-term contracts and having to do auditions for orchestras, Angela told me:

> That makes you crazy somehow [. . .] Somehow, it is like, so this, this anxiety, that you are left with nothing, and that you have to get by somehow, with things that you do not fancy or do not enjoy, just so that you get by.

Similarly, Judith talked about the fears experienced by freelance musicians. Though a freelancer herself, Judith talked about "her friends", rather than her own experiences, thereby distancing herself from the insecurity:

> They've always got that fear of having no money. Constant, constant thing, gotta get things cheaply because they know how much is in the account or how much isn't in the account. Um, so that can be, I suspect that is on most freelancers' minds constantly, which people in a job would not think about as much.

These statements resonate with Hesmondhalgh and Baker's (2010: 12) finding that many cultural workers speak of "nervousness, anxiety and even panic as regular part of their working lives".

However, many research participants pointed out that fears were present, but that they came and went in phases. Anke told me about a recent period of orchestral auditions and her attempts to find a permanent post, saying: "But yes, there were phases, where I had doubts and fears, not to get a job, but it hasn't been that bad. It was maybe a day or two, when I was thinking about that and then it was okay again." Instead of painting a picture of constant anxiety, several research participants portrayed their feelings about precarious work as fluctuating:

> Sometimes, you'd have loads of really exciting work, which a) was great for your finances and b) was great for your mental state, because you are excited about what you were doing and you felt like you were going somewhere.

And then literally within weeks, you might have a bout of it being very quiet, and you are just about surviving financially, and mentally you are practicing in a room on your own a lot of the time not really doing much productive. I just – I have done quite a few years that were really up and down and I really enjoyed the variety of having a freelance career, but when it was bad I found it really bad.

(Kerry)

Instead of using the term "up and down", Susan referred to her feelings as "bipolar" and Nora spoke of "peaks and troughs":

I can't give up, not now. It's really hard, you know, people look at you and "Oh, I'd give up." And I've wanted to give up loads of times, loads of times – I just thought I've had enough of this, you know, I really, I don't want to feel like this anymore, this is rubbish. But then the next morning you go "Uh, ok, I'm gonna do an hour's practice." It's a bit weird, it's a bit bipolar I guess.

(Susan)

I think it has its peaks and troughs, because you go into projects and you put yourself 100 per cent into them and they are incredibly exciting and then when they finish you sort of have the crash and you don't know what's – maybe you don't know what is coming next or you have something but it's ages away.

(Nora)

These statements construct the feelings associated with precarious work as dynamic. Fears are evoked, but so is excitement, suggesting that the mental states related to precarious work are marked by highs and lows.

Arguably, these changing mental states are linked to the nature of cultural work, which, as I explore in more detail below, is experienced as deeply gratifying, pleasurable, and exciting, but also as insecure. The research participants' accounts demonstrate that it is difficult to explore the experiences of precarious work outside the work context in which they are embedded. The ups and downs associated with cultural work, including the classical music profession, seem to get intermeshed with the research participants' feelings towards job insecurity, calling for a need to analyse and embed experiences of precarity in the wider work context. More broadly, and as I show in the final sections of this chapter, the research participants frequently discussed the positive and negative aspects of precarious, cultural work in tandem, making it difficult to consider and treat them separately.

My observation that feelings towards precarious work fluctuate, and my finding that the research participants regarded insecurity and freedom differently, also highlights the need to be aware of differences among precarious workers. While most of the musicians interviewed for this study struggled to make a living and had to deal with a range of insecurities, they were also privileged in other respects, most notably through their predominantly middle-class backgrounds. As I have discussed in the previous chapter, some middle-class research participants used the trope of personal 'luck' to refer to their comparatively privileged socio-economic positions. Talking about her insecure income, Amanda told me: "I mean, I'm probably quite lucky in that you – now I know that if it was absolutely terrible, you know my parents would help me." Amanda's knowledge that her parents would be able to support her acts as a buffer against income insecurity. Indeed, and as I have argued elsewhere, class privilege in the classical music profession is not only related to economic capital and the ability to fall back on an affluent family, but is also linked to social capital, such as having good networks (Scharff, 2017), and cultural capital, especially in relation to familiarity with classical music (Bull and Scharff, 2017; see Bourdieu, 1986 on different forms of capital).

In the context of the research participants' discussion of precarious work, not all had the feeling that they could fall back on the security of a middle-class background. Christine, who was from a lower middle-class background, stated she could not rely on her family for financial support and instead emphasised the importance of having "good credit, knowing that you could get a loan or get a credit card or something that would help you if you really really couldn't – was stuck for money in a really bad way". Amanda's and Christine's statements foreground the role of class background in negotiations of precarious work, especially in relation to the dimension of economic capital. These contrasting accounts resonate with the findings of other studies on precarious work in the cultural and creative industries. As Sam Friedman et al. (2016: 9) have demonstrated in the context of acting, being from a middle-class background can "provide [. . .] insulation from much of the precariousness of the labour market". Although Amanda and Christine face similar challenges, Christine was arguably more vulnerable to the insecurity of the classical music profession as she could not fall back on her parents' financial support.

The role of positionality in experiences of precarity did not only come to the fore in relation to class, but also in relation to issues around migration. Like Amanda, Amy mentioned the importance of a supportive family, but then moved on to discuss her citizenship:

> I do think family is quite important . . . And even now, sometimes, I feel like a little kid, if I'm like "Oh God, what am I gonna do about paying my rent?" and my mom will be like "Do you need money?", and it's sort of like a big thing . . . I think the thing is – because I'm not a UK citizen, there is no prospect of getting any kind of government hand-out if I'm unemployed or anything, so I just have to keep on getting work, basically.

In this case, class background intersects with citizenship and positions Amy variously in relation to her vulnerability to precarious work. While she can fall back on her parents for financial support, her status as a non-UK citizen means that she does not have any recourse to public funds. These observations demonstrate that the research participants differ in their vulnerability to precarious work. In the context of my study, class background and citizenship most notably affected experiences of precarious work.

Responses to precarious work: silencing, 'wilful ignorance', and acceptance

As can be seen from the accounts I have provided so far, the research participants openly discussed their feelings about their working lives with me, including their fears and anxieties. At the same time, they pointed out that they would rather not share experiences of insecurity with other musicians. When I asked Ashley whether she discussed her difficulties with others, she said: "No, it's not really discussed, it's unwritten rules." Later on, Ashley told me "you don't really want people to know that you are not busy." Eve answered the same question in a similar way, telling me: "Actually, I don't really talk to anyone about money. I think that's again keeping your cards close and not wanting to admit that actually, things are very difficult." Nora echoed these statements, saying that she would discuss her experiences with "very close friends", but not with colleagues:

> I guess within the environment you don't – you wouldn't – I wouldn't like particularly for people to think of me: "Oh gosh, Nora is really – for instance, nearly really depressed, she doesn't have any work she's this or that", you know, that whole series of – that's not sort of the face that you want to present, I suppose.

Through these statements, Ashley, Eve, and Nora tell me about the "unwritten rules" (Ashley) of the game and thereby present themselves as insiders of the classical music profession. Their statements suggest that weaknesses and difficulties are not shared among colleagues. To be sure, there were some exceptions and Monika told me that she discussed her fears openly with her peers. "As you can tell, I am a very inquiring and talkative person. That means, I do also speak about these things." On the whole, however, insecurities – both personal and financial – seemed to be silenced in the work context (see also Help Musicians, 2014).

The silencing of insecurities seems to tie into the wider process of the individualisation of failure. In the previous chapter, I pointed out that injuries were common among musicians, but not openly talked about. Instead, they were overwhelmingly presented as the outcome of the wrong technique, reflecting the individualisation of failure in neoliberalism. Similar processes seem to be at play in the silencing of money worries and work insecurity. If there is no open communication about these issues, difficulties associated with precarious work may be seen as individual problems. Jette told me that a friend of hers had recently made her aware that stories of success, and not failure, were widely shared, leading to a sense that one was the only one to experience difficulties. "If you somehow have the feeling that you don't have much success, you only feel that yourself, that you do not have anything to do. And you only hear about the others when they have something to do." By contrast, Emilia remembered a rare occasion where she spoke to someone about the insecurities associated with work in classical music, stating: "it's quite nice to realise that they have the same thoughts as you. And coming to the same conclusions. But it's still not like, it's not that easy to talk to other musicians about that sort of thing." These statements suggest that concerns relating to precarious work are not openly talked about, at least not among colleagues. The silencing of difficulties makes it hard to identify whether other musicians face similar problems and concerns. Rather, difficulties tend to be regarded as individual problems. As Jette reminds us, "you only feel that yourself"; instead of regarding the lack of work and a secure income as wider features of the industry, insecurities associated with precarious work are individualised.

In light of the individualisation of failure, and my detailed discussion of entrepreneurial subjectivity in the previous chapter, it is perhaps unsurprising that anger about the precarious nature of work in the classical music profession was almost absent from the research participants' accounts. Some research participants were angry about the precedence of unpaid work in the classical music sector:

> It pisses you off, well it pisses us off, because at the end, bloody hell, we did a lot of work. We do not want – Obviously, we want to get paid, we are not students anymore!
>
> (Isabella)

> I just find I get very upset about having to play for free all the time, I get very frustrated about the amount of time you have to put into it.
>
> (Liz)

> And you often get asked to do things for free. Which is upsetting, because you know, you feel bad, but it's like asking your dentist to fix your teeth for free. You know, this is our job. This is what we do. No, we don't play for free.
>
> (Ashley)

Anger is openly expressed in these statements about the expectation to work for free. Isabella is "pissed off", while Liz and Ashley express feelings of upset.

Other research participants, however, argued that doing free work was a way into the profession and an opportunity to build one's CV and reputation. Some even accepted the lack of pay because it provided them with the opportunity to play music:

> So I think sometimes you have to say, okay, I am not going to get paid for this, but the rewards I'll reap for doing it, and the exposure and the networking and the buzz it will generate, it is worth investing time in. So I think it is payment in a way, but in a different kind, it is just not – it's not a monetary payment.
>
> (Janine)

And you know, some gigs you do free just for the love of it, or because of the contacts. Or because it might lead to something, you know, when you are a student especially. You do all kinds of things for no money and you gradually build up and you start saying 'no' to things like that.

(Judith)

I am actually quite happy, always, also when I play concerts for free I don't care. I just want to play music [. . .] It's a pity because you screw up the market by doing it, which is really bad.

(Kara)

As these statements illustrate, unpaid work is regarded and constructed variously by the musicians interviewed for this study. To some, the expectation to work for free is a source of anger, while others engaged in the practice. Importantly, even those who worked for free problematised it, most notably Kara who pointed out "you screw up the market by doing it." I read her statement as indicating that the willingness to work for free undercuts other workers and brings wages down for everybody.

Based on these accounts, the practice of playing for free could be understood in at least three different, and not necessarily mutually exclusive, ways: first, as a form of 'hope labour', discussed above, where research participants engage in unpaid work in the hope that they will reap some benefits in the future. Second, working for free could also be read as a form of "sacrificial labor" (Ross, 2003: 10), where nonmonetary rewards are accepted as partial compensation for work. Lastly, and discursively, the research participants' acceptance of unpaid work could be seen as part of the wider '"art-versus-money"' (Taylor and Littleton, 2012: 84) discourse, which posits that a choice has to be made between financial success and creative work. Judith's and Kara's statements about playing for free because you "love" it or because it makes you "happy" could be interpreted in this light. The practice of playing for free can thus be read in various ways. Crucial to my argument, several research participants were angry about the prevalence of unpaid work in classical music. Mostly, however, anger was absent from the research participants' accounts (see chapter four).

Instead, some research participants displayed a form of 'wilful ignorance' when engaging with the precarious nature of their chosen profession. Many stated that they tried "not to worry too much" (Carolyn) about the uncertainties characterising the working lives of musicians. While they told me about the feelings associated with their work, they also made it clear that they preferred not to think about insecurities in a lot of detail. When I asked Kristina how she dealt with job insecurity, she replied: "At the moment, I don't know, I have like a deep calmness. But I do not want to think about it at all." In talking about her aspirations to find work in London, Emilia also told me that she preferred to reassure herself: "sort of keep your head down in an ignorant bliss, and keep going – just everyone is in the same boat, it's fine, it's okay!" When I asked her: "Why do you say ignorant bliss?" she responded: "I guess it's reassuring yourself, like – trying not to think about just how difficult things are sometimes, because if you did, there would just be no energy left to do any work [Laughs] – from worrying about things."

In these statements, Carolyn, Kristina, and Emilia construct themselves as actively choosing not to engage with dire employment prospects. Significantly, they do not portray themselves as passively exposed to circumstances beyond their control. Nor do their responses suggest that they are unaware of the precarious nature of the classical music profession. Arguably, they present their chosen 'ignorance' as an active act and deliberate choice of disengagement. As Angela McRobbie (2015) has pointed out, young people working in the cultural and creative industries demonstrate a high degree of self-reflexivity. The occupational cultures characterising the cultural and creative industries are "known to young people well in advance" (McRobbie, 2015: 79). I therefore read the 'ignorance' described here as a deliberate coping strategy, rather than an indication of the research participants' lack of awareness.

In addition to the attempt not to worry, acceptance was mentioned as another strategy to cope with precarious work. When Esmeralda told me how she felt about unpaid work, she stated: "I think that's the way it is now. So I mean I'm used to it." Equally, Liz told me that she would like "more stability", but then moved on to say: "But I think . . . it's probably not gonna happen, so I just need to become more content with the way things are." Echoing this sentiment, Carolyn answered my question about how she coped with the emotional stress of job insecurity by saying: "Yeah, I think just accepting that it goes up and down." As Morgan et al. (2013: 411) have demonstrated in their research on young, creative workers, "[m]ost creative aspirants accept that their chosen fields are inherently precarious", which resonates with Scott Burrows's (2013: 393) finding on young people who "accept precarious forms of work as a matter of course". According to Helen Kennedy (2012: 48), precarious working conditions "feel increasingly normal to those workers who have never known anything else". My study supports the idea of precariousness as the 'new normal' (Taylor and Luckman, in press).

Dealing with precarious work: an entrepreneurial attitude

The research participants' attempts not to worry and to accept precarious working conditions should not be equated with passivity. In parallel with my argument that the research participants presented themselves as actively choosing not to engage with job insecurity, they portrayed themselves as actively dealing with the ups and downs of precarious work by exhibiting an entrepreneurial attitude (see also Bergvall-Kåreborn and Howcroft, 2013; Brophy and de Peuter, 2007; Burrows, 2013; McRobbie, 2010; McRobbie, 2015). Indeed, and in addition to the processes described in the previous chapter, the research participants constructed themselves as entrepreneurial subjects in and through their engagement with precarious work. They, for example, presented themselves as flexible and versatile in the never-ending search for work. Christine told me that she built up her clients for her compositions, while also "singing Jazz at weekends to help my income". Equally, Hope stated:

> I worked out quite early on that if you have lots of fingers in lots of pies, if something dries up it's not the end of the world. Conversely, I have friends who kind of put all their eggs in one basket, and if an orchestra starts ringing they kind of let everything else slip away so that they can do that. And I have seen instances with particular friends, suddenly that orchestra stops phoning, and then you've got nothing.

In this statement, Hope presents herself as versatile and therefore able to cope with job insecurity. She does so by portraying herself as different from "friends who kind of put all their eggs in one basket" and instead emphasises the need to pursue several lines of work.

The research participants' flexibility did not only encompass different types of work, but also geographical location, specifically a willingness to move to different cities and/or countries. Carolyn moved to Berlin in order to enjoy lower living costs, stop teaching, and free up time for her work:

> I almost had to turn down [work] because I didn't have enough time and I was still teaching, so then it made sense to think about living somewhere else. And I had been to Berlin and really loved the city, so I thought "Oh, okay", so maybe realising it's much more reasonable to live here.

Apart from moving, one research participant had changed her instrument in order to play a less competitive one. Esmeralda had played the violin but then changed to viola, telling me:

> It was easier for me, also in terms of looking for a job in an orchestra. Normally, it's easier or I mean there are less people. It's still lots of good people but still it's less than violin players. I just decided.

In these accounts, flexibility is not presented as a burden, but as something that the research participants take on freely (see also Morgan et al., 2013). By showing self-initiative and a willingness to be flexible, they adopt an entrepreneurial attitude.

This flexibility did not, however, translate into spontaneity or recklessness. The research participants emphasised the need to plan – particularly financially – and presented themselves as responsible. Faith stated: "I don't know how other musicians are, but I am very very careful with money. I save a lot, because I always think you never know when something is gonna happen." Similarly, when I asked Linda how she coped with job insecurity, she said:

> I just try to plan really meticulously and be really sensible, so sort of financially it's just – I work out my budget really carefully and then

basically sort of make sure that I'm living on what I need to live on, and not any more.

By presenting themselves as accountable for their actions, Faith and Linda construct themselves as entrepreneurial subjects who manage their working lives through careful financial planning.

The research participants also exhibited an entrepreneurial attitude towards precarity by embracing risk (see chapter four; Neff et al., 2005; Neff, 2012). Reflecting on her feelings towards precarious work, Annabel stated: "I tend to see myself as somebody who finds all of this great. And that it's also totally courageous and totally exciting, risky, but above all exciting, heroic, and exciting." When I asked Esther how she liked not knowing when the next gig is, she replied: "I like that. I love it actually. It's quite the challenge. I don't have anything next Saturday, actually, but most possibly I'll get a phone call. It's exciting." Others, such as Elena, embraced risks by pointing out that the notion of security is 'elusive':

> I thought I better start adjusting to this insecurity now, to learn to live with it, so that I can live with it without any problems later on than standing here at 50, and no longer knowing where do I get my money from, my rent? I basically decided for myself that life is insecure anyways, and then I better start to work on this now, to build something up, than having to do it later.

Annabel, Esther, and Elena embrace risk by stating that they find it heroic and exciting or by arranging their lives according to the belief that security is elusive. Again, I do not read their statements as indicating passivity or lack of reflexivity and awareness; the research participants accept risk and uncertainty, but do so in a proactive and knowing way by dubbing it exciting or by being prepared to "work on this now" (Elena).

The research participants' entrepreneurial attitude to precarious work did not lead to political mobilisation. To be sure, the research participants were active, but their energies were not channelled into forms of resistance. Instead, their high level of activity was directed at managing their working lives self-responsibly, which resonates with the findings of other studies on precarious, cultural work (Arvidsson et al., 2010; Armano and Murgia, 2013; Bain and McLean, 2013). Indeed, the research participants' entrepreneurial outlook also chimes with McRobbie's (2015) recent analysis of the incitement to 'be creative' which calls upon young people, and especially young women, to become "creative entrepreneurs" (11) and to do away with the securities and benefits associated with mainstream employment. In this context, entrepreneurialism "functions to solve the problems thrown up by the decline of the employment society for an aspirational sector of the workforce" (153). In fact, McRobbie (107) argues that the encouragement to be creative instigates "a new labour regime marked by self-enterprise". As can be seen from the research participants' accounts, the challenges of precarious work are addressed through entrepreneurialism, specifically the emphasis on flexibility, careful financial planning, and risk-taking.

While McRobbie (111) emphasises the disciplining force of the incitement to be creative, her analysis also highlights "the lines of flight, and the possibilities for movement on the part of young women as something more than individualization process and entrepreneurship of the self". McRobbie locates the capacity for resistance to the new work regime in inter-generational relations and memory "where lines of flight connect past parental struggles with the day-to-day experiences of their children in the modern work economy" (93). Crucially, McRobbie (163) points out that memories are not always "inherently radical" and that they can also lead to conservative politics. Nevertheless, while her account offers a strong critique of the incitement to 'be creative', it also highlights "ambivalence and tension" (2015: 93).

McRobbie's reference to ambivalence resonates with Hesmondhalgh and Baker's (2011: 19) finding that "worker experiences of creative labour are highly ambivalent". While McRobbie's and Hesmondhalgh and Baker's work are embedded in different theoretical trajectories, they both highlight ambivalence in cultural workers' experiences. Hesmondhalgh and Baker (2011) document the difficult aspects of cultural work, including high levels of casualisation, long working hours, and fierce competition. However, they also foreground elements of good work, such as the "pleasurable absorption" (Hesmondhalgh and Baker, 2011: 132) experienced by musicians. In order to explore this ambivalence in more detail, the next section of the chapter homes in on the pleasures that the research participants derived from their work. I show that the positive aspects of cultural work were deeply intertwined with its negative aspects, highlighting the need to trace the complexities of subjective experiences of precarious, cultural work.

Playing music: love, passion, and 'being in the zone'

In discussing their feelings towards precarious work, many research participants spoke about their love and passion for playing music. This passionate attachment motivated them to pursue a line of work that was precarious, badly paid, and insecure. According to Ashley, "the good most certainly outweighs the bad":

> So everyone is scrambling around, a bit nervous. So yeah, it's a bit of a bad time to be a musician, I think. But, likewise, when you are actually doing it, it's the best job in the world! And you can't believe you get paid for doing, you know . . . It's not just what you love, because it's what you have invested so much into, and so, you know, you get to see the benefits. Yeah, it's the best thing ever.

Lauren echoed Ashley's sentiment by pointing out that she was privileged to do something she loved:

> I get up in the morning and get paid to do something I really love doing, all day, every day. I love that, that's a real privilege. And I don't think there are many people in the world who can say that, which is – that is really cool.

Similarly, Sasha said that being a musician

> is a great way to make a living. I mean everyone will tell you that it's not a stable job or an easy living at times, but I mean it is a thousand times better than so many other things you could be doing, in terms of the variety and the people that you mix with, and obviously the opportunity to perform, and I really do love playing the trumpet. So it's a great thing to do!

Ashley, Lauren, and Sasha's statements are heightened in emotional tone and full of positive affect. They all emphasise the "love" they feel for playing music and communicate a sense of privilege that they are able to do this work. As Stephanie Taylor and Karen Littleton (2012: 111) have pointed out, the claims of love for one's work function discursively "to validate the choice of a creative career, particularly if it might appear to an outsider not to be very successful. They can elevate the status of creative work to a vocation."

Indeed, several research participants expressed their passionate attachment to being a musician by contrasting it with other, and allegedly more 'mundane' lines of work, such as office jobs. Liz told me that she was "overall happy" that she "changed from being in an office to being a musician. I do enjoy the work that I do almost all of the time." Describing moments of absolute absorption in music, Hope also indicated that an office job would not fulfil her:

> When that happens, you are sort of reminded why you do it, because I know that personally speaking I wouldn't get that same high from having an office job or being a solicitor or doing something else. Maybe they do in their professions, but the opportunity and the possibility of having that is what makes you – as well as obviously the love of the music, is what spurs you on to do it.

Esther similarly contrasted being a musician with having another job, stating that it would not satisfy her:

> I think being a musician is a special thing. I think what I get from being a musician I cannot get from another job. Maybe being a dancer is similar, but I need that sort of spiritual feeling, that sort of thing that music gives me. It's a very special feeling.

These statements construct the work of a musician as different from an "office job" and, more importantly, as "special" and fulfilling in a way that other work is not. As McRobbie (2015: 161) has pointed out, "artists and creative people are also led to believe their work is exceptional and unique", contributing to the 'lifted out' status of cultural work as different from other forms of work. According to McRobbie, the representation of cultural work as special can have depoliticising effects because it brushes over continuities with other, allegedly more mundane forms of work and establishes hierarchies between people who work in 'mundane' and 'special' fields.

Perhaps even more relevant to the accounts presented here is McRobbie's (2015) notion of 'passionate work'. This concept is based on Jacques Donzelot's account of pleasure in work "as a force that acts to reduce the likelihood of labour organization, in this case specifically for young female subjects in post-feminist times who are expected, or normatively required to participate in waged labour" (McRobbie, 2015: 107). The research participants' enthusiastic statements about their love for playing music and the special nature of their work resonate with McRobbie's argument and we could read their emotional investments in playing music as a form of 'passionate work'. However, McRobbie portrays passionate work as "inherently individualistic" (107). Yet, in analysing the research participants' accounts, I found that they sometimes linked moments of heightened pleasure in work to an intense connection with their audience, thus breaking with an individualist narrative. This dynamic came to the fore in the research participants' accounts of what it is like to 'be in the zone'. In the following, I discuss the research participants' portrayals of being in the zone, thus providing a different and slightly more optimistic reading of pleasures in work.

All of the research participants experienced states of "pleasurable absorption" (Hesmondhalgh and Baker: 132) and moments of being in the zone, which Tim Jordan et al. (2017) describe as performing in a distinctive, unusual, pleasurable, and highly competent way (see also Banks, 2014).[3] When research participants were discussing these experiences, the atmosphere in the interview often changed palpably and there was a sense of intense concentration and focus, but also of pleasure and absorption. Indeed, and as I have already alluded to when discussing Hope's statement about not wanting an office job, several research participants stated that being in the zone spurred them on to be musicians. According to June, being in the zone was addictive:

> And even though through my troubles and through considering walking away from this very difficult, fickle, tumultuous career path, I don't know what I would do if I couldn't find that, that lift and that – it's, you are transported out of yourself, it's an out of body experience, and you are for that moment in time or for however long that experience lasts for you, whether it's the whole opera or a certain part of the opera or whatever, nothing else in the world matters.

Using the language of love rather than addiction, Nora said she fell in love with the state of being in the zone and that this motivated her to be a musician:

> When I witnessed that for the first time I was just so overwhelmed and so awed that it was something I wanted to keep very close and something that felt very special. So I think it's that extremity that I love about it, and you reach that each time you have it with the music – unless someone is conducting it really badly or something, but you feel you are reaching a very special state. I am repeating myself there but . . . And that's sort of what I fell for, I suppose.

Echoing June's and Nora's sentiments, Ricarda also told me that experiences of special or heightened states made it all "worth it":

> It's kind of the best thing ever [. . .] If you are playing some of your favourite music and you're feeling good, you know, you're feeling physically in control and relaxed, then it's just a very homogenous, very organic experience, very natural, very beautiful. You just think: "Thank God, I did put in all those years! And thank God I stuck to my guns and stayed on the road that was sometimes stony." Um, 'cause then it's all worth it. And, sounds ridiculous – it's just a huge part of who I am and – I don't know – makes me happy.

These statements resonate with the experiences reported by the musicians interviewed in Hesmondhalgh's and Baker's (2011) study and more generally illustrate the affective intensity, pleasure, and satisfaction commonly associated with cultural work. Crucially, several research participants portrayed states of being in the zone as a key motivation to work as a classical musician.

The descriptions of being in the zone were remarkably similar and highlighted features that have been described elsewhere, such as a sense of "timeless time" (Hesmondhalgh and Baker, 2011: 133; see also Marotto et al., 2007). Elena described being in the zone as "simply being. You are in the moment, or I am in the moment and it simply flows." Jeanette told me that she "completely forgets time" when she is in the zone. Equally, Sonja described the state as "an alertness and a forgetting of time." Research participants also referred to physical changes, including an adrenalin rush, goose bumps, and hair on the back of the neck standing up. In this context, some research participants used sexual metaphors (see also Atkinson, 2006). Isabella described being in the zone in the following way: "it's the same as when you have a boyfriend and it is the first time you touch his hand, or whatever, or the first time when you kiss someone" and Jeanette likened it to "really good sex". Other research participants compared the physical changes of being in the zone to taking drugs. Kira stated that being in the zone was probably "like the feeling you get from taking drugs" while Ashley described it as "the purest form of escapism [. . .] I think it's what people are looking for if they are taking drugs and things."

Most pertinent to this chapter's overarching argument about the complex experiences associated with precarious, cultural work were the research participants' statements that being in the zone was closely connected to an ability to communicate with the audience. Alice stated that being in the zone "feels like there is a connection of energies between the stage and the audience. It's like a big amalgamation of energy and – like I give it out and they give it back to me." Similarly, Amanda told me that when you are in the zone, "you can create with an audience, between performer and audience, this sense of shared understanding and a shared experience", which echoed with Esmeralda's claim that being in the zone allowed her to "reach" the audience. Isabella reported similar feelings when she told me that moments of being in the zone could make her tearful: "I had moments I had tears in my eyes from my own playing, not because I am vain and I love my own playing, but because it touched me so much, and it connected me so much."

To be sure, some research participants problematised these claims. Annegret, for example, pointed out that she mainly sought moments of being in the zone for her own enjoyment: "I believe that you mainly do it for yourself. I mean, many people always say: 'Obviously, I also play for my audience', but I obviously do a lot for myself." While Annegret's statement was an exception, several participants pointed out that whether or not one could be in the zone depended on the performance situation (Elena). Sasha, for example, stated that other thoughts and feelings could get in the way, which meant she was not always in the zone:

> I mean, when you play your best you are [in the zone], but obviously sometimes you are just thinking. You know, nerves get in the way. Or, you know, thinking about other things, like life stuff or boring things, things you shouldn't be thinking about, distractions. So yeah, not always, unfortunately. If only!

These statements caution against elevating being in the zone to an idealised status. Musicians cannot always be in the zone and some may not use it as an opportunity to communicate with the audience.

Nevertheless, I have discussed these statements at length because the endeavour and ability to communicate with an audience emerged as a distinctive pattern, which, crucially, has also been identified in other research on musicians as cultural workers (see for example Hesmondhalgh and Baker, 2011). More to the point, the desire to communicate with an audience as an important aspect of being in the zone was discussed in the wider context of what motivates musicians to pursue their work, despite its insecure and precarious nature. Having described the research participants' entrepreneurial responses to precarious work in the previous section, I now wish to highlight their desire to connect with their audience because it breaks with an individualist narrative and paints a more complex picture of the various ways in which musicians respond to and cope with precarious work. As I hope to have shown through my discussion of the pleasures involved in playing music and, more specifically, being in the zone, responses to precarious work are not exclusively individualist and entrepreneurial. Arguably, the desire to communicate with the audience represents a 'line of flight' (McRobbie, 2015) and a response to precarious, cultural work which breaks from the entrepreneurial logic outlined above. While these motivations may not have given rise to more collective forms of resistance to precarious work – at least not in the context discussed here – they challenge the otherwise rather individualist outlook displayed in the interviews.

Beyond pleasure: additional perks of being a musician

The research participants' passion for playing music was not only linked to an ability to communicate with the audience, but also to an opportunity for self-expression. Emilia decided she wanted to become a musician when she realised that playing her instrument offered her the opportunity to express herself: "I was quite shy when I was younger, still am a bit. And it was just like a way of expressing myself or something." Interestingly, Sophie told a very similar story about her decision to pursue music professionally:

> There were moments when I had the impression that I can really speak with the instrument. Perhaps it sounds a bit turgid, but – it is also about the age, when you are fourteen/fifteen and then you suddenly have the impression you can express something.

Isabella echoed Emilia's and Sophie's sense that playing music can be an avenue for self-expression:

> And music is in a way, is the way I can say absolutely everything. People don't understand that that is me, they think it is the music, but for me, everyone has doubts, like: "Maybe it will not work out? I do or do not know what to do?" You bring all of this to the stage. You go to talk, you go to interact, you go to influence people to think about their own stuff.

In this statement, Isabella refers to music as "the way I can say absolutely everything" and, in line with my argument above about the importance of communicating with an audience, ends her reflections by talking about interacting and influencing the people who listen to her playing.

Here, I do however want to focus on music as a vehicle for self-expression as it also seems to have a gendered dimension. Sasha told me:

> The only time that I really feel like I'm myself is when I'm on stage, and when I'm performing, and then it's like, I suppose, it's 'you intensified'. But for me, the opportunity to perform is sort of the only opportunity you have in life to sort of make people listen and . . . yes, speak to them on some level that's just so much deeper than what we're doing now.

Similar to her peers, Sasha represents the performance situation as an occasion to speak and to do so in a way that is "deeper" than other forms of conversation. Crucially, Sasha also uses the expression "to make people listen". Later on in the interview, she said:

> And you know, I've got real issues about being heard – which is obviously stupid, but as a musician – But I think as a girl, I think I wasn't ever heard. I wasn't ever pushed forward.

In this second statement, Sasha refers to the gendered dimensions of "being heard", which chimed with an impression I had from listening to the research participants' accounts: namely, that there was something meaningful about going on stage and making the audience listen, and that the appeal of performing had a gendered dimension.[4] While Sasha was the only one who explicitly stated that she "wasn't ever heard" as a girl, I read Emilia's, Sophie's, and Isabella's statements in a similar light. Playing an instrument, performing, and having a 'voice' may be particularly attractive to women who may be given these opportunities less frequently in other spheres of life due to, for example, expectations that women are modest, as discussed in chapter two. Crucially, I do not argue that performance situations as described by the research participants disrupt gendered norms. The desire to communicate with an audience, for example, can also be read as a performance of femininity (see chapter two), which may break with individualist rhetoric, but not with common portrayals of women as 'natural' communicators. Equally important, my analyses of inequalities in the classical music profession (see chapter two) caution against presenting the performance situation as solely empowering.

I highlight the pleasure derived from self-expression because it provided yet another motivation for the research participants to pursue an often "difficult, fickle, tumultuous career path" (June). In addition to the love and passion for music, the pleasures derived from being in the zone and communicating with the audience, the ability to self-express seemed to be another positive aspect of being a musician. These different motivations were made relevant in discussions about the precarious nature of the classical music profession, indicating that the research participants considered them as crucial elements of their work. More to the point, the negative and positive components of being a musician were intermeshed in the research participants' accounts and hard to separate.

Even though I adopt a Foucauldian framework, which has been charged for underplaying the complex interplay between the positive and negative aspects of cultural work (Hesmondhalgh and Baker, 2011; Kennedy, 2012; Taylor and Littleton, 2012), I hope to have demonstrated that both aspects are not only present in subjective accounts of cultural work, but that they are deeply intertwined. In their talk about the precarious nature of work in classical music, the research participants referred to the pleasures involved in their line of work. At the same time, when sharing the intense joys they derived from playing music, they drew attention to otherwise difficult aspects of the classical music profession. By highlighting these interconnections, my analysis has attempted to represent the research participants' experiences in all their complexity and explored how this plays out in the context of negotiations of precarious, cultural work.

Conclusion

This chapter has drawn on a wide range of personal accounts to shed light on the research participants' experiences of precarious work. The first analytical section showed that precarious work reshapes time in two distinct ways: the sense that all time can be put to productive use blurs the boundaries between work and leisure while the insecurity of precarious work makes it difficult to predict the future.

Although the research participants shared similar views of these temporal dimensions, their feelings about precarious work varied over time, ranging from fear to excitement. Far from being associated with a homogenous affective register, feelings about precarious work seem to fluctuate and depend on a range of factors, such as the degree of freedom associated with the work on offer and precarious workers' positioning. As the third section of this chapter demonstrated, silencing, 'wilful ignorance', and acceptance were common responses to precarious work. Indeed, and as outlined in the fourth section, the research participants exhibited an entrepreneurial attitude towards precarious work by emphasising flexibility, foresight, and risk-taking.

As the final two sections of this chapter however argued, the research participants' discussion of the difficult aspects of precarious work, as well as their entrepreneurial attitude, has to be analysed in the wider and highly ambivalent context of precarious, cultural work. In discussing their working lives, the research participants drew attention to the intense joys and pleasures they derived from playing music, from being in the zone, and, more specifically, from communicating with their audience and from being offered a platform for self-expression. As I hope to have shown, the research participants oriented to both the positive and negative aspects of precarious, cultural work in their accounts. These aspects were difficult to separate, pointing to the complexities surrounding subjective experiences of precarious work in the cultural and creative industries. The notion of 'ambivalence' grasps these tensions well, foregrounding both the hardships associated with precarious, cultural work, but also the satisfaction associated with it. Maintaining my focus on subjectivity, the next and final chapter animates Raymond Williams's (1977) notion of 'structures of feeling' to explore how urban contexts affect experiences of cultural work. In addition to exploring cultural workers' subjectivities in relation to inequalities (see chapters two and three), entrepreneurialism and neoliberalism (see chapter four), precarious and cultural work (this chapter), the final chapter analyses the interplay between subjectivity, cultural work, and urban contexts.

Notes

1 But note that Lorey also refers to the 'double meaning' of precarity, especially in her recent work (2015: 103) where she points out that "[m]odes of subjectivation are not always subsumed into normative political and economic calls for flexibility, mobility and affective and creative work."

2 To be sure, there are organisations that help musicians who struggle with injuries. The Royal Society of Musicians of Great Britain, for example, seeks "to provide immediate financial assistance to musicians unable to work due to accident, illness or old age". It is a charity run by musicians for musicians and more information can be found here: www.royalsocietyofmusicians.org/.

3 Certainly, the phenomenon of 'being in the zone' has been researched from a range of perspectives, and has also been referred to as 'flow' (Csikszentmihalyi, 1990) moments, or 'peak performance' (Marotto et al., 2007). I draw on Jordan et al.'s work in this context, as it understands being in the zone as a social and collective experience.

4 In her research on classical music education, Anna Bull (2015) also found that young, female singers experienced the making of a loud sound as giving them a sense of power. Crucially, however, Bull describes how this sense of empowerment was constrained by a strongly gendered and institutional context, which undermined the singers' empowered voices. Bull's analysis thus cautions against portraying the performance situation as solely empowering. Indeed, my analysis of inequalities in the classical music profession (see chapter two) similarly highlights a range of gendered constraints that female musicians have to negotiate when performing. The appeal of self-expression should, therefore, not be considered in isolation from the wider industry context.

References

Anderson, B. (2007). *Battles in time: The relation between global and labour mobilities.* Working Paper No. 55, University of Oxford, Oxford Centre on Migration, Policy and Society.

Armano, E., & Murgia, A. (2013). The precariousnesses of young knowledge workers: A subject-oriented approach. *Global Discourse, 3*(3–4), 486–501.

Arvidsson, A., Malossi, G., & Naro, S. (2010). Passionate work? Labour conditions in the Milan fashion industry. *Journal for Cultural Research, 14*(3), 295–309.

Atkinson, P. (2006). *Everyday arias: An operatic ethnography.* Lanham, MD: AltaMira Press.

Bain, A., & McLean, H. (2013). The artistic precariat. *Cambridge Journal of Regions, Economy and Society, 6*(1), 93–111.

Banks, M. (2014). Being in the zone of cultural work. *Culture Unbound: Journal of Current Cultural Research, 6*(1), 241–262.

Banks, M., Ebrey, J., & Toynbee, J. (2014). *Working lives in Black British jazz: A report and survey.* Accessed 1 December 2016. Available at: www.cresc.ac.uk/sites/default/files/WLIBBJ%20NEW%20FINAL.pdf

Banks, M., Gill, R., & Taylor, S. (2013). *Theorizing cultural work: Labour, continuity and change in the creative industries.* London: Routledge.

Bennett, D. (2008). *Understanding the classical music profession: The past, the present and strategies for the future.* Farnham: Ashgate.

Bennett, D. (2016). Developing employability and professional identity through visual narratives. *Australian Art Education, 37*(2), 100–115.

Bergvall-Kåreborn, B., & Howcroft, D. (2013). 'The future's bright, the future's mobile': A study of Apple and Google mobile application developers. *Work, Employment and Society, 27*(6), 964–981.

Blair, H. (2001). 'You're only as good as your last job': The labour process and labour market in the British film industry. *Work, Employment & Society, 15*(1), 149–169.

Bossen, A. (2012). *Einkommenssituation und Arbeitsbedingungen von Musikschullehrkräften und Privatmusiklehrern 2012.* Berlin: Verdi Fachgruppe Musik. Accessed 1 December 2016. Available at: www.miz.org/dokumente/2012_verdi_umfrage.pdf

Bourdieu, P. (1986). The forms of capital. In J. Richardson (Ed.), *Handbook of theory and research for the sociology of education* (pp. 241–258). New York: Greenwood.

Bourdieu, P. (1999). *The weight of the world: Social suffering in contemporary society.* Oxford: Polity.

Brophy, E., & de Peuter, G. (2007). Immaterial labour, precarity, and recomposition. In C. McKercher & V. Mosco (Eds.), *Knowledge workers in the information society* (pp. 177–191). Lanham: Lexington Books.

Bull, A. (2015). *The musical body: How gender and class are reproduced among young people playing classical music in England.* Unpublished PhD thesis, Goldsmiths, University of London.

Bull, A., & Scharff, C. (2017). 'McDonalds' music' versus 'serious music': how production and consumption practices help to reproduce class inequality in the classical music profession. *Cultural Sociology.* Accessed 20 July 2017. Available at: http://journals.sagepub.com/doi/pdf/10.1177/1749975517711045

Burrows, S. (2013). Precarious work, neo-liberalism and young people's experiences of employment in the Illawarra region. *The Economic and Labour Relations Review: ELRR, 24*(3), 380–396.

Butler, J. (2004). *Precarious life: The powers of mourning and violence.* London: Verso.

Csikszentmihalyi, M. (1990). *Flow: The psychology of optimal experience.* New York: Harper & Row.

de Peuter, G. (2014). Beyond the model worker: Surveying a creative precariat. *Culture Unbound: Journal of Current Cultural Research, 6*(1), 263–284.

DOV (2014). *Deutsche Orchester: Abbau Ost schreitet voran.* Berlin: Deutsche Orchestervereinigung. Accessed 1 December 2016. Available at: www.dov.org/pressereader/items/deutsche-orchester-abbau-ost-schreitet-voran-1260.html

Ettlinger, N. (2007). Precarity unbound. *Alternatives: Global, Local, Political, 32*(3), 319–340.

Friedman, S., O'Brien, D., & Laurison, D. (2016). 'Like skydiving without a parachute: How class origin shapes occupational trajectories in British acting'. *Sociology* (February) [published online before print].

Gill, R., & Pratt, A. C. (2008). In the social factory? Immaterial labour, precariousness and cultural work. *Theory, Culture & Society, 25*(7–8), 1–30.

Gregg, M. (2011). *Work's intimacy.* Cambridge: Polity.

Gregg, M. (2013). Presence bleed: Performing professionalism online. In M. Banks, R. Gill, & S. Taylor (Eds.), *Theorizing cultural work: Labour, continuity and change in the creative industries* (pp. 122–134). London: Routledge.

Help Musicians UK (2014). *Professional music in the UK: Health and wellbeing survey.* London: Help Musicians UK. Accessed 1 December 2016. Available at: https://issuu.com/helpmusiciansuk/docs/help_musicians_uk_health_and_wellbe?e=10405134/8971874

Hennekam, S., & Bennett, D. (2017). Creative industries work across multiple contexts: Common themes and challenges. *Personnel Review, 46*(1), 68–85.

Hesmondhalgh, D., & Baker, S. (2010). 'A very complicated version of freedom': Conditions and experiences of creative labour in three cultural industries. *Poetics, 38*(1), 4–20.

Hesmondhalgh, D., & Baker, S. (2011). *Creative labour: Media work in three cultural industries.* London: Routledge.

Ikonen, H-M. (2013). Precarious work, entrepreneurial mindset and sense of place: Female strategies in insecure labour markets. *Global Discourse, 3*(3–4), 467–481.

Jordan, T., Woodward, K., & McClure, B. (2017). *Culture, identity and intense performativity: Being in the zone.* London: Routledge.

Kalleberg, A. L. (2009). Precarious work, insecure workers: Employment relations in transition. *American Sociological Review, 74*(1), 1–22.

Kennedy, H. (2012). *Net work: Ethics and values in web design.* Basingstoke: Palgrave Macmillan.

Kuehn, K., & Corrigan, T. F. (2013). Hope labor: The role of employment prospects in online social production. *The Political Economy of Communication, 1*(1), 9–25.

Lorey, I. (2011). Virtuosos of freedom: On the implosion of political virtuosity and productive labour. In G. Raunig, G. Ray, & U. Wuggenig (Eds.), *Critique of creativity: Precarity, subjectivity and resistance in the 'creative industries'* (pp. 79–90). London: MayFlyBooks.

Lorey, I. (2015). *State of insecurity: Government of the precarious.* Translated by A. Derieg. London; New York: Verso.

Luckman, S. (2013). Precarious labour then and now: The British Arts and Crafts Movement and cultural work revisited. In M. Banks, R. Gill & S. Taylor (Eds.), *Theorizing cultural work: Labour, continuity and change in the creative industries* (pp. 19–29). London: Routledge.

Marotto, M., Roos, J., & Victor, B. (2007). Collective virtuosity in organizations: A study of peak performance in an orchestra. *Journal of Management Studies, 44*(3), 388–413.

McRobbie, A. (2010). Reflections on feminism, immaterial labour and the post-Fordist regime. *New Formations, 70,* 60–76.

McRobbie, A. (2015). *Be creative: Making a living in the new culture industries.* Cambridge: Polity.

Mitropoulos, A. (2005). Precari-Us? *Republicart,* 3. Accessed 1 December 2016. Available at: www.republicart.net/disc/precariat/mitropoulos2001_en.htm

Morgan, G., Wood, J., & Nelligan, P. (2013). Beyond the vocational fragments: Creative work, precarious labour and the idea of 'Flexploitation'. *The Economic and Labour Relations Review, 24*(3), 397–415.

Murgia, A., & Selmi, G. (2012). "Inspire and conspire": Italian precarious workers between self-organisation and self-advocacy. *Interface: A Journal for and about Social Movements, 4*(2), 181–196.

Musicians' Union (2012). *The working musician.* London: Musicians' Union. Accessed 1 December 2016. Available at: www.musiciansunion.org.uk/Files/Reports/Industry/The-Working-Musician-report

Neff, G. (2012). *Venture labor: Work and the burden of risk in innovative industries.* Cambridge, MA; London: MIT Press.

Neff, G., Wissinger, E., & Zukin, S. (2005). Entrepreneurial labor among cultural producers: 'Cool' jobs in 'hot' industries. *Social Semiotics, 15*(3), 307–334.

Neilson, B., & Rossiter, N. (2008). Precarity as a political concept, or, Fordism as exception. *Theory, Culture & Society, 25*(7–8), 51–72.

Precarias a la deriva (2004). Adrift through the circuits of feminized precarious work. *Feminist Review, 77*(77), 157–161.

Quinlan, M. (2012). The 'pre-invention' of precarious employment: The changing world of work in context. *The Economic and Labour Relations Review, 23*(4), 3–23.

Rogaly, B. (2008). Migrant workers in the ILO's global alliance against forced labour report: A critical appraisal. *Third World Quarterly, 29*(7), 1431–1447.

Ross, A. (2003). *No-collar: The humane workplace and its hidden costs.* New York: Basic Books.

Ross, A. (2008). The new geography of work: Power to the precarious? *Theory, Culture & Society, 25*(7–8), 31–49.

Rossiter, N., & Neilson, B. (2005). From precarity to precariousness and back again: Labour, life and unstable networks. *Fibreculture Journal, 5.* Accessed 1 December 2016. Available at: http://five.fibreculturejournal.org/fcj-2022-from-precarity-to-precariousness-and-back-again-labour-life-and-unstable-networks/

Rowlands, L., & Handy, J. (2012). An addictive environment: New Zealand film production workers' subjective experiences of project-based labour. *Human Relations, 65*(5), 657–680.

Scharff, C. (2016). Gender and neoliberalism: Young women as ideal neoliberal subjects. In S. Springer, K. Birch, & J. MacLeavy (Eds.), *The handbook of neoliberalism* (pp. 217–226). Abingdon, Oxon; New York Routledge.

Scharff, C. (2017). Inequalities in the classical music industry: The role of subjectivity in constructions of the 'ideal classical musician'. In C. Dromey & J. Haferkorn (Eds.), *The classical music industry*. London: Routledge.

Schulz, G. (2013a). Bestandsaufnahme zum Arbeitsmarkt Kultur. In G. Schulz, O. Zimmermann & R. Hufnagel (Eds.), *Arbeitsmarkt Kultur: Zur wirtschaftlichen und sozialen Lage in Kulturberufen* (pp. 27–201). Berlin: Deutscher Kulturrat.

Schulz, G. (2013b). Arbeitsmarkt Kultur: Eine Analyse von KSK-Daten. In G. Schulz, O. Zimmermann & R. Hufnagel (Eds.), *Arbeitsmarkt Kultur: Zur wirtschaftlichen und sozialen Lage in Kulturberufen* (pp. 241–322). Berlin: Deutscher Kulturrat.

Schulz, G., Zimmermann, O., & Hufnagel, R. (2013). *Arbeitsmarkt Kultur: Zur wirtschaftlichen und sozialen Lage in Kulturberufen*. Berlin: Deutscher Kulturrat.

Sennett, R. (1998). *The corrosion of character: The personal consequences of work in the new capitalism*. New York; London: W. W. Norton.

Standing, G. (2011). *The precariat: The new dangerous class*. London: Bloomsbury Academic.

Taylor, S., & Littleton, K. (2012). *Contemporary identities of creativity and creative work*. Farnham: Ashgate.

Taylor, S., & Luckman, S. (Eds.). (in press). *The 'new normal' of working lives: Critical studies in contemporary work and employment*. Basingstoke: Palgrave Macmillan.

Toynbee, J. (2013). How special? Cultural work, copyright, politics. In M. Banks, S. Taylor, & R. Gill (Eds.), *Theorizing cultural work: Labour, continuity and change in the creative industries* (pp. 85–98). London: Routledge.

Tsianos, V., & Papadopoulos, D. (2006). Precarity: A savage journey to the heart of embodied capitalism. *EIPCP: European Institute for Progressive Cultural Policies*. Accessed 1 December 2016. Available at: http://eipcp.net/transversal/1106/tsianospapadopoulos/en/base_edit

Vosco, L. F. (2009). *Managing the margins: Gender, citizenship, and the international regulation of precarious employment*. Oxford: Oxford University Press.

Waite, L. (2009). A place and space for a critical geography of precarity? *Geography Compass, 3*(1), 412–433.

Williams, R. (1977). *Marxism and literature*. Oxford: Oxford University Press.

Chapter 6

Structures of feeling in two creative cities

London and Berlin

This chapter retains the book's focus on subjectivity by asking what it feels like to pursue cultural work in London and Berlin. As I will demonstrate, both cities have vibrant cultural and classical music sectors and yet, they are also characterised by different material conditions, particularly in relation to the cost of housing. London's high rents and property prices contrast sharply with the relative affordability of housing in Berlin. By focusing on the ways in which material conditions shape cultural work, and how this plays out in two urban contexts, this chapter builds on Kirsten Forkert's (2013) analysis of artistic lives in London and Berlin. In her study, Forkert (2013: 7) asks: "What kinds of art practices, projects, ways of working and ways of being an artist do these very different conditions make possible?" This chapter adds to and complements her insightful analysis by animating Raymond Williams's (1977) notion of 'structures of feeling'. Distinct from "more formal concepts of 'world-view' or 'ideology'", structures of feeling are "concerned with meanings and values as they are actively lived and felt" (Williams, 1977: 132). The notion of structures of feeling attempts to grasp "characteristic elements of impulse, restraint, and tone; specifically affective elements of consciousness and relationships" (132). In this chapter, I use the concept 'structures of feeling' to explore the emotional underpinnings of doing cultural work in specific urban settings. As I will argue, cultural work is experienced differently in Berlin and London and material conditions play a key role.

I begin with a brief discussion of Berlin's particularity, highlighting a range of factors such as the consequences of reunification. The main focus of the first section, however, is on the cultural and creative industries in Berlin and London. Citing a range of reports, this section provides an overview of the cultural and music sectors in London and Berlin. This is less to advance instrumentalist arguments about the economic contributions of the 'creative industries', than to contextualise the accounts of the research participants by describing the industry contexts in which they work. In part related to the size and importance of the cultural sectors in Berlin and London, both cities have been branded and marketed as 'creative cities' and the second section of this chapter explores this policy discourse critically. As I show, the notion of the 'creative city' is used variously and yet Richard Florida's (2002) ideas have been prominent, also in relation to cultural policymaking in Berlin and London. This is despite robust criticisms of the creative city narrative, especially in relation to its neoliberal underpinnings and the role it plays in widening inequalities.

The overview of Berlin's and London's cultural sectors, as well as the discussion of the two cities' positioning as creative, provides a starting point for my analysis of the structures of feeling in Berlin and London. As I will show, there was a feeling of cosmopolitanism and openness in both cities. Life in London, however, was overwhelmingly portrayed as hard because of its high living and housing costs. In order to navigate London's high housing costs, research participants had a range of living arrangements, which were frequently temporary and gave rise to a sense of insecurity. While some research participants had moved away from London to escape high housing costs, many felt that this was not an option. London was constructed as a happening place for musicians where freelance work was readily available, which meant that moving away from the city was regarded as risky in terms of access to work. However, the construction of London as a happening place also meant that there was a sense of excitement about being at the centre of the classical music industry, at least nationally. London's structure of feeling was thus characterised by a sense of hardship, insecurity, inescapability, and excitement. By contrast, life in Berlin was portrayed as affordable. Indeed, research participants celebrated Berlin's low living costs and rents. Yet, insecurity also formed an element of the structure of feeling in Berlin. Many research participants noted that things were about to change, mentioning rising rents, stagnating wages, and increased competition amongst musicians. The structure of feeling in Berlin was thus marked by a sense that life was affordable and even 'luxurious', but also that change was immanent, giving rise to a feeling of insecurity.[1]

The cultural and creative industries in Berlin and London

Since the fall of the Wall, Berlin has undergone a series of transformations. As in other cities, neoliberal policies are pronounced and Berlin is increasingly characterised by growing social heterogeneity and more de-localised urban lifestyles and consumer cultures (Bernt et al., 2013). Yet, and as I will demonstrate in the subsequent paragraph, Berlin is also special (Bernt et al., 2013). In order to contextualise the accounts of the research participants who were based in Berlin, it is worth reviewing the processes that have marked Berlin's transformation since reunification.

According to urban researchers Matthias Bernt, Britta Grell and Andrej Holm (2013), four factors have characterised Berlin's development since the fall of the

Wall. First, there are ongoing inequalities that have resulted from the East West division and subsequent unification, including, for example, the displacement of East German residents from gentrifying neighbourhoods such as Prenzlauer Berg. Post unification, up to 80 per cent of residents moved out of desirable inner city areas, adding to a sense of injustice about the handling and consequences of reunification. Second, Berlin's economic base has been eroded and it is now the German city with the highest unemployment rate and the only European capital with a GDP that lies below the national average. The end of subsidies to West Berlin, the dissolution of the East German government, as well as the shrinking of East Berlin's industrial base have weakened Berlin's economy.

In addition, and third, Berlin experienced an economic crisis in the early 2000s as a consequence of the so-called banking scandal, which has resulted in 'austerity urbanism' (Peck, 2012) where the aim of subsequent city governments has been to achieve a balanced budget. Lastly, and despite the rise of austerity urbanism, Berlin's urban policy-making has had a history of 'careful urban renewal', which sought to avoid the displacement of low-income populations from the inner city, to preserve a socially mixed city, and to involve citizens in local politics. While the reality of urban policy-making has frequently diverged from this ideal, the assumptions underpinning the policies of 'careful urban renewal' have had a lasting influence on Berlin's political culture. In addition to and in conjunction with these transformations, Berlin has also seen developments that are not locally distinct, such as the internationalisation of real estate speculation and the growing importance of the local cultural sector (Bernt et al., 2013). In the context of this chapter's focus on Berlin and London as creative cities, it is the latter trend that I will discuss in detail.

Berlin's urban economic development has been marked by low growth rates and high unemployment. One sector that has done well, however, is the cultural sector (Colomb, 2012a; Krätke, 2013 [2004]; Manske and Merkel, 2008). Since the mid-2000s, there has been a dramatic increase in the number of people who work in the so-called 'creative industries': around a quarter of Berlin's entire employment growth has been in this sector (Berlin Senate, 2014a). As I pointed out in chapter one, a fifth of all Berlin businesses are active in the creative industries (Berlin Senate, 2014a) and one out of 11 jobs is in the cultural sector (DiW, 2013). By comparison, only one out of 31 jobs is in the creative industries in Germany (DiW, 2013). In the context of the classical music profession, it is also worth mentioning that Berlin benefits from considerable public support for culture and the arts, which amounts to around €400 million (Berlin Senate, 2014b). With a budget of €9.5 billion nationwide, Germany's expenditure on the cultural sector is world leading and these subsidies give a boost to Berlin's cultural landscape, including the classical music sector.

Berlin boasts three opera houses (Berlin State Opera, Deutsche Oper, Komische Oper) each with an autonomous choir, orchestra, and corps de ballet, as well as world leading symphony orchestras such as Berlin Philharmonic and

Staatskapelle Berlin, a further eight renowned orchestras, and numerous ensembles and choirs (Berlin Senate, 2015; see also Grésillon, 1999). Music education is vibrant in Berlin, with 155 music schools with a total of 540,000 registered students, and prestigious higher education institutes such as Hanns-Eisler School of Music Berlin and Berlin University of the Arts (Berlin Senate, 2014a). Berlin's opera houses and concert halls are among the city's leading employers and provide jobs to nearly half of those working in the music industry (Berlin Senate, 2014a). Crucially, Berlin is not only known for its well established classical music sector, but it is indeed home to a very wide range of music genres. According to Ingo Bader and Albert Scharenberg (2013 [2009]: 247), the music industry has become an important part of the urban economy and Berlin is now "one of the most important cities for electronic music worldwide". Berlin's electronic music scene, its vibrant subculture of temporary clubs and bars, as well as its image as youthful and hip have all contributed to Berlin's cultural boom. Music, then, plays a key role in Berlin's cultural sector.

London too has a vibrant cultural sector. In 2014, there were 795,800 jobs in the creative economy[2] in London or, to put it differently, 16.3 per cent of total jobs in the capital (GLA, 2015a). This compares to 7.4 per cent of the total number of jobs in the rest of the United Kingdom (GLA, 2015a). Similar to Berlin, the growth rate of London's cultural and creative industries is outstripping more conventional sectors of the economy and may even be less prone to recession (Pratt, 2010). In the period between 2009–2012, the creative industries showed relatively higher growth than London's economy as a whole (GLA, 2015a). The music, performing and visual arts sector, for example, grew by 2.2 per cent between 2009 and 2012 (GLA, 2015a). As in other cities, culture is becoming a more significant part of the urban mix (Pratt, 2012). It is said to play a key role in urban tourism with eight out of ten visitors stating that heritage and culture is the main reason for their visit (GLA, 2014). To put this in context, London is the capital for music tourism in the United Kingdom with 1.8 million music tourists and £67 million generated each year from musical theatre and classical music sales to London tourists (GLA, 2014).

Indeed, a report on the economic impact of London's conservatoires argued "London represents probably the world's largest classical music agglomeration" (LSE, 2012: 40). The city has a vibrant music education sector. Over 200, 000 young people learn how to play a musical instrument with over 75 per cent being taught through borough music services (GLA, 2014).[3] London and its outskirts are also home to specialist music schools such as Purcell School and the three choir schools of St Paul's Cathedral, Westminster Abbey, and Westminster Cathedral. There are several prestigious conservatoires, including the Royal Academy of Music, The Guildhall School of Music and Drama, the Royal College of Music, as well as Trinity Laban Conservatoire of Music and Dance. In addition, many other London universities host music departments with a range of undergraduate and postgraduate courses. Similar to Berlin, the orchestral landscape is lively.

A high number of London orchestras are members of the Association of British Orchestras, which indicates that they are established groups providing work to professional instrumentalists and giving regular performances (Laing and York, 2000). Prestigious orchestras include the BBC Symphony Orchestra, the London Symphony Orchestra, the London Philharmonic Orchestra, and the Royal Philharmonic Orchestra. Apart from orchestras, many opera companies are based in London (Laing and York, 2000) of which the English National Opera and the Royal Opera are probably the best known.

According to recent estimates by the Greater London Authority, the 'music, performing & visual arts' sector provided 92, 800 jobs in 2014, which compares to 191, 500 in the rest of the United Kingdom (GLA, 2015a). An earlier study by David Laing and Norton York (2000: 1) explored the value of music in London, demonstrating that music "creates added value of over £1 billion and the London music business has net foreign earnings of over £400 million per annum". Crucially, classical music forms just one sub-sector of the wider music industry. Similar to Berlin, London features a number of different music genres. Problematically, however, public subsidies of classical music are disproportionally high. "Classical concerts and opera together account for 10–15 per cent of the total annual ticket sales in London, yet classical music (including opera) attracts about 90 per cent of the available public subsidy" (Laing and York, 2000: 32; see also Monk, 2014; Warwick Commission, 2015). I would like to clarify, therefore, that my discussion focused on the classical music sector – as compared to other music sectors – to contextualise my research participants' accounts. This is not to underplay the diversity of musical genres or to foreclose important questions about public subsidies (see Bull and Scharff, 2017). Significantly, these questions tie into wider arguments about inequalities in the classical music profession and the cultural and creative industries (see chapter two). Instead of focusing on these questions here, I situate Berlin's and London's cultural and creative industries, and particularly their classical music sectors, in the context of wider debates about the creative city.

Berlin and London as creative cities

The notion of the creative city has been used in different ways in writings, debates, and urban policies around the world (Pratt, 2010). Indeed, and following Andy Pratt and Thomas Hutton (2013: 90), "it makes more sense to consider the creative city a field of policy rather than one particular policy as the ideas have been fragmented and recombined many times in different places." Nevertheless, certain themes reoccur in debates about the creative city, which have been pertinent to cultural policy-making in Berlin and London in recent years. In particular, Florida's (2002) work on the creative city, popularised in *The Rise of the Creative Class*, has proven influential (Peck, 2011). Building on earlier entrepreneurial models of urban governance, which focused on the provision of infrastructure, subsidies, and amenities to attract highly mobile corporations, creative city policies aim at appealing to highly skilled individuals through the creation of diverse and tolerant communities (Catungal et al., 2009). This policy approach supports the cultural and creative industries as a motor of economic development, particularly in order to attract investment and human capital. Crucially, the creative city narrative has been critiqued extensively for its instrumentalist outlook, neoliberal underpinnings, and the ways in which it fosters processes of gentrification and widens existing class, race, and gender inequalities (see, for example Bodirsky, 2012; Catungal et al., 2009; Colomb, 2012a; b; Jakob, 2010; Leslie and Catungal, 2012; McLean, 2014; Peck, 2005; Pratt, 2010; 2011). Despite these criticisms, city leaders around the world have embraced Florida's ideas enthusiastically. Reworking older arguments of urban entrepreneurialism in politically seductive ways (Peck, 2005), the creative city narrative has also shaped cultural policy-making in Berlin and London.

In Berlin, governing and opposition parties have promoted the notion that mobilising creative potential can be a means for addressing various economic and social problems, related to deindustrialisation, high levels of unemployment, and social polarisation (Bodirsky, 2012). The creative city narrative entered the local marketing discourse for the first time in the year 2000, and the left-wing coalition government (2001–2011) subsequently adopted various policy measures to promote Berlin as a creative city (Colomb, 2012a; b; Novy and Colomb, 2013). These measures attempted to support new business start-ups or create urban environments that meet the appeal of cultural and creative industries. They targeted the cultural and creative industries as an economic sector in its own right, as a means to attract (young) urban tourism, and as a location factor for the knowledge economy (Colomb, 2012a). As a 2014 report by the Berlin Senate (Berlin's city government) demonstrated, support for the cultural and creative industries remains a key policy objective both in Berlin, but also nationally (Berlin Senate, 2014b).

Despite the continuing popularity of the creative city narrative, it is worth pointing out that the growth of the cultural and creative industries in Berlin has not been the outcome of specific policy measures. As Claire Colomb (2012a: 232) has argued, it "has been facilitated by the availability of affordable working and living spaces, by a tolerant and liberal culture inherited from the 1970s and 1980s, and fed by pre-existing concentrations of cultural producers, artists and networks of alternative culture (e.g. the techno music scene)" (see also Bader and Scharenberg, 2013 [2009]). Against this backdrop, it is notable that the creative city discourse has continued to be influential, as can be seen from the 2014 report by the Berlin Senate, discussed above. The ongoing influence of the creative city discourse is particularly noteworthy in light of existing criticisms. As research on the effects of creative city policies in Berlin has demonstrated, they reinforce social and ethnic boundaries (Jakob, 2010), conform to neoliberal values, and feed into gentrification processes that, for example, create 'diverse' neighbourhoods where 'difference' has no place (Bodirsky, 2012).

In comparison to Berlin, London seems to have a slightly longer history of championing its cultural and creative industries, going back to the late 1980s and increasing in intensity since the first DCMS *Creative Industries Mapping Document* was published in 1998 (Foord, 2008). Similar to Berlin, "the main focus of policy makers and politicians has not been on cultural production, but on place marketing and consumption: namely the instrumental use of culture and creativity to attract 'real' (high tech manufacturing) jobs" (Pratt and Hutton, 2013: 89). A statement by former Mayor of London, Boris Johnson (GLA, 2014: 11), reflects this instrumentalist stance: "Our culture and creative talent is central to promoting London as a place to visit, work and study and to attracting foreign investment and multinational companies."

Florida's arguments and the creative city narrative have also been taken up in the field of classical music. The aforementioned report (LSE, 2012) on the economic impact of London's conservatoires draws on Florida's ideas. The report echoes an instrumentalist approach to culture by foregrounding the role that conservatoires play in training professional musicians whose performances generate ticket sales and attract tourists. It argues that the conservatoires form part of London's music industry eco-system, which in itself is an essential component of London's creative economy that, in turn, contributes substantially to economic growth in London and the United Kingdom. While the report also highlights the potential social contributions of conservatoires through outreach projects, it does not consider the lack of diversity amongst conservatoire students (see chapter two), criticisms of substantial public support for classical music (Laing and York, 2000; Warwick Commission, 2015), and the precarious working conditions characterising the sector (see chapters one and five). The lack of attention to issues around inequalities and working conditions chimes with the neoliberal agenda of creative city discourses. As in the case of Berlin, the creative city narrative continues to be influential in London (see, for example, GLA, 2014, discussed above), despite existing critiques. Having outlined the industry and policy contexts in which the research participants' work is embedded, the next section will provide a detailed discussion of Williams's notion of structures of feeling and discuss commonalities in how cultural work was experienced in London and Berlin.

Structures of feeling: London and Berlin as cosmopolitan

As I stated in the introduction to this chapter, Williams's (1977: 132) notion of structures of feeling attempts to grasp "characteristic elements of impulse, restraint, and tone; specifically affective elements of consciousness and relationships". Experience is central to the concept of structures of feeling (Longhurst, 1991; Williams, 1977); "what seems to interest Williams is the very basic idea, yet very complex phenomenon, of the lived presence" (Sharma and Tygstrup, 2015: 1). Indeed, Devika Sharma and Frederik Tygstrup (2015: 2) usefully suggest that Williams complements "the analysis of the social and material infrastructure of reality with a third layer: that of affective infrastructure". The attention to affect and feeling usefully maps onto this book's focus on subjectivity.

The notion of structures of feeling speaks to this chapter's more specific concern with the feelings that underpin cultural work in particular urban settings. Williams's concept lends itself to analyses of what it is like to be in a particular place. As Williams (2001 [1961]: 63) himself explained, "[t]he most difficult thing to get hold of, in studying any past period, is this felt sense of the quality of life at a particular place and time" or, as Stuart Hall (1993: 351; emphasis in original) put it, exploring "the way meanings and values were *lived* in real lives, in actual communities". Indeed, several scholars have pointed to the importance of the concept of structures of feeling in understanding the patterning of experience in particular places (Jackson, 1991). As Mark Banks (2007: 148) has argued, the notion

> offers theorists a potential tool for dismantling some of the complexities of local social formations, in so far as it offers a way of thinking about localities as more than simply 'labour markets', but as places possessed of more intangible and ethereal socializing structures.
>
> (2007: 148)

Ian Taylor et al. (1996) explored the local structures of feeling in two cities (Manchester and Sheffield). This involved "an attempt to listen closely to the voices of people living in these two cities – hearing their troubles, fears and anxieties as to 'what's happening to our city'" (1996: 14). The foci on feelings and on listening closely work well with my analytical framework informed by critical discursive psychology and recent modifications of this approach (see chapter one). My focus on patterns in talk speaks to Williams's insistence that he is discussing a structure, a "set" (1977: 132) and something that is in some sense organised. As the subsequent sections will demonstrate, the research participants' talk about living and working in Berlin and London was definitely patterned. It contained specific "elements" (132), which, through analysis, come together to elucidate the structures of feeling in London and Berlin.

Research participants in both places spoke about a feeling that London and Berlin were cosmopolitan. According to Ricarda, "Berlin is feeling quite cosmopolitan" where "you meet people from all over the world" (Gesche) and where "everybody comes from all over the world to play music" (Gudrun). Esther echoed these sentiments when sharing her feelings about living in London:

> I do like it here. It is quite cosmopolitan. I just like this place, to be honest. I can't really see myself living somewhere else, maybe in Rome, but I do like this cosmopolitanism. It is very open and very liberal.

The sense of openness was also something that Kara picked up on when discussing her experiences of freelancing with London orchestras. Kara, who then lived in Berlin but who had studied in London, stated: "I do really like the opportunities you can get there, how easily you can freelance there in the orchestras, how open they are to foreigners, as I'm not English."

The feelings of cosmopolitanism and openness were also tied to a sense of greater freedom. Faith felt that London was "very free in the sense that I feel that – like in comparison with [East Asian country] I don't feel so judged here. You have the freedom to do a lot of things." The sense of being able to do what you want was equally pronounced in Berlin: "there are a lot of people who do it their way and who manage because it is much more normal to do that" (Annabel). Annabel linked this to "the people, and to the inspiration, and to the environment and also the acceptance" of Berlin. Clarissa echoed this sentiment:

> I believe that everybody here can do what they want and I think that's the great thing about this city. So you don't dash against certain societal prejudices. I mean, yes definitely. And this is also the great thing about the city, so that everything is really possible.

These statements celebrate London's and Berlin's openness. Clarissa's statement is particularly celebratory with the repeated casting of Berlin's openness as a "great thing".

The research participants' sense of Berlin as cosmopolitan, open, and free may reflect the city's tolerant and liberal culture inherited from the 1970s and 1980s. But their statements also chime with the creative city narrative discussed above which constructs Berlin as a tolerant place that attracts talent from all over the world. Indeed, Berlin's city marketing campaigns in the 1990s explicitly stressed "the 'cosmopolitan' and 'world open' character of 'The New Berlin'" (Colomb, 2012a: 248). However, and as Colomb (2012a) goes on to argue, these early marketing campaigns did not home in on the multi-ethnic mix of ordinary neighbourhoods or the contribution of existing migrant communities to the cultural life of the city. Instead, they focused on a global, mobile elite of professionals such as Sir Simon Rattle who was appointed artistic director of Philharmonie Berlin and chief conductor of the Berliner Philharmoniker in 2002. These marketing strategies gradually changed in the 2000s and began to emphasise Berlin's ethnic diversity. Again, however, diversity was promoted as a location factor for creative entrepreneurs and the hype around it contrasted with the city government's actual management of ethnic-cultural diversity (Colomb, 2012a; see also Bodirsky, 2012; Jakob, 2010).

Reading the research participants' comments about Berlin and London's cosmopolitanism in light of some of their statements about diversity in the classical music sector (see chapter three) further complicates the celebratory accounts offered here. While I do not want to dispute that the structures of feeling in both cities are marked by a sense of cosmopolitanism, openness, and tolerance, it is worth drawing attention to some of the tensions that remain unacknowledged in these celebratory statements. The portrayal of Berlin and London as cosmopolitan seems to parallel the research participants' depiction of the classical music profession as 'international' and 'very open' (see chapter three). As I argued in chapter three, however, references to the classical music industry's openness and internationalism figured as cover terms that brush aside existing ethnic and racial inequalities. Thus, there seem to be interesting parallels between the portrayal of London and Berlin as cosmopolitan and tolerant, and the research participants' depiction of the classical music profession as international and open. In both accounts, racial and ethnic inequalities remain unacknowledged.

London: hard, happening, and seemingly impossible to escape

While the structures of feeling in London and Berlin converged around the sense of a prevailing cosmopolitanism, there were also marked differences, notably around the feeling that life was hard and expensive in London, and easy and cheap in Berlin. When I asked the research participants what it was like to live and work in or around London, they overwhelmingly responded that it was difficult. Amanda compared life in London to other places in the United Kingdom, describing it as "hard" several times:

> I think it's harder. I was at a wedding in the summer in Wales, and my friend who was getting married, she is a harpist, so I was sitting at a table with all harpists, but they were mostly like older, kind of 50s, so they made their careers in Wales. And I don't know, one of them said to me it's so hard in London. And it is hard.

Perhaps unsurprisingly, high living costs were frequently referenced in portrayals of life in London as difficult. When telling me about her experience of living in London, Eve said it's "hard, very hard. At the minute I have no money, I am not going to lie. I am struggling a lot." Sasha told me that she really "struggled" to live off her income and Ashley emphasised that "we really do have to watch the pennies, to be honest, especially if you want to stay in London." Susan echoed these sentiments when she said: "Someone I know uses that phrase that you are always running to stand still in London because financially, you know, it's tricky. It's really expensive, and rent is ridiculous, and – it's hard, really hard."

Apart from its high living costs, London was constructed as a "tough" (Saaga) place to live due to the amount of travelling required, especially for freelance musicians:

> It's tricky as a freelance musician. I think most of my colleagues would say we constantly have to take on work even though we are really really tired. And sometimes you might go for two weeks straight without one day off. Which is horrific. Especially because I think a lot of us end up travelling a lot. This is not just travelling within London, but out of London. It could be two/ three hours one way and back again, so you are going off doing a rehearsal and . . . So, you know, it's pretty difficult.
>
> (Kim)

Lauren told me, "I can spend two and a half hours travelling in a day. If I have got three or four different jobs in different places, much more than that." Kara also felt that, apart from the high living costs, travel made life hard in London. Reflecting on the fact that she had to travel across the city to teach private students and that they would not reimburse her travel expenses, she stated: "This is really a no-go in London. There is no way that you will get travel expenses. That's what makes life hard there; if it would be a tiny bit smaller." In these statements, life in London is overwhelmingly constructed as hard, suggesting that a sense of hardship constitutes a central element of the structure of feeling in London. This resonates with Forkert's (2013: 57) findings on artistic lives in London where "[t]he overall impression was of lives that were difficult to sustain, particularly in the long-term."

As Forkert (2013) reminds us, it is a truism that London is an extremely expensive place to live and high housing costs are a crucial factor. As the *Housing in London* (GLA, 2015b) report has demonstrated, housing costs have risen substantially. "Between 2005 and 2014 average private rents in London rose 29%" (75) and "[t]he median rent for a privately rented home in London (excluding any cases where the tenant receives Housing Benefit) is £1,350, more than twice as high as the median in England as a whole" (76). Equally, "[t]he affordability of owner occupation is at its worst ever level in London, while in the UK as a whole houses are still a little more affordable than they were before the recession" (57). There is thus a stark difference between housing costs in London and elsewhere in the country. In this context, it is perhaps no surprise that 24 per cent of young adults (aged between 20–34) in London live with their parents and that this percentage has increased rapidly in recent years (GLA, 2015b). Low to middle earners have been priced out of the city centre (GLA, 2015c) and, as the centre becomes richer and leaves behind outer districts, social inequalities increase.

Several factors have led to the rise in housing costs in London, such as the decline of council housing as well as the shift towards higher levels of owner-occupation in the 1980s and 1990s (Forkert, 2013). According to Forkert (2013: 52), the "shift from council or private tenancy towards owner-occupation was both productive and symptomatic of a property speculation boom which began in the early 1990s and continued until the financial crisis". The property boom has had several consequences, including high rents and property prices, as well as social and generational inequalities where the younger generation is particularly hard hit by high housing costs. Within the wider context of the branding and positioning of London as a creative city, high housing costs pose a particular dilemma. Apart from adding to social inequalities, they are also "driving out culture and creativity by making cities unaffordable for many local artists and cultural producers" (GLA, 2015c: 8). More specifically, "gentrification, based upon the initial spark of cultural capital of art, often results in the demise of that very art and cultural practice" (Pratt, 2011: 127). This dilemma has been well documented and been described as "one of the major paradoxes of the rise to prominence of place marketing strategies" (Colomb, 2012a: 266). Even celebratory policy documents, such as GLA's reports *Cultural Metropolis* (2014) and *World Cities Culture Report*

(2015c) have acknowledged "that while there are considerable property demands for housing, education and other services, artists make an important contribution to London's creative economy and cultural distinctiveness, and need workspace to be able to do this" (GLA, 2014: 91). Reflecting the creative city narrative's instrumentalist outlook, the reports highlight artists' economic contribution rather than other benefits of a vibrant cultural life in a city. Cultural workers, including the research participants interviewed for this study, are caught up in these dynamics and have to make various arrangements to reduce living costs.

In line with the trend described above of young Londoners living with their parents, some of the research participants had not yet moved out. Kim, for example, told me:

> I'm lucky, I live with my parents. I pay rent, but I probably, to be honest, especially in the area I live in, in [middle-class North London neighbourhood], I probably don't pay as much as people in [middle-class North London neighbourhood] would pay, so I'm very lucky. And at the moment, I actually haven't paid this month's rent to my parents because I'm having trouble working and also paying for my course. So, you know, it is tricky.

However, most research participants rented. Due to high property prices, as well as low and irregular incomes, home ownership was out of reach for most.[4] Renting in the private sector also proved difficult, given that renters enjoy comparatively little protection in the United Kingdom with regards, for example, to rent rises or the duration of tenancy agreements (Hill, 2015). Due to this situation, the research participants had to find other solutions, such as relying on the (probably rare) goodwill of landlords or landladies. Liz and Holly told me:

> The good thing with my landlady as well is that she's quite wealthy, and she doesn't really need – she doesn't need to charge me – you know, she's happy for the amount of rent that I pay, and she can make improvements to the house – but you know she's got a lot of investments and she's not looking to make money out of me. But then you think "well what would happen if I would have to leave, if I had to go back to kind of paying real market rates?" I certainly couldn't buy a house – because yes, the bank might lend me, if I can show them three years' worth of freelance income they would probably lend me, but they would only lend me three times my salary. So you might be able to buy a parking space or something but . . . and also, I would feel very worried to have a mortgage, because I just can't know from year to year, so yeah, there is a lot of insecurity.
>
> (Liz)

> I live in a shared flat, but it is incredibly reasonable, but, as in rent-wise, and I think it is because my landlord is an artist and he is an incredibly prolific artist, and all of his children are musicians, and I just get the impression

that they have an understanding of how difficult it is to be a musician [. . .] I think if I wasn't living here, I would be living at home, which would be a nightmare. Yeah, actually, I don't know what I would do. I don't know what I would do if – well, I do know. I would be living at home, which wouldn't be, that would be awful.

(Holly)

Liz and Holly had special arrangements that enabled them to pay less rent and to pursue cultural work in London. As the statements show, however, the arrangements are precarious, tying into a sense of "insecurity" (Liz) where Holly would not know "what to do" if the arrangement changed (see also chapter five). As arrangements, the living situations were temporary. The underpinning structure of feeling was not only that life in London was hard, but also uncertain.

An alternative way of negotiating high housing costs was to move away from London. Kelly had moved to East Anglia because she could not afford to live on her own in the city. Christine had also moved out of London, telling me that the suburb she lived in "is quite an expensive place to live still, but still not as expensive as London, so yeah, it is a very popular place if you commute". Jane had moved away and noted "a lot of my colleagues, the older we get, into our 30s, people are moving out of town and commuting in a bit more rather than living in rough areas, because it is not a really well-paid job". While these research participants had moved away to avoid high living costs, the majority felt that they had to live and work in the city, as this was where the work was, particularly for freelancers. According to Sasha, "London is the only place in England that you can freelance in." Janine shared this sentiment by saying "if you want to be involved in lots of ensembles and things you need to be in London." Linda confided that she would not be able to move away "because, although obviously London is expensive, it's also where the work is, so if I lived somewhere cheaper I wouldn't get enough work, so I'd probably be in exactly the same situation." Equally, Lauren said

London is probably the only place where I could do my job [. . .] Maybe New York, there will be a scene big enough there to do the kind of work that I do. I'm not sure. Without contacts, it would be very difficult. So London is where the work is.

In these statements, London is constructed as a happening place for musicians, but also as the only place where work, and in particular freelance work, can be pursued. And while some research participants had moved away from London to benefit from lower housing costs, they commuted back into the city to pursue all, or at least some aspects, of their work.

The sense that London offered work meant that many research participants felt they did not have the option of moving elsewhere. This was sometimes experienced as stifling. According to Isabella, "London is a huge place where you meet people and you need that, because without that you are nowhere. You feel strangled very often as you don't know what to do financially." Eve also found life in London was "stressful" and went on to say:

> If one was ever to get work it would be here. So I have to just sort of rely on that, this is the right place, it is just difficult for everyone right now. Sort of having to keep your head down in an ignorant bliss, and keep going, just everyone in the same boat. It's fine, it's okay!

London's vibrant music scene combined with high living costs made some research participants feel "strangled" (Isabella) where the only option is to keep "your head down in an ignorant bliss" (Eve, see also chapter five). To be sure, London's vibrancy was also experienced as exciting. In discussing her working life in London, Nora said, "it does feel that you are sort of certainly at the centre of it [. . .] I definitely feel it is the right place to be now." Apart from being at the centre of things, Lauren felt there was a sense of possibility in London:

> I feel like there is possibility here that isn't in other places, and that if you are available and ready for those opportunities, you can take them, you know. And where else are you gonna get that kind of feeling? It's cool – it's really cool.

Similar to accounts of other cultural workers (see, for example, Taylor and Littleton, 2012), Lauren's statement celebrates the opportunities available in the city.

As the interview extracts demonstrate, a further element of the structure of feeling in London was a sense of inevitability. London was portrayed as a happening place for musicians that offered work. Some experienced this as limiting their options because they felt they could not move away, while others found London's vibrancy exciting or had taken the step to move out of the city. Arguably, the structure of feeling in London consisted of at least four elements: a sense that life in London is cosmopolitan, hard, and insecure but also, somehow, unavoidable as a musician, whether this was experienced positively or negatively. As we will see in the next section, a sense of hardship was much less pronounced in the structure of feeling in Berlin. Berlin was equally constructed as a happening place for musicians, but one that was almost luxuriously cheap.

Berlin: happening and affordable, but changing

When I asked Kira what it felt like to live in Berlin, she said that she was "happy to be in Berlin. There is so much culture on offer." Indeed, Annegret told me that she had always wanted to go to Berlin:

> As a musician you can always see or do new things here. In a way, for everything you could do, there is an audience somewhere or the opportunity to

perform, or to listen. If I wanted to, I could go to three concerts every day, no matter – the most diverse genres ever. Yes, there is simply a lot one can do. And we, as students also have a big spectrum of freelance opportunities [Mucken] available to us where we can play.

Zola echoed these sentiments by stating:

In terms of classical music, there is definitely a lot going on, you have three huge opera houses and huge four to five orchestras, and lots of ensembles, lots of opportunities and lots of soloists coming and going. You can pretty much hear anyone here, like every week there comes Lang Lang, and there goes Domingo, you can hear everyone.

Interestingly, Berlin was primarily constructed as a happening place because of the various cultural activities on offer. While Annegret and Zola mentioned freelance opportunities, the emphasis on work was less pronounced. Having named the high number of big orchestras in Berlin, Kristina went on to say, "that's a lot. You can always go to a concert or to some performances. I don't think that you'd get bored." Similarly, Monika felt that "you can have so many experiences in Berlin. And I think, especially if you are an artist, somehow, it's very inspiring." In comparison to the research participants' construction of London's cultural vibrancy as offering work, Berlin's cultural scene was portrayed as vibrant because of what could be consumed and experienced. There are several possible explanations for why the research participants portrayed London and Berlin's vibrant cultural sectors in contrasting ways. Arguably, one explanation is that concerns about making a living were less at the forefront of the structure of feeling in Berlin due to the city's low living costs.

When I asked Jette about her feelings about living in Berlin, she said:

I find it quite luxurious, in Berlin, if I compare it to other cities. In Berlin, you can somehow, at least still at the moment, have lunch at every corner for four or five Euros and nowhere is going out as cheap as it is in Berlin.

Monika felt that Berlin "was still pretty comfortable to live" and, according to Gesche, living in Berlin had many advantages: "It is cheap, studying is cheap, you can live well here." As I indicated in chapter one, the research participants came from a range of countries. Gesche was one of several research participants who had moved to Berlin from abroad and who emphasised the differences in rents between Berlin and other cities.[5] Lorraine, who had moved to Berlin from the United States, said that "the city is so lively and compared to other cities you can live very reasonably". Stefanie had also moved to Berlin from the United States and said she could "absolutely live" on her scholarship money (€750 a month):

Funnily, I'm paying basically the same for rent here as I was paying in [small town in the Midwest of the United States], which is absolutely ridiculous. If

I were living in New York or Boston, I mean I would be paying four times as much or more. And in terms of living expenses it is really astoundingly affordable now.

Kira echoed the sentiment that living costs "can't get any better than that, right? So, London is different, Paris too, I believe. When I tell people about the rent I pay, they are like 'what?'" These statements portray Berlin as cheap and affordable, especially in comparison to other cities internationally.

In fact, several research participants compared Berlin's living costs favourably to those in London. Arguably, they drew this comparison because they knew that my study explored the working lives of musicians in both cities. When I asked Gudrun about her experiences of living in Berlin, she said: "For now, it's still the case that Berlin is not very expensive to live in. I imagine that it is much more difficult in London to get a cheap flat." As I demonstrated in the previous chapter, Carolyn had actually moved from London to Berlin in order to focus on her work:

I live on my own, so I'm paying less to live on my own than with four people in London. And I couldn't carry on to do that in London. I had to move to live on my own, I knew for my [work] I had to give up teaching, and I just could not really envisage that I could do that in London at the moment on what I earn. So for me it was such a gift, it was almost a no-brainer really.

Another research participant, Ricarda, had also moved to Berlin from London. She was one of the few research participants who had a permanent orchestral position and told me:

Honestly, I'm feeling like I hit the jackpot really 'cause I get to live somewhere gorgeous and it's not expensive [. . .] There's, I feel London has always some kind of a compromise, which in Berlin you don't necessarily have to have. So I'm very happy here.

Interestingly, Sophie also had a permanent orchestral post in Berlin and used the same metaphor of hitting the jackpot:

So I would say, honestly, I believe, it is pretty much a paradise. Because you can live well in the city on the income and because we play in great concert halls [. . .] And yes, I believe, it's great, I believe that most feel that it's really, like hitting the jackpot, really. And if you hear, so for example about London, how difficult it is for them and that, for example, they have to work on the side. This is all voluntary for us.

These statements establish a stark contrast between London and Berlin and position Berlin as inexpensive (see also Forkert, 2013). Ricarda and Sophie use a particularly positive metaphor by describing their life in Berlin as "hitting the jackpot". As opposed to the majority of research participants who worked as freelancers (see chapters one and five), Ricarda and Sophie both had permanent, well-paid jobs in orchestras. However, it was not only orchestral musicians who lauded Berlin's affordability. Students and freelancers also described life in Berlin as "luxurious" (Jette), "comfortable" (Monika), a "gift" (Carolyn), and difficult to top (Kira). In this context, it is worth recalling that most research participants were from a middle-class background (see chapter one). While living costs in Berlin are comparatively low – especially in relation to London – the research participants' middle-class backgrounds probably contributed to a sense that Berlin was affordable.

Those participants who had moved to Berlin from abroad seemed to be particularly smitten by its affordability. As Andrej Holm (2013: 181) has argued, Berlin and particularly certain neighbourhoods, such as the borough of Neukölln, have been presented as a "global destination for young international artists and other creatives". The portrayal of Berlin as a great city for artists shines through the research participants' accounts. This positioning of Berlin is linked to wider processes of gentrification that seem to be increasingly "driven by an international creative class" (Holm, 2013: 181). This means that local rents are determined by comparison to other places, such as New York, Boston, London, or Paris, to name the cities that the research participants mentioned. According to Holm (2013), this has resulted in the displacement of the urban poor, particularly in neighbourhoods that are hyped internationally, such as Berlin's Neukölln. Almost all of the research participants lived in gentrifying or gentrified areas, such as Prenzlauer Berg, Kreuzberg, and Neukölln. As Holm's analysis suggests, their celebratory accounts about Berlin's affordability have to be placed in the wider context of gentrification. Indeed, and as the following section will demonstrate, processes of gentrification have also had an effect on the subjective experiences of the research participants. They sensed that change was taking place, which qualified their feelings about Berlin's favourable living conditions and added another element to the structure of feeling.

The celebratory statements about Berlin's low living costs often went hand in hand with claims that change was happening or immanent, particularly in terms of increasing rents. Having stated that Berlin was a "comfortable" place to live, Monika went on to say:

> Rents are increasing rapidly. If I compare what I paid for my room in our flat share three years ago to now . . . We just rented out one of the rooms, the ad, which we wrote – it's no comparison. It is really unbelievable how rents are increasing and how demand is rising and how many people are simply looking for a place to live for months and can't find anything. But still, I believe, in comparison to other big cities, it is still relatively comfortable.

Annabel, too, stated that one could live on "very little" in Berlin but added that this was changing: "And you do notice that the pressure is increasing, that rents are getting higher, that everybody is struggling a bit, that there are cuts everywhere."

There was a sense that this change had happened rapidly. Kristina felt that rents had "exploded" and, as Astrid pointed out, housing costs had risen considerably "even during the relatively short amount of time that I've lived here".

According to Holm (2013), rents in Berlin were comparatively low in the period between the early 1990s and the mid-2000s. This was due to a range of factors, such as public subsidies, house building, publicly owned housing, and rent control. "This has completely changed. Berlin's rent levels are definitely on the up now and despite the still sobering overall economic situation the city shows the most intensive rent increases in Germany" (Holm, 2013: 172). The main reason for this is a shift in Berlin's housing policies, which saw cuts to subsidies and a decrease in house building. This combined with rising numbers of households and led to intense pressure on the housing market. On average, since 2003, rents have increased by 23 per cent (Holm, 2013). This applies to existing tenancy agreements. Where new tenancy agreements were formed, rent hikes were even higher (Holm, 2013; see also Berliner Mietspiegel, 2013; Forkert, 2013; McRobbie et al., 2016; Uffer, 2013). As one consequence of these developments, talk about gentrification has entered daily parlance amongst Berliners, but also the media and political debates (Holm, 2013; see also Bernt and Holm, 2009). Similar to debates about high housing costs in London, cultural workers' livelihoods are considered to be under threat. As stated in a recent report on Berlin's cultural sector (Berlin Senate, 2014a: 86): "Rather than many artists and creative artists seeing themselves as pioneers reclaiming spaces, they now tend to feel driven [sic] by the real estate market." As I have discussed in the context of London, gentrification processes pose a range of challenges and, in the creative city context, lead to a particular dilemma where "gentrification generally limits the opportunities for creative pioneers" (Bader and Scharenberg, 2013 [2009]: 255).

The effects of rising rents worried several research participants. Sonja had lived and freelanced in Berlin for many years and shared her concerns:

> I could and can live the way I have because living costs in Berlin are so low, have been so low. And this is currently changing. You've probably already heard this often. And what most of those who work in the creative sector earn as freelancers is not increasing proportionally. And, obviously, this leads to a widening gap, which is a bit worrying.

Elena also commented on the gap between rising rents and stagnating or low earnings. "Rents are rising very strongly, but in Berlin you earn a lot less as a freelancer than in Munich or Stuttgart, for example." Several research participants highlighted the low pay for freelance gigs in Berlin: "I believe that the fees in Berlin, or, in fact, I know, are simply really bad" (Annegret). The average fee for a gig seemed to be around €150. According to Elena, "a freelance gig for little money in Munich starts at €300. In Berlin you usually play for €150." In addition, and in line with the figures presented in the previous chapter on the precarious working conditions at music schools in Berlin (Bossen, 2012), many research participants taught on a freelance basis and earned comparatively little. Research on the income of cultural workers in Berlin has actually demonstrated that "earnings of Berlin's creative workforce continue to lag behind those in other regions" (Berlin Senate, 2014a: 82). Despite rising living costs, the income of cultural workers has increased "very little" in the time period between 2005–2011 (2014a: 83).

In the context of the research participants' discussion of changes that were taking place in Berlin, several also commented on rising competition amongst musicians, which they attributed to a constantly growing number of musicians living and working in Berlin. According to Elena, "there are very very many opportunities in Berlin. But there is also an incredibly high number of musicians." Jasmin found:

> Berlin is incredibly convenient, if you are a musician. But, I don't know, somehow, this also attracts many to come to Berlin, many musicians. Even though, the more musicians who come here, the worse it gets. Everybody knows that, but somehow, nobody leaves. So, it is getting more expensive, but it is still really relatively cheap in comparison to other cities.

Gudrun also commented on Berlin's popularity amongst musicians:

> This has the advantage that you find people who play all sorts of genres. On the other hand, there are probably also better musicians at every corner, who play at a lower price. So it has different aspects. But if you play in a club or somewhere, you basically don't make anything.

These statements illustrate that the research participants had mixed feelings about Berlin's status as a music hub. Berlin's vibrant music sector was said to attract skilled musicians but also, according to the research participants, meant rising competition and undercutting. More generally, and as I discussed in chapter one, growing numbers of music graduates as well as fewer orchestral jobs have led to increased competition for work in the classical music sector (Gembris and Langner, 2005; Mertens, 2012 [2005]). Rising rents, low earnings, and intensifying competition gave rise to a feeling that Berlin's affordability may not last. A sense of immanent change and related insecurity thus constituted a further element of the structure of feeling in Berlin. Notably, the structures of feeling in London and Berlin both contained an element of insecurity, linked to precarious living arrangements in London and a sense of immanent change in Berlin.

Conclusion

This chapter has explored the structures of feeling in London and Berlin. More specifically, it asked what it felt like to do cultural work in the two cities. The chapter began with a brief discussion of the particularity of Berlin, noting, for example, the lasting effects of the reunification on Berlin's urban economy. The main focus of this chapter's opening section was, however, on the status of London and Berlin as creative cities. Having provided an overview of the cultural and music sectors in both cities, I homed in on debates about the creative city and the influence of Florida's ideas on urban policies around the world. As my discussion of policy initiatives in London and Berlin has shown, both cities adopted the creative city narrative, despite existing criticisms of its neoliberal and instrumentalist outlook, as well as the role it plays in widening inequalities.

Against this backdrop, the chapter drew on Williams's notion of structures of feeling to grasp what it feels like to live and work in London and Berlin. As my analysis has shown, the structures of feeling were different in London and Berlin. Both places were described as cosmopolitan, but in London, a feeling of hardship was central along with a sense of insecurity about temporary living arrangements. Some experienced London's vibrancy and status as a music hub as exciting, while others felt that it was almost impossible to escape London and its high living costs. Berlin, by contrast, was overwhelmingly described as cheap, comfortable, and sometimes even luxurious. Nevertheless, a sense of insecurity also constituted an element of the structure of feeling in Berlin. Due to rising rents, stagnant or low wages, and intensifying competition amongst musicians, there was a fear that Berlin's favourable living conditions were about to change. In short, there was a sense of cosmopolitanism, openness, and vibrancy in London and Berlin. London was portrayed as a hard place to live and this portrayal contrasted with affirmative accounts of Berlin as affordable. And yet, insecurity seemed to permeate the accounts of the research participants in both cities, linked to precarious living arrangements in London and a sense that cultural workers' ideal living conditions were about to change in Berlin.

What are we to make of these differences in the structures of feeling in Berlin and London? First, and very much resonating with Forkert's study (2013), the material conditions of particular urban settings shape subjective experiences of cultural work. This may be a truism, but it is worth highlighting in the context of the prevalence of creative city narratives that tend to foreground 'buzz' at the expense of dealing with much more challenging political questions about work opportunities, wage levels, and housing costs. Second, my analysis of structures of feeling and the finding that there were local specificities chimes with Pratt's (2011: 123) call for "a more nuanced and subtle approach of creativity, culture and cities, one that is *situated* and not universal". By attending to the affective aspects of cultural work in Berlin and London, this chapter sought to provide a nuanced account of subjective experiences in relation to cultural work and the ways this plays out in particular urban settings.

Having explored the role of subjectivity in the context of persisting inequalities in the cultural and creative industries (see chapter two), the ways in which the research participants made sense of ongoing inequalities (see chapter three), the contours of entrepreneurial subjectivity (see chapter four), and subjective experiences of precarious work (see chapter five), this chapter approached the interplay between subjectivity and cultural work in the classical music profession by focusing on the ways in which urban settings affect cultural workers' structures of feeling. As such, I hope that this chapter has embedded the research participants accounts, discussed throughout this book, in their wider urban and national contexts. In the next and final part, the conclusion, I will summarise my key arguments and contributions, discuss the study's limitations, and point to some ways in which the concerns raised in this book – especially the persistence of inequalities – may be addressed.

Notes

1 As this introduction to my chapter demonstrates, my analysis of structures of feeling is not exhaustive. Other, important themes, such as that of resistance to neoliberal urban policies of which the creative city narrative forms part, remain unexplored. In Berlin, for example, there has been growing opposition to growth-oriented urban policy agendas (Bernt et al., 2013; Dohnke, 2013; Novy and Colomb, 2013; McRobbie, 2015), leading to questions of whether forms of resistance constitute another element of the structure of feeling in Berlin. I do not address these issues here because my empirical material did not contain sufficient data on this issue.
2 "The Creative Economy [. . .] encompasses people with creative occupations working in the creative industries, as well as workers with creative occupations working in any other industry, and also people in a non-creative job working in a creative industry" (GLA, 2015a: 4).
3 The report also highlighted "the patchiness of music education provision, with just ten per cent of London's secondary schools being responsible for almost half of all the students taking music qualification" (GLA, 2014: 79). This pertains to the wider issue of inequalities in music education and training (see chapter two).
4 To my knowledge, two research participants owned a property in London. They had managed to do so with their parents' financial support.
5 The rate of home ownership in Germany is comparatively low at around 42 per cent (Palmer, 2011), which is why I do not discuss home ownership in the context of the research participants' feelings about living in Berlin.

References

Bader, I., & Scharenberg, A. (2013 [2009]). The sound of Berlin: Subculture and global music industry. In M. Bernt, B. Grell, & A. Holm (Eds.), *The Berlin reader: A compendium on urban change and activism* (pp. 239–260). Bielefeld: Transcript.

Banks, M. (2007). *The politics of cultural work*. Basingstoke: Palgrave Macmillan.

Berlin Senate (2014a). *Third creative industries report: Development and potential.* Accessed 1 December 2016. Available at: www.berlin.de/projektzukunft/uploads/tx_news/KWB13_Inhalt_engl.pdf

Berlin Senate (2014b). *Kulturförderbericht 2014 des Landes Berlin.* Accessed 1 December 2016. Available at: www.berlin.de/sen/kultur/kulturpolitik/www.berlin.de/sen/kultur/kulturpolitik/

Berlin Senate (2015). *Musikwirtschaft in Berlin.* Accessed 1 December 2016. Available at: www.berlin-partner.de/fileadmin/user_upload/01_chefredaktion/02_pdf/publikationen/Musikwirtschaft_de.pdf

Berliner Mietspiegel (2013). *Berliner Mietspiegel 2013*. Berlin: Senatsverwaltung für Stadtentwicklung und Umwelt. Accessed 1 December 2016. Available at: www.stad tentwicklung.berlin.de/wohnen/mietspiegel

Bernt, M., Grell, B., & Holm, A. (Eds.). (2013). *The Berlin reader: A compendium on urban change and activism*. Bielefeld: Transcript.

Bernt, M., & Holm, A. (2009). Is it, or is not? The conceptualisation of gentrification and displacement and its political implications in the case of Berlin-Prenzlauer Berg. *City*, *13*(2–3), 312–324.

Bodirsky, K. (2012). Culture for competitiveness: Valuing diversity in EU-Europe and the 'creative city' of Berlin. *International Journal of Cultural Policy*, *18*(4), 455–473.

Bossen, A. (2012). *Einkommenssituation und Arbeitsbedingungen von Musikschullehrkräften und Privatmusiklehrern 2012*. Berlin: Verdi Fachgruppe Musik. Accessed 1 December 2016. Available at: www.miz.org/dokumente/2012_verdi_umfrage.pdf

Bull, A., & Scharff, C. (2017). 'McDonalds' music' versus 'serious music': how production and consumption practices help to reproduce class inequality in the classical music profession. *Cultural Sociology*. Accessed 20 July 2017. Available at: http://journals.sagepub. com/doi/pdf/10.1177/1749975517711045

Catungal, J. P., Leslie, D., & Hii, Y. (2009). Geographies of displacement in the creative city: The case of Liberty Village, Toronto. *Urban Studies*, *46*(5&6), 1095–1114.

Colomb, C. (2012a). *Staging the new Berlin: Place marketing and the politics of urban reinvention post-1989*. Oxon: Routledge.

Colomb, C. (2012b). Pushing the urban frontier: Temporary uses of space, city marketing, and the creative city discourse in 2000s Berlin. *Journal of Urban Affairs*, *34*(2), 131–152.

DiW (2013). *Struktur und Einkommen der kreativ Tätigen in Berlin*. Berlin: Deutsches Institut für Wirtschaftsforschung. Accessed 1 December 2016. Available at: www.diw. de/documents/publikationen/73/diw_01.c.430297.de/diwkompakt_2013-076.pdf

Dohnke, J. (2013). Spree riverbanks for everyone! What remains of "sink mediaspree"? In M. Bernt, B. Grell, & A. Holm (Eds.), *The Berlin reader: A compendium on urban change and activism* (pp. 261–274). Bielefeld: Transcript.

Florida, R. (2002). *The rise of the creative class*. New York: Basic Books.

Foord, J. (2008). Strategies for creative industries: An international review. *Creative Industries Journal*, *1*(2), 91–113.

Forkert, K. (2013). *Artistic lives: A study of creativity in two European cities*. Farnham, Surrey: Ashgate.

Gembris, H., & Langner, D. (2005). *Von der Musikhochschule auf den Arbeitsmarkt: Erfahrungen von Absolventen, Arbeitsmarktexperten und Hochschullehrern*. Augsburg: Wißner.

GLA (2014). *Cultural metropolis: The Mayor's culture strategy – achievements and next steps*. London: Greater London Authority. Accessed 1 December 2016. Available at: www.london.gov.uk/sites/default/files/cultural_metropolis_2014.pdf

GLA (2015a). *The creative industries in London: Working paper 70*. London: Greater London Authority. Accessed 1 December 2016. Available at: www.london.gov.uk/sites/ default/files/creative-industries-in-london.pdf

GLA (2015b). *Housing in London 2015: The evidence base for the Mayor's housing strategy*. London: Greater London Authority. Accessed 1 December 2016. Available at: www.london.gov.uk/sites/default/files/housing_in_london_2015_v3.pdf

GLA (2015c). *World cities culture report*. London: Greater London Authority. Accessed 1 December 2016. Available at: www.worldcitiescultureforum.com/publications/world-cities-culture-report-2015

Grésillon, B. (1999). Berlin, cultural metropolis: Changes in the cultural geography of Berlin since reunification. *Cultural Geographies, 6*(3), 284–294.

Hall, S. (1993). Culture, community, nation. *Cultural Studies, 7*(3), 349–363.

Hill, D. (2015). Would Ed Miliband really improve London tenants' rights and rents? *The Guardian*, 29.04.2015. Accessed 1 December 2016. Available at: www.theguardian. com/uk-news/davehillblog/2015/apr/2029/miliband-tenants-rights-and-london-rents

Holm, A. (2013). Berlin's gentrification mainstream. In M. Bernt, B. Grell, & A. Holm (Eds.), *The Berlin reader: A compendium on urban change and activism* (pp. 171–188). Berlin: Transcript.

Jackson, P. (1991). Mapping meanings: A cultural critique of locality studies. *Environment and Planning A, 23*(2), 215–228.

Jakob, D. (2010). Constructing the creative neighborhood: Hopes and limitations of creative city policies in Berlin. *City, Culture and Society, 1*(4), 193–198.

Krätke, S. (2013 [2004]). City of talents? Berlin's regional economy, socio-spatial fabric and "worst practice" urban governance. In M. Bernt, B. Grell, & A. Holm (Eds.), *The Berlin reader: A compendium on urban change and activism* (pp. 131–154). Bielefeld: Transcript.

Laing, D., & York, N. (2000). The value of music in London. *Cultural Trends, 10*(38), 1–34.

Leslie, D., & Catungal, J. P. (2012). Social justice and the creative city: Class, gender and racial inequalities. *Geography Compass, 6*(3), 111–122.

Longhurst, B. (1991). Raymond Williams and local cultures. *Environment and Planning A, 23*, 229–238.

LSE (2012). *The impact of three London conservatoires on the UK and London economies: A project for the Royal Academy of Music, the Guildhall School of Music & Drama and the Royal College of Music, with Universities UK*. London: London School of Economics and Political Science. Accessed 1 December 2016. Available at: www.lse.ac.uk/geographyAndEnvironment/research/london/pdf/LSE-London-Conservatoires-Report-FINAL-July-2012.pdf

Manske, A., & Merkel, J. (2008). *Kreative in Berlin: Eine Untersuchung zum Thema "GeisteswissenschaftlerInnen in der Kultur- und Kreativwirtschaft"*. Discussion Paper SP III 2008–401. Wissenschaftszentrum Berlin für Sozialforschung. Accessed 1 December 2016. Available at: http://econpapers.repec.org/paper/zbwwzbnew/spiii2008401.htm

McLean, H. E. (2014). Cracks in the creative city: The contradictions of community arts practice: Contradictions of community arts practice in Toronto. *International Journal of Urban and Regional Research, 38*(6), 2156–2173.

McRobbie, A. (2015). *Be creative: Making a living in the new culture industries*. Cambridge: Polity.

McRobbie, A., Strutt, D., Bandinelli, C., & Springer, B. (2016). *Fashion micro-enterprises in London, Berlin, Milan*. London: Goldsmiths University of London.

Mertens, G. (2012 [2005]). Philharmonisches Paradies? Arbeitsmarkt- und Berufssituation von Orchestermusikern. In O. Zimmermann & T. Geißler (Eds.), *Arbeitsmarkt Kultur: Vom Nischenmarkt zur Boombranche* (pp. 77–79). Berlin: Nachdruck von Beiträgen aus Politik & Kultur, Zeitung des Deutschen Kulturrates.

Monk, C. (2014). Arts council England renews funding focus on music education. *PRS Members Music Magazine*, 1.10.2014. Accessed 1 December 2016. Available at: www.m-magazine.co.uk/news/focus-funding/

Novy, J., & Colomb, C. (2013). Struggling for the right to the (creative) city in Berlin and Hamburg: New urban social movements, new 'spaces of hope'? *International Journal of Urban and Regional Research, 37*(5), 1816–1838.

Palmer, J. (2011). Brits buy homes, the Germans rent – which of us has got it right? *The Guardian,* 19.03.2011. Accessed 1 December 2016. Available at: www.theguardian. com/money/2011/mar/2019/brits-buy-germans-rent

Peck, J. (2005). Struggling with the creative class. *International Journal of Urban and Regional Research, 29*(4), 740–770.

Peck, J. (2011). Creative moments: Working culture, through municipal socialism and neo-liberal urbanism. In E. McCann & K. Ward (Eds.), *Mobile urbanism: Cities and policy making in the global age* (Vol. Globalization and community, pp. 41–70). Minneapolis, MN; London: University of Minnesota Press.

Peck, J. (2012). Austerity urbanism. *City, 16*(6), 626–655.

Pratt, A. C. (2010). Creative cities: Tensions within and between social, cultural and economic development: A critical reading of the UK experience. *City, Culture and Society, 1*(1), 13–20.

Pratt, A. C. (2011). The cultural contradictions of the creative city. *City, Culture and Society, 2*(3), 123–130.

Pratt, A. C. (2012). A world turned upside down: The creative economy, cities and the new austerity. In A. Beauclair & E. Mitchell (Eds.), *Smart, creative, sustainable, inclusive: Territorial development strategies in the age of austerity* (pp. 13–19). Seaford: Regional Studies Association.

Pratt, A. C., & Hutton, T. A. (2013). Reconceptualising the relationship between the creative economy and the city: Learning from the financial crisis. *Cities, 33,* 86–95.

Sharma, D., & Tygstrup, F. (2015). *Structures of feeling: Affectivity and the study of culture.* Berlin: De Gruyter.

Taylor, I. R., Evans, K., & Fraser, P. (1996). *A tale of two cities: Global change, local feeling and everyday life in the North of England. A study in Manchester and Sheffield.* London: Routledge.

Taylor, S., & Littleton, K. (2012). *Contemporary identities of creativity and creative work.* Farnham: Ashgate.

Uffer, S. (2013). The uneven development of Berlin's housing provision: Institutional investment and its consequences on the city and its tenants. In M. Bernt, B. Grell, & A. Holm (Eds.), *The Berlin reader: A compendium on urban change and activism* (pp. 155–170). Bielefeld: Transcript.

Warwick Commission (2015). *Enriching Britain: Culture, creativity and growth.* Coventry: University of Warwick. Accessed 1 December 2016. Available at: www2.warwick. ac.uk/research/warwickcommission/futureculture/finalreport/warwick_commission_ report_2015.pdf

Williams, R. (1977). *Marxism and literature.* Oxford: Oxford University Press.

Williams, R. (2001 [1961]). *The long revolution.* Canada, Peterborough: Broadview Press.

Key contributions, directions for further research, and recommendations

This conclusion is divided into three parts in order to revisit *Gender, Subjectivity, and Cultural Work*'s main findings and contributions, discuss directions for further analysis, and explore how we can address some of the concerns raised in this book. I begin with a summary of my contributions to existing research on inequalities in cultural work, entrepreneurialism, and precarious work. The second section charts ways in which my analysis of the interplay between gender, subjectivity, and cultural work can be taken forward. In particular, I show that my arguments can be developed further by exploring the role of subjectivity in the context of mothering, the 'aesthetic labour' (Entwistle and Wissinger, 2006; Nickson et al., 2003; Warhurst et al., 2000; Witz et al., 2003) that female cultural workers engage in, and the ways in which inequalities in classical music do not only relate to cultural production, but also consumption. The third and final section of my conclusion asks what we can do to address some of the concerns raised in this book. I briefly discuss existing research and initiatives that have challenged processes of precarisation and neoliberalisation. However, I mainly focus on the ways in which we could tackle persisting racial, class, and gender inequalities in the cultural and creative industries. In putting forward a set of recommendations,[1] I do not seek to provide a comprehensive list of proposals, but draw conclusions from my analysis of the workings of inequalities in the classical music profession.

Key findings and contributions

Inequalities in cultural work

This book brought together a wide range of studies, which have documented the lack of diversity among classical musicians in Germany and the United Kingdom. It drew on existing research, but also presented new data on the demographic backgrounds of conservatoire teachers in Germany and the United Kingdom, musicians in British orchestras, as well as students at UK conservatoires. By providing original data, *Gender, Subjectivity, and Cultural Work* addressed existing gaps in our knowledge about the demographic makeup of the classical music profession. However, I went beyond an analysis of ongoing exclusions and set out to explain the lack of workforce diversity in the classical music profession. In particular, I drew on pioneering research on inequalities in cultural work to foreground the role of subjectivity in constructions of the ideal, classical musician. In this context, I explored the gendered dynamics of self-promotion and showed that female musicians have to negotiate a range of gendered challenges when engaging in the practice, including accusations of lacking modesty, fears of not being taken seriously as an artist, and difficulties associated with 'selling yourself' in a wider, sexualised context. My findings on self-promotion are not only relevant to the classical music profession and the cultural and creative industries. They may apply to a range of work settings, especially in light of wider, cultural conversations taking place over the supposed need for women to 'lean in' (Sandberg, 2013). Self-promotion could be seen as a form of 'leaning in', but one, as I have shown, that remains circumscribed by gendered constraints.

My analysis of inequalities in the classical music profession also involved an examination of how musicians make sense of ongoing hierarchies, privileges, and exclusions. I showed that they were more open to discussing classed exclusions and that racial, and in particular gender inequalities, were talked about much more ambivalently. Gender imbalances were disarticulated through a range of rhetorical tools, including disclaimers, trivialisation, and normalisation. Crucially, my analysis did not merely document the various ways in which inequalities were talked about or silenced. It also drew on several theoretical frameworks, such as theories of individualisation, postfeminism, and neoliberalism, to make sense of the disarticulation of inequalities. As such, I demonstrated how ongoing hierarchies, privileges, and exclusions – particularly in relation to gender – become unspeakable, which provides yet another explanation for why inequalities persist in the classical music profession. As I have shown, disarticulations of inequalities have been analysed and observed in a range of work settings, within but also outside the cultural and creative industries. In this sense, my analysis has implications that reach beyond the classical music industry and the cultural sector to workplace dynamics more generally.

Entrepreneurialism

My study's innovative theoretical framework and focus on early career, female, classical musicians have enabled me to explore the experiences of individuals who appear to be entrepreneurial subjects par excellence. *Gender, Subjectivity, and Cultural Work* put young women's and cultural workers' positioning as entrepreneurial subjects centre-stage to explore how entrepreneurialism is registered and lived out. I mapped and discussed ten contours of entrepreneurial subjectivity, ranging from the understanding of the self as a business, the hiding of injuries, and the allocation of difficulties to the past to the internalisation of competition. Significantly, my analysis reframed existing accounts of competition in neoliberalism by arguing that it is not only other-directed, but also self-directed, thus working at a 'deeper' level. Further, I enriched our understanding of how exclusions play out in the context of entrepreneurial subjectivity. As I have shown, exclusionary dynamics do not only pertain to the kinds of classed, gendered, and racialised subjects that can easily lay claim to being entrepreneurial, but may lie at the heart of constitutions of entrepreneurial subjectivity. Equally important, I explored the affective register, which underpins entrepreneurial subjectivity, arguing that there is not one dominant affect, but instead a palette of emotions that entrepreneurial subjects may experience.

In presenting these arguments, *Gender, Subjectivity, and Cultural Work* has contributed to discussions on entrepreneurialism and neoliberalism in two key ways. First, based on empirical data, it explored entrepreneurial subjectivity from the ground up. Existing research, by contrast, has tended to be theoretical in focus. As such, this book has made a methodological contribution to contemporary debates on a widely discussed and timely topic. Second, I addressed questions of subjectivity, indeed of the 'psychic life' (Butler, 1997; Scharff, 2015) of entrepreneurial subjects. I use the term 'psychic life' here because it highlights my specific contribution to our understanding of entrepreneurialism. Judith Butler's (1997: 2) question, "What is the psychic form that power takes?" resonates with my interest in the psychic dimensions of entrepreneurial subjectivity. In addition, the notion of psychic life is based on the concept of subjection, which "signifies the process of becoming subordinated by power as well as the process of becoming a subject'" (2). The concept of the psychic life thus conveys the formation of subjectivities in and through power. Reflecting both of these dimensions in the term psychic life, my analysis of entrepreneurial subjectivity has not only shed light on the ways in which it is lived out on a psychic level, but has also examined how it is constituted in and through discourse.

Precarious work

A final and third set of debates that this book has contributed to relates to the issue of precarious work. My analysis of musicians' experiences of, and responses to, insecurity has highlighted a range of aspects. These include the reshaping of time in the context of precarious work, the role of workers' positioning – especially in relation to class background – in buffering uncertainties, and the affective dynamics and fluctuating feelings associated with insecure, cultural work. In fact, I showed that responses to precarious work are multifaceted and complex. The musicians exhibited an entrepreneurial attitude towards dealing with the unpredictability of their profession. However, the individualist outlook associated with this entrepreneurial mind-set was also ruptured through descriptions of being in the zone as moments that enabled a meaningful connection with the audience. More generally, my analysis showed that the pleasurable aspects of playing music – such as the highs derived from being in the zone or the ability to self-express – were deeply intertwined with some of the hardships associated with precarious work in the classical music profession. By highlighting these and other complexities, *Gender, Subjectivity, and Cultural Work* has sought to avoid a one-dimensional account of precarious, cultural work and instead brought to light both its negative and positive components.

I chose two research sites with very different material conditions to embed my analysis of precarious work in specific urban contexts. The precarious nature of cultural work was more pronounced in London, where many musicians had to rely on temporary living arrangements to navigate high housing costs and make ends meet. This gave rise to a sense of hardship and insecurity, which contrasted with the portrayal of living conditions in Berlin as affordable and almost luxurious. However, a sense of insecurity was also present in Berlin, thus cautioning against celebratory portrayals of the German capital as providing an ideal setting for cultural work. By paying careful attention to the specific, geographical, and national contexts that the musicians negotiated, *Gender, Subjectivity, and Cultural Work* adopted an international perspective. Notably, my analysis highlighted both similarities and differences in how cultural workers' location affects their sense making. While there were parallels in talk about inequalities, and entrepreneurialism, I also detected place-specific variations, particularly in relation to the experiences of living and working precariously in London and Berlin. As such, the book has provided a nuanced and situated account of the interplay between precarious, cultural work and subjectivity in specific urban and national contexts.

Directions for further analysis and study

My analysis of gender, subjectivity, and work in the classical music profession could be developed in several ways. For instance, we may revisit my discussion of gender inequalities and parenting in the cultural and creative industries. To recall, I drew attention to the difficulties of combining cultural work with having children, while cautioning against a perspective that re-cements the link between women and child rearing. However, I did not frame my discussion in terms of the interplay between parenting – and more specifically mothering – and subjectivity. As I have documented elsewhere (Scharff, 2017), the issue of mothering was on the research participants' minds, regardless of whether or not they wanted to have children, or were mothers. In particular, and supporting wider arguments for analyses of subjectivity in relation to gender and cultural work (Allen et al., 2013; Conor, 2014; Conor et al, 2015; Gill, 2014; Taylor and Littleton, 2012) and, indeed, mothering (Wreyford, 2013; 2015), the research participants feared that becoming a mother would conflict with their emotional investment in being a musician. This conflict arose both in terms of not having enough love or passion for a child, the music, and important others, but also in terms of the enormous commitment required to pursue cultural work and how this might clash with mothering. While the research participants, and especially those who were already mothers, also voiced very real concerns around practical matters, such as the cost and availability of childcare, the tensions around potentially conflicting emotional commitments of being a mother and a musician came most strongly to the fore.

Thus, we can expand debates on gender and cultural work by exploring the issue of mothering in the context of subjectivity.

My discussion of gender inequalities in the classical music profession also pointed to the various challenges that female musicians face in negotiating their femininity, appearance, and sexuality. I explored these difficulties in my analysis of the gendered dimensions of self-promotion by highlighting that 'selling yourself' is not a straightforward undertaking in a wider, sexualised context. However, another productive way to think about this is in terms of aesthetic labour (Entwistle and Wissinger, 2006; Nickson et al., 2003; Warhurst et al., 2000; Witz et al., 2003), as denoting the "mobilization, development and commodification of embodied 'dispositions'" (Witz et al., 2003: 37). The concept of aesthetic labour has been developed to capture "something of the embodied *work* some workers have to do to maintain their bodies for particular forms of employment (emphasis in original)" (Entwistle and Wissinger, 2006: 776). For example, several opera singers that I interviewed argued that it was increasingly important to look good on stage and one told me that she had recently lost a lot of weight in order to compete for roles more easily. This embodied work (and singing, of course, is itself a very embodied practice), raises the question of aesthetic labour in the classical music profession. Surely, this labour takes on different forms in various contexts and may be less pronounced in the lives of orchestral musicians and more of a feature of soloists' and opera singers' work.

Recently, Ana Sofia Elias, Rosalind Gill, and I (Elias et al., 2017) have sought to expand the notion of aesthetic labour and coined the term 'aesthetic entrepreneurship' to grasp more of the features that characterise contemporary concerns over appearance and the ways they intersect with femininity and work. In particular, we brought the concept of aesthetic labour into dialogue with feminist analyses of beauty, as well as Foucauldian notions of entrepreneurialism, to foreground the dimension of subjectivity. Like the entrepreneurial subject at work, the aesthetic entrepreneur is autonomous and self-regulating in the pursuit of the 'right look'. Preoccupations with appearance and the body constitute yet another project that the entrepreneurial subject embarks on. When mapping the contours of entrepreneurial subjectivity, I discussed the various dimensions of work on the self. They were spiritual, psychological, but also bodily. The lens of 'aesthetic entrepreneurship' could provide a useful theoretical framework for exploring these issues in more detail and tracing how they play out in relation to gender, but also race and class.

Finally, my analysis of inequalities in the classical music sector can be taken forward by attending to issues of consumption. Elsewhere, Anna Bull and I (Bull and Scharff, 2017) have shown that the links between inequalities, production, and consumption came to the fore in the research participants' discussion of their family backgrounds. Middle-class research participants used the term 'musical family' to describe an upbringing where classical music was practiced and consumed at home. By contrast, research participants from lower middle-class or working-class backgrounds reported that classical music was unfamiliar; it was not listened to at home and the research participants struggled to garner their parents' support to pursue a career as a musician. Notably, all research participants described 'being from a musical family' as a professional advantage, thereby ges-turing to the links between production, consumption, and class privilege. As Dave O'Brien and Kate Oakley (2015; see chapter one) have argued, an analysis of pro-duction *and* consumption is key to understanding the relationship between culture and social inequality. Exclusions in the classical music sector do not only play out in the realm of production, but also in the context of consumption (e.g. Bennett et al., 2009; Warwick Commission, 2015). Addressing issues of consumption can thus deepen my analysis of inequalities in the classical music industry.

I could discuss more avenues for future research, but I am limiting myself here to the dimensions that I set out to explore. As I have shown, my analysis in rela-tion to gender and, more specifically femininity in the classical music profession could be developed further by exploring the interplay between mothering and subjectivity. Another and additional way of expanding my focus on gender and subjectivity is to employ the notion of aesthetic entrepreneurship to grasp some of the links between entrepreneurialism and work on the body. Lastly, we could widen the scope of my examination of inequalities in classical music to include issues around consumption. There are thus multiple directions for further analy-ses of gender, subjectivity, and work in the classical music profession. Instead of discussing these ensuing questions in more detail, I want to use the following and final section to present a number of recommendations for addressing some of the concerns raised in this book.

Recommendations: addressing inequalities in cultural work

My analysis has brought to the fore a range of issues and I do not have recom-mendations for addressing all of these concerns. Certainly, my aim has not been to explore what can be done to counteract inequalities, processes of neoliberalisa-tion and precarisation, or to design cultural policies that would democratise the cultural sector. These aims would exceed the scope of a book and other studies as well as initiatives already engage with these issues. In relation to precarious work, for example, the research project 'Cultural Workers Organise'[2] explores how so-called flexworkers in the arts, communication, and cultural industries confront precarity or the financial and social insecurity associated with unstable employ-ment. More specifically in the context of music, the Musician's Union launched the campaign 'Work not play'[3] to support fair pay for professional musicians. And Germany features an insurance scheme for freelance cultural workers, the Kün-stlersozialkasse,[4] which covers health insurance, pensions, and nursing care insur-ance. The scheme is obligatory for freelance cultural workers and offers some protection against the insecurities related to precarious work.

Equally important, there has been resistance to neoliberal urban policies, par-ticularly in Berlin (Bernt et al., 2013; Dohnke, 2013; Novy and Colomb, 2013; McRobbie, 2015). In light of the poor social and economic outcomes of neolib-eral development, cultural workers mobilised to defend particular urban spaces and influence urban policy-making. Research and political activism have thus variously engaged with issues of precarisation and neoliberalisation. While I am not aware of studies or initiatives tackling some of the more problematic features of the psychic life of neoliberalism, processes of neoliberalisation have been challenged in the context of urban policy-making.

In relation to the issue of inequalities, I believe that my analysis of exclusions in the classical music profession points to some ways in which the lack of diversity could be addressed. First, it is important to collect data on the demographic background of the cultural workforce, including musicians who work in classical music. As chapter two has shown, several studies have been conducted and my original data has addressed some existing gaps. However, keeping this information up to date seems crucial. Available and accessible data provides an informed understanding of the demographic makeup of the cultural sector workforce and highlights good practice as well as areas for improvement and intervention. Such data would make visible existing inequalities and, over time, generate an evidence base for longitudinal research to identify changes and continuities. Existing initiatives, such as the various studies cited in chapter two, have done important work to document inequalities in the classical music sector. Cultural sector organisations could collect data on the demographic background of the workforce themselves, and do so routinely and voluntarily. The League of American Orchestras, for example, recently published a report on racial/ethnic and gender diversity in the orchestra field (League of American Orchestras, 2016). Similar initiatives could be pursued by relevant organisations in Germany and the United Kingdom.

Second, and as my discussion of the unspeakability of inequalities in chapter three has shown, ongoing exclusions have to be discussed openly. An informed and open engagement with inequalities in the classical music sector, and the cultural sector at large, will lead to greater understanding of why they matter. Debates about inequalities will also challenge prevalent myths of individual success, talent, and merit by fostering an understanding that some obstacles and opportunities are not down to the individual. Increased awareness of the wider *social* forces that shape working lives may help musicians and the wider cultural sector workforce to cope with the high demands of their profession. Undoubtedly, there are several initiatives that have put inequalities on the agenda. In London, the charity London Music Masters[5] has held several public discussions on gendered, racial, and classed exclusions in the classical music sector. The Southbank Centre also hosts breakfast meetings on 'Women in Classical Music', which focus on particular aspects of the profession – such as composition – but also provide a platform for networking with other women in the sector, as well as for sharing ideas and best practice. And BBC Radio 3 recently organised a conference on the lack of ethnic diversity among composers,[6] in addition to reporting on equality issues in other programmes, such as *Music Matters* or *The Essay*.[7]

I welcome these initiatives, and have actively taken part in some of them. My third recommendation, however, is to provide structural solutions to structural issues. Inequalities reflect wider patterns and cannot, therefore, be addressed on an individual level. Research has demonstrated that formal arrangements work well to address inequalities. To recall, the switch to blind auditions in US orchestras can possibly explain 25 per cent of the increase in the percentage of female players in the orchestras from the 1970s to 1996 (Goldin and Rouse, 2000; see chapter two). Due to the informality of large segments of the classical music sector, it is not feasible to introduce blind auditions in all contexts. The available evidence does however suggest that they can successfully be implemented in institutionalised settings (such as conservatoires and orchestras). The introduction of quotas also helps to increase the representation of minority groups. Quotas can be applied to a range of contexts, including, but not limited to: commissions, scholarships, concert programming, conductors, and composers. These more formal measures would work in tandem with more informal ways to address inequalities, such as the initiatives I described in the previous paragraph, as well as mentoring schemes or professional development courses aimed at under-represented groups. The programme Women Conductors@Morley (2016), for example, offers a course for young aspiring women conductors and provides them with guidance in the essential technical skills of conducting. These, and other, more informal interventions should not, however, replace more formal ones, such as blind auditions and quotas.

Conclusion

I began this conclusion with a summary of the book's key contributions and subsequently charted ways to develop my analysis further. In particular, I argued that we can take forward research and debates on gender, subjectivity, and cultural work through an exploration of attitudes towards mothering, the ways in which work on the body intersects with entrepreneurialism, and the links between inequalities, production, and consumption. The final section of the conclusion drew attention to the wider concerns that my study has raised, such as the outcomes and effects of inequalities as well as processes of neoliberalisation and precarisation. While I made it clear that I did not set out to address these concerns, I gestured towards some existing studies and initiatives, most notably in relation to precarious work and neoliberal urban policies. Finally, I drew conclusions from my analysis of inequalities to put forward several recommendations for tackling exclusions in the cultural sector workforce. On the whole, *Gender, Subjectivity, and Cultural Work* has made several important contributions to our understanding of a range of contemporary issues – including inequalities in the cultural and creative industries, entrepreneurialism and neoliberalism, as well as precarious, cultural work in creative cities – and thus laid the groundwork for further research, debate, and ongoing exchange of ideas.

Notes

1 I presented some of these recommendations in my 2015 research report *Equality and Diversity in the Classical Music Profession*, available at: http://blogs.kcl.ac.uk/young-female-and-entrepreneurial/files/2014/02/Equality-and-Diversity-in-the-Classical-Music-Profession.pdf

2 For more information, see: https://culturalworkersorganize.org/
3 For more information, see: www.worknotplay.co.uk/
4 For a detailed discussion of the scheme's remit and history in German see: Schulz, 2013. For a short summary in English, see: www.bbk-kulturwerk.de/con/kulturwerk/front_content.php?idart=3194&idartlang=3572&idcat=174&changelang=7
5 For more information, see: www.londonmusicmasters.org/
6 For more information, see: www.bbc.co.uk/programmes/b0801hkr
7 See, for example: www.bbc.co.uk/programmes/b072j0qv

References

Allen, K., Quinn, J., Hollingworth, S., & Rose, A. (2013). Becoming employable students and 'ideal' creative workers: Exclusion and inequality in higher education work placements. *British Journal of Sociology of Education, 34*(3), 431–452.

Bennett, T., Savage, M., Bortolaia Silva, E., Warde, A., Gayo-Cal, M., & Wright, D. (2009). *Culture, class, distinction.* Abingdon, Oxon; New York: Routledge.

Bernt, M., Grell, B., & Holm, A. (Eds.). (2013). *The Berlin reader: A compendium on urban change and activism.* Bielefeld: Transcript.

Bull, A., & Scharff, C. (2017). 'McDonalds' music' versus 'serious music': how production and consumption practices help to reproduce class inequality in the classical music profession. *Cultural Sociology.* Accessed 20 July 2017. Available at: http://journals.sagepub.com/doi/pdf/10.1177/1749975517711045

Butler, J. (1997). *The psychic life of power.* Stanford, CA: Stanford University Press.

Conor, B. (2014). *Screenwriting: Creative labour and professional practice.* London: Routledge.

Conor, B., Gill, R., & Taylor, S. (Eds.). (2015). *Gender and creative labour* (Vol. 63). Chichester: Wiley.

Dohnke, J. (2013). Spree riverbanks for everyone! What remains of "sink mediaspree"? In M. Bernt, B. Grell, & A. Holm (Eds.), *The Berlin reader: A compendium on urban change and activism* (pp. 261–274). Bielefeld: Transcript.

Elias, A. S., Gill, R., & Scharff, C. (Eds.). (2017). *Aesthetic labour: Rethinking beauty politics in neoliberalism.* Basingstoke: Palgrave Macmillan.

Entwistle, J., & Wissinger, E. (2006). Keeping up appearances: Aesthetic labour in the fashion modelling industries of London and New York. *The Sociological Review, 54*(4), 774–794.

Gill, R. (2014). Unspeakable inequalities: Post feminism, entrepreneurial subjectivity, and the repudiation of sexism among cultural workers. *Social Politics: International Studies in Gender, State and Society, 21*(4), 509–528.

Goldin, C., & Rouse, C. (2000). Orchestrating impartiality: The impact of "blind" auditions on female musicians. *The American Economic Review, 90*(4), 715–741.

League of American Orchestras (2016). *Racial/ethnic and gender diversity in the orchestra field: A report by the League of American Orchestras with research and data analysis by James Doeser, Ph.D.* New York: League of American Orchestras. Accessed 1 December 2016. Available at: www.ppv.issuelab.org/resources/25840/25840.pdf

McRobbie, A. (2015). *Be creative: Making a living in the new culture industries.* Cambridge: Polity.

Nickson, D., Warhurst, C., Cullen, A. M., & Watt, A. (2003). Bringing in the excluded? Aesthetic labour, skills and training in the 'new' economy. *Journal of Education and Work, 16*(2), 185–203.

Novy, J., & Colomb, C. (2013). Struggling for the right to the (creative) city in Berlin and Hamburg: New urban social movements, new 'spaces of hope'? *International Journal of Urban and Regional Research, 37*(5), 1816–1838.

O'Brien, D., & Oakley, K. (2015). *Cultural value and inequality: A critical literature review.* Swindon, Wiltshire: Arts and Humanities Research Council. Accessed 1 December 2016. Available at: www.ahrc.ac.uk/documents/project-reports-and-reviews/cultural-value-and-inequality-a-critical-literature-review/

Sandberg, S. (2013). *Lean in: Women, work, and the will to lead.* London: WH Allen.

Scharff, C. (2015). The psychic life of neoliberalism: Mapping the contours of entrepreneurial subjectivity. *Theory, Culture & Society, 33*(6), 107–122.

Scharff, C. (2017). Inequalities in the classical music industry: The role of subjectivity in constructions of the 'ideal classical musician'. In C. Dromey & J. Haferkorn (Eds.), *The classical music industry.* London: Routledge.

Schulz, G. (2013). Arbeitsmarkt Kultur: Eine Analyse von KSK-Daten. In G. Schulz, O. Zimmermann, & R. Hufnagel (Eds.), *Arbeitsmarkt Kultur: Zur wirtschaftlichen und sozialen Lage in Kulturberufen* (pp. 241–322). Berlin: Deutscher Kulturrat.

Taylor, S., & Littleton, K. (2012). *Contemporary identities of creativity and creative work.* Farnham: Ashgate.

Warhurst, C., Nickson, D., Witz, A., & Cullen, A. M. (2000). Aesthetic labour in interactive service work: Some case study evidence from the "new" Glasgow. *Service Industries Journal, 20*(3), 1–18.

Warwick Commission (2015). *Enriching Britain: Culture, creativity and growth.* Coventry: University of Warwick. Accessed 1 December 2016. Available at: www2.warwick.ac.uk/research/warwickcommission/futureculture/finalreport/warwick_commission_report_2015.pdf

Witz, A., Warhurst, C., & Nickson, D. (2003). The Labour of aesthetics and the aesthetics of organization. *Organization, 10*(1), 33–54.

Women Conductors@Morley (2016). *Women conductors @ Morley: Phase 1 report and press coverage prepared for Arts Council England by Marion Friend MBE.* Accessed 1 December 2016. Available at: http://royalphilharmonicsociety.org.uk/images/uploads/Women_Conductors_@_Morley_Phase_1_report_with_press.pdf

Wreyford, N. (2013). The real cost of childcare: Motherhood and flexible creative labour in the UK film industry. *Studies in the Maternal, 5*(2). Accessed 1 December 2016. Available at: www.mamsie.bbk.ac.uk/articles/abstract/2010.16995/sim.16926/

Wreyford, N. (2015). *The gendered contexts of screenwriting work: Socialized recruitment and judgments of taste and talent in the UK film industry.* Unpublished PhD thesis, King's College London.

Index

Acker, J. 60
affect/affective 4, 6, 114, 128–9, 142, 161, 165, 170, 176, 189, 196
aesthetic labour 7, 194, 198
aesthetic entrepreneurship 198–9
age 14, 20, 22, 25, 27, 43–4, 47–8, 61, 142, 163
Ahmed, S. 92
Alexiadou, N. 17
Alford, R.R. 22, 124
Allen, K. 2, 13, 15, 28, 42, 61, 63, 70, 116, 118, 197
Allmendinger, J. 49, 55
Amable, B. 113, 129
Anderson, B. 145
Antrag der Abgeordneten 42–3
anxieties 128–9
Armano, E. 140, 157
Armstrong, V. 20
art, commerce, and femininity in self-promotion 70–2
Arts Council England 20, 50
Arvidsson, A. 157
Atkinson, P. 20, 161
audience 58, 69, 90, 141, 160–5, 183, 196; connection with 160, 196
auditions, blind 64, 201
austerity urbanism 172

Bachtrack 50
Bader, Ingo 173, 175, 187
Bain, A.L. 15, 62–3, 105, 157
Baker, G. 20, 61, 106
Baker, J. 10, 18, 113, 116
Baker, S. 2, 10, 12–14, 63, 140, 143, 148–9, 158, 161–2, 164
Banks, M. 1, 3, 10–17, 21, 61, 71, 125, 143, 160, 177

Bansel, P. 16–17, 116
Bartleet, B-L. 20, 23, 55, 57
Bates, V.C. 49
Bauman, Z. 85, 98
Beckles Willson, R. 20
being in the zone 11, 21, 141, 158–62, 164–5, 196
Bennett, D. 3, 13, 20–2, 24, 55, 106, 124, 140, 142, 144
Bennett, T. 25, 86, 199
Berardi, F. 18, 116–17, 125
Bergvall-Kåreborn, B. 155
Berlin 170–1, 188–90; as cosmopolitan 176–9; as creative city 174–6; cultural and creative industries in 171–4; as happening and affordable, but changing 183–8
Berliner, M. 187
Berlin Senate 12, 172–3, 175, 187–8
Bernt, M. 171–2, 187, 199
Bielby, D.D. 15, 43
Bielby, W.T. 15, 43
Binkley, S. 18, 116–17, 121
Blair, H. 14, 22, 60, 145
Blamey, J. 42, 45–6, 48
Blech, V. 56
Boas, T. 114
Bodirsky, K. 175, 178
Bork, M. 20–2, 44
Born, G. 20, 23, 46
Bossen, A. 21, 43, 55–6, 140, 144, 187
Bourdieu, P. 89, 114, 126, 141, 151
Brah, A. 19, 86
Bröckling, U. 16, 18, 115–18, 125
Brophy, E. 140–2, 155
Brouillette, S. 65
Brown, W. 2, 10, 16, 23, 99, 113–15, 119, 129

Bruni, A. 18, 116
Bull, A. 20, 23, 46, 59, 61, 63, 86, 89, 151, 166n4, 174, 198
Burchell, G. 10, 16, 115, 125
Burke, J.P. 61
Burrows, S. 155
Butler, J. 68–9, 120, 141, 196

Cameron, D. 26
Carpos, F. 20, 60, 96
Catungal, J.P. 175
class: classical music as luxury hobby and 86–91; entrepreneurial subjectivity and 116; experiencing and disavowing racial prejudice and middle-class privilege 91–5; music education and 46, 59, 88–9; self-invention and 115–16
class backgrounds: of classical musicians 50–1, 63–4, 86–91; conservatoire students 46, 89–90; of cultural and creative workers 43–4
classical music profession 1–2, 27–8; additional perks of 162–4; business skills in 23, 117–20; combining parenting with 63; defined 7n1; demographics of musicians studied in 25–6; directions for further analysis and study 197–9; gendered dynamics of self-promotion in 65–75; horizontal segregation 5, 43–4, 51, 55, 57, 75; jobs in academia 21; in London and Berlin, study of 3–4; love and passion for 158–62, 165n3; making sense of persistence of inequalities in 59–65; orchestra jobs 21, 28, 28–9n7, 55–6; pleasure derived from 21–2; as precarious workers 143–4; underrepresentation of women in 49–50; researching gender, subjectivity, and work in 20–1, 25–7; vertical segregation 23, 41, 43, 55–7, 96, 106–7
Colomb, C. 172, 175, 178, 180, 199
competition 3, 6, 10, 17, 114, 124, 129–31, 133, 142, 158, 171, 188–9, 195; competition as self-directed 3, 6, 114, 129–31, 133, 195
composition, overrepresentation of men in 51, 53
Comunian, R. 22, 55
Conant, A. 20
conductors, female 55–8
Conor, B. 1–2, 10, 12–13, 15, 22, 28, 59–60, 63, 197

conservatoires 22–3, 28n3; private school students and 46–7, 89; race and ethnicity of applicants to 48–9; class backgrounds of students in 46, 89–90; teachers 52–3, 54–5; women in 45
consumption 15, 19, 133, 176, 194, 198–9, 201
Corrigan, T.F. 145
Cottrell, S. 7n1, 20–2, 26, 60–1
Coulangeon, P. 43, 51
Coulson, S. 17
Crawshaw, P. 125
Creative Blueprint 50
creative city 1, 171, 174–6, 178, 180–1, 187, 189
Creative Industries Mapping Document 176
Crenshaw, K. 19, 86
Crouch, C. 114
cultural and creative industries 2, 11–13, 27–8; higher education and 61; home-based workers in 62–3; inequalities in 14–16, 41–4; making sense of persistence of inequalities in 59–65; parenting by workers in 61–2
creative labour 1, 13, 158
cultural policy 11, 17, 174–5
cultural work 1–2, 10–11; directions for further analysis and study 197–9; entrepreneurialism in 2–3, 16–20, 28n6; inequalities in 14–16, 41, 194–5, 199–201; key findings and contributions 194–7; neoliberalism and 16–20; recommendations for addressing inequalities in 199–201; scholarly research on 13–14

Dardot, P. 18, 114, 116–17, 121, 125, 129
Davies, B. 16, 17–19, 116–17
de Peuter, G. 13–14, 140–3, 155
DeNora, T. 57
Devine, K. 20, 46
Dex, S. 14
DiAngelo, R. 92
difficulties, survival of 122–3
disability 14–15, 20
disarticulating: structural constraints in entrepreneurialism 126–8; inequalities 127
discourse: analysis 5, 11, 26; entrepreneurial 23; artistic 129
discursive psychology 26, 177

diversity: in the cultural and creative
industries 10–28; in the classical music
profession 14–16, 41, 50; *see also*
inequalities
Dohnke, J. 199
Donzelot, Jacques 160
Doolin, B. 17
du Gay, P. 10, 16–17, 115, 119
Duggan, L. 114

East Asian musicians: as "others" 64;
stereotypes of 59; *see also* ethnicity
and race
Edley, N. 15, 26, 88
education, music: higher 61; class and 46,
59, 61, 88–9
Edwards, P. 62
Ehrenberg, A. 18, 116
Ehrenreich, B. 122
Eikhof, D. 12, 15, 43, 60, 65
Eikhof, D.R. 15, 22, 59–60
Elias, A.S. 7, 19, 198
Ellemers, N. 104
Elliott, C.A. 64
entrepreneurialism 2–3, 10–11, 28n6,
113–14, 195–6; constant 119–20; in
cultural work 16–20; in dealing with
precarious work 155–8; disarticulating
structural constraints in 126–8;
embracing risks, learning from knock-
backs, and staying positive in 120–2;
gendered dynamics of self-promotion
and 65–75; hiding injuries in 123–5;
negotiating competing discourses in
125–6; surviving difficulties in 122–3
entrepreneurial subjectivity 3, 7n2, 133–4;
anxieties in 128–9; contours of 117–19;
literature on 114–17; race and 116; class
and 115–16
Entwistle, J. 7, 17, 194, 198
Erel, U. 24
ethnicity and race: classical musicians and
50–1, 59; conservatoire staff and 57;
cultural and creative industries workers
and 43; entrepreneurial subjectivity and
116; music education and 47–9
Ettlinger, N. 140, 142
Everett, M. 60, 63

Feher, M. 119
femininity: art, commerce, and 70–2;
performing modesty and 67–70;
physical appearance and 57–9

feminism 99
Fenwick, T.J. 17, 126
Finnegan, R. 20
Florida, R. 171, 174, 176
Foord, J. 176
Forkert, K. 4, 24, 170, 180, 185, 187, 189
Foucauldian approach to neoliberalism 2,
10, 16, 113–15
Foucault, M. 2, 10, 16, 113–15
Frankenberg, R. 92
Friedman, S. 44, 60, 151

Gane, N. 115
Gans-Morse, J. 114
Garland, C. 114
Garnham, N. 12
Garrick, J. 17
Geißler, T. 12
Gembris, H. 20–2, 26, 124, 188
gender 85–110; *see also* femininity;
hierarchies; inequalities; women
Germany 10–12, 15, 21, 24–5, 42–3, 45,
49–51, 53–8, 99–100, 144, 172, 187,
194, 199–200
Gershon, I. 115, 117–18, 121
Gilbert, J. 114–15
Gill, R. 2, 7n2, 10, 13–15, 17–19, 24, 28,
42, 59, 61–3, 68, 86, 97, 100, 102–4,
113, 116, 126, 130–1, 140, 142, 147,
197–8
Gillet, G. 26
Gilroy, P. 116
Giroux, H.A. 114
GLA 180–1
Goldin, C. 64, 201
Gonick, M. 10, 18, 113, 116
Gordon, C. 10, 16
Gould, E. 106
Gray, A. 17
Green, L. 20, 23, 45–6, 54, 59
Gregg, M. 14, 146
Grell, B. 171
Grésillon, B. 173
Grugulis, I. 15, 60

Hackman, J. 49, 55
Halford, S. 17, 125
Hall, S. 18, 114, 116–17
Handy, J. 140, 143, 147
Hardin, C. 114
Harper, S. 114
Harré, R. 26
Harris, A. 18

Harvey, D. 114
Haunschild, A. 65
Heijstra, T.M. 62
Hennekam, S. 13, 24, 106, 140
Hesmondhalgh, D. 2, 10–15, 23, 44, 63,
    140, 143, 148–9, 158, 161–2, 164
Hewitt, J. 98
Heye, A. 22, 124
hierarchies 85, 108–10; acknowledging
    gender inequalities and 95–7; classical
    music as luxury hobby and 86–91;
    experiencing and disavowing racial
    prejudice and privilege 91–5; gender
    inequalities as unspeakable and 104–8;
    performing the empowered woman
    and 97–100; postfeminist sensibility to
    100–4
Higgins, C. 106
Higgins, J. 125
Hill, D. 181
Holgate, J. 80
Holm, A. 171, 186–7
home-based workers 62–3
homophily 60
horizontal segregation 5, 43–4, 51, 55,
    57, 75
Housing in London 180
Howcroft, D. 155
Hutton, T.A. 174, 176

Ibarra, H. 60
Ikonen, H.M. 147
Independent Schools Council 46–7
inequalities 85–6, 108–10; acknowledging
    gender 95–7; and classical music as
    luxury hobby 86–91; in the classical
    music profession 2, 23–5, 41–2, 44–59;
    in cultural work 14–16, 41, 194–5,
    199–201; experiencing and disavowing
    racial prejudice and privilege 91–5;
    making sense of persistence of 59–65;
    and performing the empowered woman
    97–100; postfeminist sensibility to
    100–4; recommendations for addressing
    199–201; as unspeakable, gender 104–8
individualisation 2, 5, 85, 98, 107, 109,
    152–3, 195
insecurity of precarious work 147–52
intersectional 19, 86, 91, 108
Italian Operaismo School 28n5

Jackson, P. 177
Jakob, D. 175, 178

Jefferys, S. 15, 59, 61
Johnson, B. 176
Johnson-Williams, E. 20, 61
Jones, D. 61
Jordan, T. 11, 21, 141, 160

Kagerbauer, L. 18
Kalleberg, A.L. 142
Kehily, M.J. 18–19
Kelan, E.K. 97, 100, 102, 104
Kennedy, H. 2, 13–14, 140, 143, 155, 164
Kingsbury, H. 20
Klangzeitort 53
Kok, R.M. 20, 61
Kokot, P. 42, 76n4, 76n8, 97
Koppman, S. 60
Krätke, S. 172
Kuehn, K. 145
Kulick, D. 26

Laing, D. 174
Lamb, R. 106
Lander, R. 22
Langner, D. 20–2, 26, 127, 188
Larner, W. 114
Laval, C. 18, 114, 116–17, 121, 125, 129
Layton, L. 18, 116–17, 123, 125, 132
Leberl, J. 15, 55, 62
Leech-Wilkinson, D. 20
Lemke, T. 2, 10, 16, 113–15
Leonard, P. 17, 125
Leppänen, T. 20, 24, 49, 59, 64
Leslie, D. 175
Lewis, P. 18
Liddy, S. 106–7
Lie, A. 114
Littleton, K. 2, 10, 13–15, 17, 26–8,
    62–3, 70, 105, 126, 140, 143, 145, 148,
    154, 159, 164, 183, 197
London 170–1, 188–90; as cosmopolitan
    176–9; as creative city 174–6; cultural
    and creative industries in 171–4
Longhurst, B. 176
Lorey, I. 142–3
Luckman, S. 142, 155
Lutz, H. 86

MacDonald, R.A.R. 26
Macleod, B.A. 20, 58
Mäkinen, K. 65, 122
Manske, A. 15, 172
Marotto, M. 161
Mason, B. 47–8

Maus, F.E. 23
McAndrew, S. 54, 60, 63
McClary, S. 23
McClure, B. 42, 50–1, 55, 57
McCormick, L. 20, 23, 57–8
McGee, M. 123–4
McKay, S. 60
McLean, H. 157, 175
McManus, J. 61
McNay, L. 16, 18, 114–17, 129
McRobbie, A. 2, 10, 13–16, 18–19, 24, 28n6, 65, 73, 85, 113, 116, 119, 125, 130, 155, 160, 162, 187, 199; on cultural work as special 159–60; on hierarchies and sexism 98, 101–2; on self-enterprise in creative work 157–8
Merkel, J. 172
Mertens, G. 21, 188
Mills, J. 22, 55
Mirowski, P. 114–15, 121, 129
Mitropoulos, A. 142
modesty and femininity 67–70
Monk, C. 174
Morgan, G. 140, 156
Moss-Racusin, C.A. 68
mothering 62, 194, 197–9, 201
Moore, H. 7n2
Morgan, G. 143
Moss-Racusin, C.A. 67
Mudge, S.L. 114
Murgia, A. 140, 142, 157
Musicians' Union 143
Myles Beeching, Angela 23

Nairn, K. 125
Nash, J.C. 86
Nayak, A. 18–19
Neff, G. 17, 120, 157
negotiation of competing discourses 125–6
Neilson, B. 13–14, 140, 142
neoliberalism 2, 16, 113–14; cultural work and 16–20; feminist 99; Foucauldian approaches to 2, 10, 16, 113–15; literature on 114–17; see also entrepreneurialism; entrepreneurial subjectivity
Nettle, B. 20
networking 24, 41, 60, 75, 119, 153, 200
network sociality 14, 59–60
Nickson, D. 194, 198
Nooshin, L. 20
Novy, J. 175, 199

Oakley, K. 13, 15, 19–20, 50, 60–1, 199
O'Brien, A. 107
O'Brien, D. 13, 15, 19–20, 43–4, 50, 60–1, 68, 97, 99, 104, 199
O'Flynn, G. 116, 120
Ong, A. 114
orchestras 21, 27, 28n7; women in 55–6; black and minority ethnic musicians in 24–5, 41, 48, 50–1, 57, 59–61, 64
O'Reilly, J. 24
Orgad, S. 123
Osborne, W. 20
O'Shea, A. 18, 114, 116–17
Outshoorn, J. 74

Papadopoulos, D. 146–7
parenting 61–2
Paternoga, S. 20, 22, 45, 51, 55
pay gap: gender 43; class 44
Peck, J. 115, 172, 174–5
Perkins, R. 20, 22
Perrons, D. 15, 62
Peters, M. 17
Petersen, E.B. 116, 120
Phlewe, D. 114–15
Phoenix, A. 19, 86
physical appearance of female musicians 57–9, 104–5
Pidd, H. 106
Plan C 128
Pohlman, L. 15, 62
postfeminism 2, 5, 86, 102, 107, 109, 195; postfeminist sensibility 100–4
Pratt, A.C. 2, 10, 13–14, 17, 24, 113, 140, 142, 147, 173–5, 176, 180, 189
precarias a la deriva 142
precarious work 140–1, 164–5, 165n1, 196–7; additional perks of 162–4; debating precarity and 141–3; entrepreneurial attitude in dealing with 155–8; and love and passion for playing music 158–62, 165n3; of musicians 143–4, 165n2; responses to 152–5; temporal dimensions of 144–7; ups and downs of 147–52
Prichard, C. 17
principals, female orchestra 55–8
Pringle, J.K. 61
Proctor-Thomson, S. 63, 118
production 15, 44, 60, 133, 176, 194, 198–9, 201
prostitution 72–5
psychic life 196, 200

quotas 95, 201

race 5, 14, 18–20, 23, 28, 41, 44, 57, 59–61, 64, 85–110, 116, 127, 142, 175, 198; *see also* ethnicity and race
racial prejudice and privilege, experiencing and disavowing 91–5
Rafnsdóttir, G.L. 62
Randle, K.R. 15, 60–1, 86
Rattle, S. 178
recruitment 59–60
reputation 60–1
research: methodology 5, 10–11; interviews 86, 109; participants 2–6, 10, 17, 19, 21, 23–7, 59–61, 63–7, 69, 71–2, 75, 85–6, 100, 104, 106–8, 125–6, 150–1, 176–9
Rimmer, M. 20
Ringrose, J. 2, 10, 18–19, 113, 115–16, 132
Rise of the Creative Class, The 174
Rofel, L. 114
Rogaly, B. 143
Rose, N. 2, 16, 113–15, 118
Ross, A. 2, 10, 14, 17, 21, 113, 140, 143, 154
Rossiter, N. 14, 140, 142
Rottenberg, C. 99, 127
Rouse, C. 64, 201
Rowlands, L. 140, 143, 147
Rubin, H.J. 25
Rubin, I. 25
Rudman, L.A. 65, 67–8

Saha, A. 15, 44
Saleci, R. 18, 116, 125, 127
Salmenniemi, S. 125
Sandberg, S. 195
Scharenberg, A. 173, 175, 187
Scharff, C. 2, 10, 18–19, 24, 42, 51, 55, 57, 60–1, 68, 73, 99–100, 102, 113, 116, 124, 147, 151, 174, 196–8
Schmutz, V. 50, 58
Schulz, G. 3, 15, 21, 43, 49, 53, 55–6, 62, 140, 144
self as business 117–20
self-exploitation 14
self-improvement/self-optimisation 120, 123
self-invention 115
self-promotion: art, commerce, and femininity in 70–2; gendered dynamics of 65–75; performing modesty and

femininity in 67–70; spectre of prostitution in 72–5
Selmi, G. 142
Sennett, R. 18, 116–17, 143
Seu, B. 126
sexism 95–7, 104–8
sexual harassment 98–101, 106
Shamir, R. 114
Sharma, D. 176
Small, C. 20
social mediation of music 23
Solie, R.A. 23
Springer, S. 114
Standing, G. 142
Stedman Jones, D. 114–15
Steinpreis, R.E. 68
Stokes, R. 98
Storey, J. 17, 65, 117, 125
Stoyanova, D. 15, 60
structures of feeling 165, 170–1, 176–9
subjectivity: defined 7n2; entrepreneurial *see* entrepreneurial subjectivity; of the ideal cultural worker 62–5
Swan, E. 18, 116
Szanto, A. 22, 124

Taylor, I. 177
Taylor, S. 2, 10, 13–15, 17, 26–8, 62–3, 67, 70, 105, 126, 130, 140, 143, 145, 148, 154–5, 159, 164, 183, 197
teachers, conservatoire *52–3*, 54–5
temporal dimensions of precarious work 144–7
Thanki, A. 15, 59, 61
Thorsen, D.E. 114
Tickell, A. 115
Tindall, B. 22, 106
Toynbee, J. 71, 140
Tsianos, V. 146–7
Tygstrup, F. 176
Tyler, I. 19, 128, 132

Uffer, S. 187
United Kingdom 1–2, 4–5, 10–12, 15, 21, 24, 42–3, 45–6, 49–50, 53, 61, 86, 144, 173–4, 179, 181, 194, 200
urbanism, austerity 172
Ursell, G. 17
Usher, R. 17

vertical segregation 23, 41, 43, 55–7, 96, 106–7
Vorona, M. 125
Vosco, M. 140

Wagner, I. 20, 22, 44
Waite, L. 14–3
Wajcman, J. 62
Walkerdine, V. 2, 10, 18–19, 113, 115–16, 132
Wang, G. 20, 24, 48–9
Warhurst, C. 7, 12, 15, 22, 43, 59–60, 194, 198
Warwick Commission 15, 20, 28n4, 43, 50
Weinkopf, C. 24
Welsh, G. 47–8
Wetherell, M. 15, 26, 66, 88
Williams, C.L. 16, 68–9, 176–7
Williams, R. 4, 6, 165, 170, 176
Williams, R. 116
Wilson, G.B. 20, 26
Wimust 50
Wing-Fai, L. 59–60, 62
Wissinger, E. 7, 17, 194, 198
Wittel, A. 14, 22
Witz, A. 194, 198
women: in composition 51, 53; as conductors, artistic leaders and principals 55–8; in cultural work 14–16; gendered dynamics of self-promotion and 65–75; gender pay gap and 43; horizontal segregation 5, 43–4, 51, 55, 57, 75; inequalities in cultural and creative industries 14–16, 41–4; in music teaching 54–5; in orchestras 55–6; parenting by 61–2; percentage of conservatoire students 45; performing modesty and femininity 67–70; performing the empowered woman 97–100; physical appearance of 57–9, 104–5; postfeminist sensibility of 100–4; underrepresentation in the classical music profession 2, 10–11, 49–50; sexism against 95–7, 104–8; spectre of prostitution in self-promotion by 72–5; vertical segregation 23, 41, 43, 55–7, 96, 106–7
Wreyford, N. 1–2, 10, 13–15, 28, 60, 62–3, 86, 102, 104, 197
Wright, F. 42, 51, 55, 57

Yang, M. 20, 24, 48–9, 59, 64
York, N. 174
Yoshihara, M. 20–3, 48–9, 59, 64, 70, 74, 97, 106
young women 2–5, 10, 16–20, 26–7, 85, 98, 103, 109, 113, 116–17, 130, 132, 157–8, 195; as ideal entrepreneurial subjects 16–20

Zaza, C. 22, 124
Zimmermann, O. 12